Science Fiction by the Hour

Science Fiction by the Hour

Exploring Televised SF Through Series Episode Guides

By John Zipperer

Author info at http://www.weimar.ws.

 Portions of the episode guides appeared in different form in the digital magazine *Galaxis: The Worlds of Science and Science Fiction*, October 2011–March 2019.

ISBN 9798539220273

First paperback edition Jully 2021.

Cover art by KELLEPICS/Pixabay.
Design and layout by John Zipperer.

Printed by Amazon in the USA.

For my mother, Carol Lahey, who instilled in me a love of books and ideas.

Contents

Foreword

Spoiler Alert

In the year 2000, I was an editor at the technology magazine *Internet World*, which entailed fairly frequent travel to other cities to conduct interviews or attend conferences. That meant I had the occasional evening to spend in my hotel room; not being a partier, drinker, or club-goer, I usually grabbed dinner and spent my evenings reading or watching television. Exciting; yes, I know. But I *was* excited on one such trip when I found myself watching an episode of *Star Trek: The Next Generation* that I had somehow missed. It was like thinking you had read all of the books by your favorite author, only to visit a bookstore and stumble across one of that author's novels that you hadn't even heard about before—and you buy it on the spot.

I normally say that even a bad book is better and feels more worthwhile to me than a good movie or television program. But TV has the added ability to build connections to your soul by trying again every week with a new story, changing or deepening your relationship with the characters and the fictional world of the program. So bookaphile that I am, I still have many television programs I have enjoyed over the years, both genre and non.

When I was young—very young, like early grade school years—I was watching reruns of the original *Star Trek* series, as well as much-rarer reruns of the animated *Star Trek*, and reading the books based on each series by James Blish and Alan Dean Foster. This is a tale not dissimilar to your parents telling you they had to walk 10 miles to school each day, uphill and in four feet of snow. For back in those mid-1970s days, if you wanted to get a synopsis of a TV episode, you were pretty much relegated to poring over the tiny one-sentence descriptions in the newspaper TV listings and maybe clipping out and collecting the mini-synopses from *TV Guide*.

In later years, magazines such as *Cinefantastique* and *Starlog* would feature extensive episode guides to various series, books examining the making of particular series in detail would include episode writeups, and of course when the Internet became popular, it would host many guides to episodes of even the most arcane television shows, written by experts and nonexperts with the Internet's typical wild abandon. And into that mix came me. About a decade ago I started producing a digital-only science fiction magazine called *Galaxis* (it's German for "galaxy"). Very much in the mode of *Starlog*, *Questar*, and *Future Life*, the magazine included a mix of articles on science, SF movies and television, books, and the like. With the second issue, I started serializing my favorite series in episode guide format, and those guides make up the bulk of this book—albeit revised, expanded, and I hope improved.

CHOICES

Having been a young child during a time with a paucity of science fiction on TV and living long enough to experience the current explosion of televised SF on networks, streaming services, cable, and syndication, I appreciate a production that can tell a compelling storyline with good actors and production values. It is difficult to create a television show; find financing; get a network or syndication deal; assemble a cast, cadre of writers and producers, camera people, costume designers, set designers and everyone else behind the camera; deal with a million compromises that must be made for personal, commercial, legal, and other reasons; and then remain on the air long enough to be a commercial and creative success. Shows that somehow last for a decade or longer (*The Simpsons*, *Cheers*, *M*A*S*H*, *Friends*, and others) are exceptions that make it look easier than it is.

So in this book, I want to explore several science fiction series via their episode synopses.

I could have included in this book any number of the dozens of science fiction TV series of the past half century. But this book is a *personal* exploration of science fiction, and each of these three series meant a lot to me (plus one series that didn't mean much to anyone); they also played a very important role in the development of the genre in the past four decades. They are *Battlestar Galactica*'s first run, it's troubled sibling *Galactica 1980*, *Battlestar Galactica*'s triumphant second run, and *Star Trek: The Next Generation*. And, as a taste of things to come and as a sign of just how TV was dramatically changing and improving even after critics started declaring the "death of television," I am including my guide to the first year of the seminal series *The X-Files*.

As much as I would like you to believe that I just know everything, I rely on research and many resources to pull together something as complicated and extensive as these episode guides. In the writing of these guides, I of course relied upon viewing episodes, and I found invaluable assistance for plot details, background, fact-checking, and more from the Memory Alpha website (*memory-alpha.wikia.com*), *battlestarwiki.org*, the licensed *Star Trek: The Next Generation* magazines, the official *Star Trek* website (*startrek.com*), Wikipedia, and interviews and articles in *Cinefantastique*, *Fantastic Films*, and *Starlog*, among print sources. For recommendations of some valuable and enjoyable resources, see my epilogue.

I have enjoyed rewatching these programs, and I appreciated the ability to consult other writers' thoughts about them; but these are my descriptions and my opinions, and any errors you might find here would be mine alone. Also, here's the spoiler alert: These pages are *full* of spoilers. I am assuming you have already seen these episodes. If there are one or two here or there that you haven't already seen, I suggest you watch them before reading my comments about the episodes in question, unless you don't mind learning a few plot details ahead of time.

One other bit of last-minute housekeeping: In my episode guides herein and my notes on individual episodes, I include some interesting ideas, connections, and implications of the episode or storyline in question. I do not, however, try to include every bit of trivia known to mankind about the episode. I am not trying to compete with the many online TV show resources that include every fact about the DVD release, deleted scenes, differences between U.S. and foreign versions of the episode, and the like. I am not trying to replace those other resources; indeed, I recommend you check them out. That information can be very interesting to some, but it's not pertinent to what I'm trying to do here, which is provide a personal look at some significant science fiction television through the episode guide format, and explore what these shows were saying (or reflecting) about the state of the world at the time they aired.

I know you won't agree with all—or possibly even most—of the conclusions and other opinions in this book. That's okay; I enjoy getting other people's input, and I hope you do, too. If I can't convince, I'm happy to inform and entertain, and I think you'll still find this book to be a handy guide to the plots and ideas of these shows.

Now let's get started.

CHAPTER ONE

Battlestar Galactica 1978–1979

There are those who believe . . . that life here began out there, far across the universe, with tribes of humans who may have been the forefathers of the Egyptians or the Toltecs or the Mayans; that they may have been the architects of the Great Pyramids, or the lost civilizations of Lemuria or Atlantis. Some believe that there may yet be brothers of man who even now fight to survive, somewhere beyond the heavens.

Let's start with the first one, which was actually a failure and is still much derided by many: ABC TV's *Battlestar Galactica.* It lasted only one year, but it has been cited by producers of later science fiction (SF) television series as a source of inspiration. Despite its short life, it was something of a glorious failure. A sprawling, ambitious space opera with a huge cast; it was also a groundbreaking series in terms of budget, which was reported to be a then-unheard-of $1 million an episode, necessary to create the small-screen spectacle to attract audiences energized by *Star Wars.*

The show was canceled before a second, less expensive season could be put together (options on the table included thinning out the cast and bringing in Isaac Asimov as science advisor). But, as fans of the show know, the program's ratings hadn't dropped out of the top 20 programs of the week; the cancellation made more sense if the network bosses simply wanted to invest in a less-expensive program. They had gone big with *Galactica,* but they proved not to have the courage of their convictions.

The show's creator, Glen A. Larson, was influenced by some of the biggest pop cultural phenomena of the 1970s when he developed *Battlestar Galactica,* which premiered in 1978. The studios behind *Star Wars* and *Battlestar Galactica*—20th Century Fox and Universal, respectively—fought fierce multi-year legal battles trying to punish each other for various violations. Fox went after Universal for what it saw as unfair competition from *Galactica*; one of the concessions Larson made was that the laser pistols in his series wouldn't shoot bolts of light-colored energy but would instead make a noise and viewers would see the explosion take place elsewhere. If that seems like a silly thing for Fox to insist on, it at least demonstrates the ridiculous tit-for-tat that the legal battle became. Universal counter-sued, claiming Fox had stolen from its early 1970s SF film *Silent Running*—and on and on. Each side won a victory here or there, but it was basically an exercise in lawyerly income-generation. It didn't affect the fans, except for those of us who liked seeing laser beams.

Though the Fox lawsuit argued that Larson stole ideas from *Star Wars*, he arguably owes more to a Swiss writer named Erich von Däniken. Von Däniken's 1968 book *Chariots of the Gods?* and his following books (*Return to the Stars*, *Gods from Outer Space,* and others) fed an enduring obsession among people who bought his line of thinking about the possibility that ancient astronauts had visited Earth and influenced human destiny. Larson, already a successful television producer when he managed to get a deal with ABC to make his expensive series, was heavily influenced by von Däniken, his own faith, and other mythological tales about human origins.

In the media frenzy that followed the breakthrough success of that other influence, *Star Wars*, Larson revised a series plan he had been working on for years and got the network's commitment to what was originally to be a series of spectacular television movies.

ALTERNATE POSSIBILITIES

Many film and TV properties undergo dramatic evolution from early concept to final presentation. Things change as producers navigate tight budgets, studios, networks, lawyers, and plain ol' creative evolution. *Galactica* too underwent significant changes over the years before it came to the small screen. Some changes were improvements, some were lamentable.

Galactica kind of existed long before it actually existed—and it could have ended up any number of ways in its final form. Larson told interviewers that he had come up with the original idea for what would eventually become *Battlestar Galactica* back in 1968, when he put together *Adam's Ark*. A Mormon, Larson wanted to tell biblical stories but place them in space, on other planets. So in *Adam's Ark*, the humans are fleeing the destruction of Earth and are looking for humans elsewhere in the universe. "It was kind of the reverse of *Galactica*," Larson told *Starlog*'s Karen E. Willson in 1980. "All the great people from this planet were leaving Earth and going someplace else because of an imminent prediction of disaster. They were tricked into going in this particular thing, which complicates the situation."

A decade later, when *Galactica* would finally materialize, that storyline would be reversed. Humans fled the destruction of the Twelve Colonies and searched for Earth. In the series that hit small screens in 1978, human ancestors had lived on the planet Kobol, from which they emigrated to colonize 13 planets. The religious themes were still there and would really come to the forefront in the "War of the

Gods" episode.

In his informative 2012 essay "Earth Star: A Monograph on the 1977 Vision of Battlestar Galactica," Steven O'Donoghue describes the *Galactica* that could have been, before it was heavily refined to become the series we know. But even relatively late in development, changes occurred. O'Donoghue includes a synopsis of a November 1977 script for the pilot movie, "Saga of a Star World":

> In the Seventh Millennium of time, the Twelve Colonies of Man hope to end a protracted war with a race of reptilian cyborgs. But the Cylons ambush the humans and destroy their civilization. A single battlestar, the *Galactica*, escapes with a fleet of ships. They travel to the planet Carillon, where the insectoid Ovions lull them into a false sense of security with offers of food and fuel. With Commander Adama captured by the traitor Baltar, the Cylons launch an all-out attack in an attempt to wipe out the last vestiges of humanity. The Colonials escape the trap and flee into deep space.

That description sounds very much like the three-hour movie aired on ABC, with some obvious caveats: the Cylons became full automatons instead of cyborg reptiles (thereby somehow making it less violent or scary when the Cylons were destroyed on a show that aired fairly early in the evening), and Adama was not captured by Baltar. Of course, the reptilian Cylons were also present in the *Galactica* novelization released by Berkley Books; those books also mentioned an early idea of Larson's: the rag-tag fugitive fleet of humans was made up of a couple hundred thousand ships, not the 220 they were whittled down to because the filmmakers didn't think they could show that many ships on screen. (That was a silly change to make. They never showed 220 ships, either; it was always just a small shot of a portion of the fleet, so they could just as well have said there were 220,000 ships if they wanted.)

The success of *Star Wars* and the legal battles between the two studios played a role in some other changes, such as the aforementioned laser guns or the inclusion of the word "star" somewhere in the title (hence *Battlestar Galactica*, though the August 1978 issue of *Starlog* notes that the series had been announced under many names, including *Earth Star*, *Star Worlds*, and *Battle Star* [sic] *Galactica*) or the changing of some names from things too reminiscent of *Star Wars* character names to Egyptian and Greek names, such as "Apollo."

Most of the changes made in its setting, storyline, and characters resulted in a better, more dramatic *Battlestar Galactica* series. Yes, I'd have preferred the laser beams (darn lawyers!) and 220,000-ship fleet (darn producers) and less kiddie-friendly elements (darn network), but in general making the series about humans looking for Earth rather than fleeing from it gave the series an added layer of (rather literal) otherworldliness. (Coincidentally, that was the same thing added when George Lucas located his adventures "a long time ago in a galaxy far, far away.")

And, of course, the show became a weekly show instead of a series of televised films. That resulted in a rush to create scripts, some of them subpar. It would not be the last time that the network's demands played a dubious role in *Galactica*'s life and death.

The show premiered to great fanfare and media attention. For example, critic Tom Shales, previewing the fall TV schedule on September 10, 1978, looked at network lineups including such new shows as *Taxi*, *WKRP in Cincinnati*, *The Paper Chase*, and others, and concluded, "There is only one unanimously certified sure-thing, ABC's lavish *Star Wars* superclone, *Battlestar Galactica*."

Its cast included celebrated veterans such as Lorne Greene working alongside younger talents such as Richard Hatch and Dirk Benedict. Special effects genius John Dykstra created the SFX. The budget was an estimated $1 million per hour, then a record amount for a television series—though the number is somewhat misleading; it is more accurately an average of the budget and includes a lot of costs amortized across the life of the series. "There were a lot of figures thrown around at the beginning, like a million dollars an hour," creator Larson told interviewer James Delson in the February 1979 issue of *Fantastic Films*. "Now it's more like three-quarters of a million per hour. We're not going to change costumes on our principals, so the more shows the lower the cost for the entire series."

ATOMIC REACTION

The critical reaction was, well, critical. Isaac Asimov, for example, wrote that it was a rehash of too many scenes we'd already watched in *Star Wars*; similar criticisms came from *The New York Times*, *The Hollywood Reporter*, and others.

In the end, only 24 hours of *Battlestar Galactica* were created before ABC killed it. Whatever the reason, the show's premature demise ended the experiment.

While it lasted, Larson's *Galactica* had served as a commentary on then-current events, arguably from a political perspective that would be flipped on its head a quarter-century later for its revival series. In the late 1970s, the world was still in the grip of the Cold War, and President Carter was trying to push through SALT II nuclear reductions during the last throes of U.S.–Soviet detente. Against that backdrop, *Galactica* depicted the uniformity and slave-like life of the Cylons (read: Soviet Russians) vs. the flawed but freedom-loving humans. If the new, SyFy-era *Battlestar Galactica* used the Cylons and the humans to comment critically on Western society, the ABC-era *Galactica* used the Cylons to comment on the Soviets and went much lighter in its criticism of the West.

The original show did, however, show the failings of the humans; the greed (of Sire Uri and others) and the inability to unite against an existential threat (such as when the tired human refugees are lured into trying to make peace with the Cylons at Carillon). A writer for Soviet newspaper *Izvestia* objected to the series as a dramatic attack on the SALT talks, representing a "perverted interpretation of the enemies of the treaty from the family of Washington hawks."

Whatever one thinks about the Soviet critique, there have been many fair criticisms of *Battlestar Galactica* (some of which I'll share in my episode recaps), but there have also been many unfair ones. For example, the show was criticized as not having character development. Yet consider Apollo growing over the series from hotshot fighter pilot to surrogate dad of Boxey to Sheba's boyfriend. Starbuck moves from being a womanizer to pretty much exclusively Cassiopeia's man. Cassiopeia—for the network censor's sake, but nonetheless—switches professions from a "socialator" (a mix of prostitute and geisha) to a med tech. Athena takes on responsibilities with the fleet's children. Baltar admittedly does not change. But even his character does more than just sit in his basestar command chair issuing orders; he goes from basestar lord to *Galactica* prisoner to renegade all over again.

Another unfair criticism is that the show was nothing but Cylons attacking every week. The Cylons were in a lot of episodes, but they dropped off toward the end of the series, and the *Galactica* met other aliens, pleasant and not-so-pleasant.

In April 1979, Tom Shales revisited his earlier prediction that *Galactica* would be a sure-fire hit in a column titled "Countdown for 'Rattletrap Galactica'": "To broaden the appeal of the program still further, it ironically or not is becoming less and less a science fiction series. Now, with series star Lorne Greene riding herd over his sons and the *Galactica*'s arkful of transients, the program's plots have degenerated into stock domestic drama—a Ponderosa of the cosmos. *Galactica* could have been the first smash hit in television to make it on visual spectacle, but that angle has been largely jettisoned in favor of meat, potatoes and corn."

Perhaps the most unfair criticism also is answered by the beguiling possibilities of what *Battlestar Galactica* could have become in a second and even third year on the air. Far from being a never-ending search for a mythical planet, in just 24 TV hours, *Galactica* showed us the birthplace of humanity, a race of advanced beings who help the fleet toward Earth, television transmissions from Earth, and other big steps forward.

Some shows that are doomed to cancellation go into a tailspin toward their end. *Galactica* arguably did not; instead, the series started off strong, suffered through some poor scripts in the middle, but then completed its sole TV season on a high note. As Larson told Karen E. Willson in his July 1980 *Starlog* interview, "The original *Galactica*, I think, started off just right. It's like an airplane that takes off from an aircraft carrier—it sort of dips before it really gets going. *Galactica*, by its sheer weight and expectations, took a natural dip as it left the carrier deck. Then I think it started to climb. We did better stories and concentrated more on the characters."

See if you agree.

Creator and Executive Producer: Glen A. Larson
Broadcaster: ABC

Studio: Universal
Supervising Producers: Leslie Stevens, Michael Sloan
Producers: John Dykstra, Don Bellisario, Paul Playton, David O'Connell
Special Effects Coordinator: John Dykstra
Effects Unit Supervisors: David M. Garber, Wayne Smith
Music: Stu Phillips
***Galactica* theme music by:** Stu Phillips, Glen A. Larson
Art Director: John E. Chilberg II
Captain Apollo: Richard Hatch
Lieutenant Starbuck: Dirk Benedict
Commander Adama: Lorne Greene
Lieutenant Boomer: Herb Jefferson, Jr.
Lieutenant Athena: Maren Jensen
Cassiopeia: Laurette Spang
Lieutenant Sheba: Anne Lockhart
Count Baltar: John Colicos
Colonel Tigh: Terry Carter
Boxey: Noah Hathaway
Flight Sergeant Jolly: Tony Swartz
Greenbean: Ed Begley, Jr.
Flight Officer Omega: David Greenan
Imperious Leader (voice): Patrick Macnee
Imperious Leader (body): Dick Durock
Lucifer (voice): Jonathan Harris
Muffit the Daggit: Evie the chimp

Saga of a Star World

Writer: Glen A. Larson. **Directors:** Richard Colla, Alan Levi. **Airdate:** September 17, 1978.

One thousand years earlier, the ever-expanding Cylon Alliance tried to fight and enslave one planet too many. The humans of the Twelve Colonies came to the aid of that planet's population and freed them from Cylon tyranny, but it resulted in a human-Cylon war that lasted for a millennium. A fleet of powerful battlestars served as the foundation of the Colonies' strength. The Cylons came to realize they would have to defeat the humans if the Alliance was to be safe from their interference. And eventually, a Cylon Imperious Leader decides to just get it over with by dispatching with the humans altogether.

With the help of the traitorous human Count Baltar, the Cylons convince the humans that they finally want peace. As the battlestar fleet gathers at the rendezvous point to sign the peace treaty, the human leaders—led by President Adar and the Council of Twelve—all seem to believe the time for peace has arrived, except for the *Galactica*'s commander, Adama, who does not trust the Cylons or Baltar. When a patrol from his ship encounters a Cylon fleet in hiding, Adama is still unable to convince Adar to see the light until it is too late. "Too late" begins with the viper flown by his son, Zac, being shot apart just short of the fleet. The *Galactica* manages to launch its viper squadrons in time to put up some resistance to the swarms of Cylon fighters, but one by one, the other battlestars are destroyed. Adama realizes the rendezvous point was merely a ruse to get the Colonial fleet away from the home worlds, so he pulls his ship out of the fight and heads to his home world of Caprica, only to find it reduced to rubble.

The Cylon surprise attack has hit all of the Colonies, with only a relative handful of humans surviving out of the billions who once flourished there. Adama orders the *Galactica* to gather up survivors who are able to get aboard anything that is spaceworthy. A total of 220 ships form the battlestar's "ragtag fleet." Among the rescued humans is the Caprican journalist Serina, and grief-stricken Apollo (still mourning his brother's death) finds himself falling for her.

Adama struggles to lead the fractious political leaders on the newly reconstituted Council of Twelve, where his chief antagonist is Sire Uri, a corrupt and influential politician. But Adama is able to convince them to go to the planet Carillon in an effort to escape the Cylons and find food and fuel. Carillon is rich in Tylium, the fuel that powers the fleet, but first warriors Apollo, Starbuck, and Boomer must clear a path through a space minefield.

The mine-shooting accomplished, the fleet approaches its destination. Once on Carillon, the *Galactica* officers find the large insect-like Ovions willing to supply their needs, even while they entertain the humans at a lavish casino. Uri and his supporters decide that Carillon's so wonderful that the humans can stop running and should come to an accommodation with the Cylons; but once again, Adama trusts neither the Cylons nor the human appeasers. When the Cylons are revealed as the power behind the Ovions, and the Ovion taste for human morsels comes to light, the Colonials are forced to fight their way off the planet.

President Adar: As we approach the seventh millennium of time, the human race will at last find peace, thanks to you.

Well, not so much, Adar.

Notes: There are some tantalizing differences between this TV movie and the novelization, both of which were written by creator Glen A. Larson (who shares the book's byline with Robert Thurston). In the book, the Cylons were a living race of beings, not the robots they became in the TV series. Also, as noted above, the number of ships in the human survivor fleet for the TV series is a small fraction of the size it is in the novel. In the books, we also see a much more conflicted Commander Adama, one who resigns the presidency of the Council of Twelve, who feels somewhat ashamed to have fled the battle at the armistice site to head to Caprica, who feels isolated from his allies and even from his family throughout much of the novel.

With the scaling down that needs to be done for television, as well as the dumbing down that needed to be done for the show's early evening broadcast slot, some of the more adult angles of the book are nowhere to be seen in the film or the series. One that did make it, the character Cassiopeia's career as a "socialator"—which we're invited to interpret as being a high-class prostitute—was quickly changed in the series to make her a proper nurse.

This three-hour TV movie cost anywhere between $7 million and $20 million, depending on how you account for the expenses of a drawn-out production and how you amortize sets and special effects that were then used for the series. Universal recouped some of the money by successfully releasing this TV movie theatrically.

Lost Planet of the Gods (Parts I & II)

Writers: Glen A. Larson, Don Bellisario. **Director:** Chris Nyby, Jr. **Airdates:** September 24, 1978 & October 1, 1978.

Captain Apollo and Serina are getting married, but "happily ever after" is not quite their destiny. It's not such a great time for the viper pilots at Apollo's bachelor party, who are all put out of action by a disease (except for Apollo and Starbuck, who are out on patrol). The sick warriors are put into cryo-pods while the doctor tries to find a cure.

Meanwhile, someone we thought was killed in the previous *Galactica* outing, Count Baltar, is spared at the last minute and given his own Cylon basestar and a not-altogether-trustworthy adjutant—the sparkly headed Lucifer—and a pat on the rear end as he goes away to try to finish off the human race.

Commander Adama, who is researching ancient legends about Kobol, the birthplace of humanity, takes a break to order Apollo to train colonial civilians as temporary replacements for the stricken warriors. Surprise of surprises (or cliché of clichés), the replacements are women, including Apollo's new bride, Serina. The only other healthy male pilot, Starbuck, is captured by Cylons during a patrol. The *Galactica*'s fleet finally finds a planet at the end of a long void in space (and don't bother questioning exactly what a void in space is); the planet is the legendary Kobol. A landing party, including Adama, enters a giant pyramid, where they discover Baltar. The traitor tries to strike a deal with Adama, who naturally does not trust him.

Meanwhile, Starbuck is returned to the humans.

Starbuck: Hey, it's against regulations to hug a junior officer. Unless you mean it.
Apollo: We thought you were dead.
Starbuck: Yeah, well, what's a little basestar to an old war jock like me?
Apollo [*Laughs, then becomes serious.*]: Basestar?
Second warrior: There's a basestar coming?

Starbuck: No, not coming. Waiting. For orders. Didn't Baltar show? He's the one who got me free. . . . He's come to offer peace. Do you believe it?
Apollo: I believe we'd better get off this planet before Baltar's forces get here.

But Baltar's plan is undercut by Lucifer, who launches an attack on the humans. The airstrikes on the pyramid disturb Adama's attempt to read ancient writings about the location of the thirteenth tribe of humans. The Cylons are fought off by—quelle surprise—the female warriors (who disprove all the naysayers) as well as the recuperating male warriors. But there's still one more surprise in store: When the humans finally have to flee the pyramid, Serina is shot by a Cylon.

Notes: If Glen Larson wanted to show Colonial warriors walking amidst the pyramids in a production he was making today, he might very well use CGI. In 1980, he might have used Magicam, which Carl Sagan used to walk "in" the Library of Alexandria in his *Cosmos* science series. Even back in 1978, he might have settled for model pyramids and forced perspective to place the actors amid the monuments. Instead, he flew a crew to the actual Egyptian pyramids and filmed actual people actually walking amidst the actual monuments.

That is what a humongous budget can buy you.

Actor Jane Seymour reprised her role as Serina in this two-part special to finish off her character's story arc. As she later told interviewers, she did not expect to be in any further *Galactica* storylines after the "Saga of a Star World" pilot for the simple reason that her character died in that movie. She was therefore startled when the producers asked her to be in "Lost Planet of the Gods." She told Alan Brender in *Starlog*'s November 1980 issue that Serina was dying of a cancer-like disease in the script she had shot; but when it was edited for the final cut, that entire sickness storyline was removed. When she was asked to be in the series, she only consented to reprise the role for this episode if she got more money and a good storyline. She should have demanded they let her play Serina as a zombie.

The discovery of humanity's birthplace on Kobol was reprised in the reimagined *Battlestar Galactica* a quarter century later, in a story arc beginning with "Kobol's Last Gleaming."

The Lost Warrior

Writers: Don Bellisario, Herman Groves. **Director:** Rod Holcomb. **Airdate:** October 8, 1978.

The X-Files and *Battlestar Galactica* both had the large-budget, highly produced "mythology" episodes, and then they also had their stand-alone episodes. Some of *X-Files*' stand-alones were gems in and of themselves. *Galactica* fared more poorly in this respect, especially early in the show's life, with stories such as this one that evince hasty writing and could have been written for pretty much any science fiction program by people who thought SF was merely a western in space.

After being attacked on viper patrol, Captain Apollo crash lands on the planet Equellus. On that frontier outpost, he is befriended by a boy named Puppis and his widowed mother, and he learns that the locals are under the control of a strongman and his henchman, Red Eye.

Puppis' mother: You'd better get back in your ship and leave. Quickly.
Apollo: I'd like nothing better, but I'm out of fuel.
Puppis' mother: Well, then we're going to have to hide it. It and you.
Apollo: Cylons?
Puppis: What are Cylons?
Apollo: Well, if you don't know, then there aren't any around.

Not so fast, Apollo. The henchman turns out to be a Cylon centurion that had also crash landed on the planet, suffering damage in the process that makes him think the strongman, Lacerta, is the Cylon Imperious Leader. Apollo decides to take on the Cylon in a duel, using the Colonial weapon of Puppis' dead father, a Colonial Warrior who had been killed by Red Eye.

After defeating the Cylon (and thus driving Lacerta out of town), Apollo takes fuel from the crashed ship of Puppis' father (apparently everyone crashes on this planet; they should build a spaceport) to get his viper back in space and return to the fleet.

Notes: In 1978, *Battlestar Galactica* didn't just invade the airwaves; its merchandise also took over the store shelves. *Star Trek* fans had to wait years before the full impact of their favorite show was realized in many licensed spinoffs that they could buy. But when *Galactica* premiered in 1978, the designers, manufacturers, and retailers were already geared up to sell a wide assortment of toys, books, and other items, and that list would only grow over the ensuing couple of years.

It continues today, of course, and licensed spinoffs from the 1978–79 TV series got a new lease on life from the popularity of Syfy's reimagined series. Some fans dug out their old *Galactica* paraphernalia to relive old memories; others realized that they had thrown away or given away those items two or three decades ago, and they began scouring eBay to find replacements. If you are one of those regretful former owners, or if you think about the original series spinoffs and feel drawn into pleasant memories of your childhood, you have lots of things from which to choose.

Marvel Comics produced a comic book that was as short-lived as the TV show; it lasted only 23 issues, but it also produced an over-sized Marvel Super Special and a two-volume reprint of the first two storylines in paperback form.

In 1979, Berkley published *Battlestar Galactica: The Photostory*, a lavishly photo-illustrated paperback that is a collectors' item. The *Photostory* of the three-hour premiere movie features hundreds of full-color photos that are bright and clear, a much better presentation than you'll find in most of the photo-books that were popular at the time, many of which included blurry or grainy photos. But you'll see similar dedication to using highest-quality photos on the cover of the Parker Brothers *Battlestar Galactica* board game and the 1979 and 1980 wall calendars from Stancraft Products.

Berkley also published 14 novels based on the show, with the first ten adapted from television episodes and the remaining four based on original stories. (Appearing out of continuity is the fifth book, *Galactica Discovers Earth*, which is based on the first episode of the *Galactica 1980* spinoff series; with book number six, the series returned to focusing on the original show.) The books, which were also published in foreign editions, carried creator Glen A. Larson's byline, which was shared with Ron Goulart, Michael Resnick, Robert Thurston, or Nicholas Yermakov. Particularly in the *Saga of a Star World* premiere novelization, the books offer a somewhat different take on the *Galactica* universe; as noted earlier, for example, the Cylons are living beings, not robots.

Galactica books also appeared in non-novel formats. The *Battlestar Galactica Space Flight Activity Book* from Grosset & Dunlap appeared in 1978, but it is not to be confused with the *Battlestar Galactica Activity Book* from Wonder Books, published the same year and filled with puzzles and other games; and to make things more confusing, Grosset published the *Battlestar Galactica Adventure Activity Book*, filled with pictures for coloring. The next year, Windmill Books and E.P. Dutton & Co. came out with the *Encyclopedia Galactica*, a resource with information on the TV series.

The model kits—of vipers, battlestars, Cylon raiders, and basestars—were a particular favorite for hands-on fans. Created by Monogram (which later merged with Revell), the detailed ships were of good quality and were fine replications of the ships in the TV show (though I have to note that my viper's left wing kept dropping off, a problem I'm not entirely convinced was caused by the modeling skills I possessed at the age of 12). The kits were so good, they were even used in some on-screen shots in the series, such as a model kit raider in the background of a basestar's interior garage.

The licensed *Galactica* spinoffs kept coming: Larami Corp.'s *Battlestar Galactica* Cylon Bubble Machine featured a sorta-Cylon-shaped statue atop a bottle of bubble-making liquid. And still more: T-shirts, action figures, posters, jigsaw puzzles, photo trading cards, radio-controlled spaceships, rocket toys, Colorforms kits, vinyl records, wrist watches, folders, wallets, bagatelle games, lunchboxes, *The Battlestar Galactica Scrapbook*; *The Battlestar Galactica Storybook* (a children's version of the novelization), disco versions of the music, talking daggit doll, water glasses, jackets, rain coats, underwear, yarn kits, belts, pajamas, paper cups, napkins, paper plates, table cloths, birthday cake decorations, bed sheets, sleeping bags, curtains, blueprints, Cylon-head AM radio, and much more.

They can all be found for sale somewhere on the internet, so you can burn a hole in that Visa card or empty your PayPal account if you want to recapture the autumn of 1978.

The Long Patrol

Writer: Don Bellisario. **Director:** Chris Nyby, Jr. **Airdate:** October 15, 1978.

Starbuck gets away from romancing Cassiopeia and Athena—separately but at the same time—by going on a mission to test a new super-viper, but he wears a sleek new non-Colonial uniform so as not to tip off any Cylons or Cylon allies he might run into. While on a test run ahead of the fleet, he finds a space shuttle being harried by a fighter ship. He defends the shuttle and then follows it down to a planet's surface. The shuttle turns out to be a smuggler's ship, and Starbuck is accused of smuggling Ambrosia. Thrown in prison, Starbuck finds that the other prisoners are descendants of criminals. The colony, Proteus, was established to provide fuel and Ambrosia to the Colonies, but it fell out of contact with the human worlds over the years. Starbuck helps the prisoners escape their jail and entertains ideas of getting rich on all of the liquor that has been bottled but gone unused over the years.

Meanwhile, the *Galactica* finds that the prototype viper—now flown by the real smuggler—is broadcasting an old Colonial signal. Worried that the Cylons might pick up the signal and find the *Galactica* and its fleet, they track the fighter ship themselves. Unfortunately, their fears are confirmed when the Cylons show up and attack the Proteus colony. Starbuck's get-rich-quick idea is lost when the Ambrosia is destroyed in the attack, but his consolation is rescue by the *Galactica*.

Starbuck [*to waiter*]: You don't happen to have a room with a better view? There's a sanitation ship right off our beam. Not exactly appetizing scenery.
Athena: A sanitation ship? Where?
Starbuck: It must have drifted back. Uh, I think there's a first-orbit cadet at the controls.

Notes: If Apollo is stuck on a planet last episode, this time it must be Starbuck's turn.

At the end of this episode, when Starbuck is back aboard the battlestar, Boxey draws a picture of how he had been told Earth's star system looks. Starbuck recognizes it from a drawing he had seen in Proteus' prison, where someone had drawn it. This is taken to be another hint that the fleet is on the right path in its search for the Thirteenth Tribe.

The ship's talking computer, named C.O.R.A., is Siri-like in its ability to annoy. Note also that Larson would go on to create the *Knight Rider* series, which featured a talking computer in an automobile.

Tasha Martel (also known as Arlene Martel), who portrays the prisoner known as Adultress 58, is a familiar face to genre viewers, having appeared in the "Amok

Time" episode of the original *Star Trek*, the "Demon with a Glass Hand" episode of *The Outer Limits*, and the "What You Need" episode of *The Twilight Zone*, as well as appearances in *The Man from U.N.C.L.E.*, *Mission: Impossible*, *I Dream of Jeannie*, and the *Star Trek* fan-created "Of Gods and Men" web production.

This episode actually begins with a dramatic concept: The *Galactica*'s fleet moves from one galaxy to another. Considering the low level of scientific literacy exhibited by the series' writers (more on which at "Fire in Space"), and the way terms such as *galaxy* and *star system* are used seemingly interchangeably, it's unknown whether we're supposed to believe the fleet has actually left the galaxy where the Twelve Colonies existed and entered another galaxy, or if the humans have simply fled one area of space for another.

And, finally, for those of you of drinking age: Ambrosia was a much-desired alcoholic drink on the series, and fans have in the years since come up with various real-world approximations of it. If you Google "Ambrosia" and "Galactica," you'll find the recipes. Also online is a photo of the label from a bottle of Ambrosia in the reimagined *Galactica* series, on which the writers or prop team included a jokey description: "Distilled and Bottled in the Bliffe Sector. This was especially difficult due to the plan[e]t's lack of barley and atmosphere. All packaging was done by hand with biosphere suits on. Not to worry; all the prisoners were treated as well as could be, considering the hostile planetary environment. For any questions concerning prisoner mortality rates, please call . . . "

Gun on Ice Planet Zero (Parts I & II)

Writers: Leslie Stevens, Michael Sloan, and Don Bellisario. **Director:** Alan Levi. **Airdates:** October 22, 1978 & October 29, 1978.

The *Galactica*'s fleet finds itself being herded toward the planet Arcta, which sports a Cylon garrison. To make matters worse, the garrison has a massive pulsar cannon that could destroy any ship in the fleet, including the battlestar. So Adama dispatches a commando team to destroy the cannon. To fill the team with the appropriate demolition experts, he must include a band of convicted criminals, who are predictably a mix of malcontents and threatening types.

Their landing on Arcta is complicated when the Cylons shoot down their shuttle, but they survive the landing and are rescued by a band of clones who work for Dr. Ravishol, the human creator of the killer canon. The good (maybe) doc doesn't want to see the cannon he created destroyed, but he is brought around to see things the Galacticans' way.

Ravishol: I have no use for war or violence in any form.
Apollo: You have a strange way of showing it. What do you call that monstrosity on the mountain—a weapon of peace?
Ravishol: It is an energy lens system designed to transmit intelligence across the

galaxy.
Apollo: Your energy lens system has fried two of my fighters.

Notes: In 1978, no one in the science fiction and fantasy worlds needed an introduction to Frank Frazetta. Frazetta, who died in 2010, was one of the most talented and influential painters and illustrators in the genre world. When the producers of the space opera extravaganza *Battlestar Galactica* pulled out all of the stops to promote their show, they enlisted Frazetta to provide some dramatic illustrations. The result was a handful of paintings that outdid the series itself in drama and fantastical imagination.

One of the paintings featured a group of beautiful female viper pilots rushing to their ships; it was used for ads in *TV Guide* (and elsewhere, I assume) promoting "Lost Planet of the Gods." Another features Commander Adama and others reacting to a wizard-like character in a medieval set piece (for "War of the Gods"). A third painting features the characters of Athena, her brother Apollo, and his pal Starbuck seemingly marooned on a planet while Cylon raiders menacingly descend. In the distance, viewers can spot a possibly crash-landed viper fighter, as well as the *Galactica* soaring above. It is this third painting that seems to have a life far beyond the others, and far beyond the typical advertising promo image. The female viper pilots painting has appeared on the hardcover edition of a *Galactica* novel by series star Richard Hatch and Alan Rodgers (2002's *Rebellion*), but it can't match the visual promiscuity of the third painting.

Frazetta's imagining of *Battlestar Galactica* is, well, vintage Frazetta. It involves unclad woman (Athena is nearly naked while the equally sexy Apollo and Starbuck are fully clothed), heroic men, and high drama. The setting is either an ice planet or a desert planet; it's not clear which, but if it's the former, Athena is going to be mighty cold. Meanwhile, the Cylon Raider looks even more sinister and threatening than it appears in the TV series. The only weak point of the painting is the main ship, the *Galactica*, which looks like it's made of wicker.

The painting appeared most widely in a two-page black-and-white ad promoting the premiere three-hour movie in *TV Guide*, which at that time was one of the largest magazines in the United States; it was also released as a poster by ABC; a poster in rock music magazine *Circus*; a wrap-around cover for the Berkley paperback novelization of "Gun on Ice Planet Zero" (renamed *The Cylon Death Machine*); a reissue of the novelization of the premiere episode, "Saga of a Star World," also featured the painting on its front cover; and cheapie SF media magazines *Star Battles* and *Space Trek* each used details from the painting on their covers.

It's not hard to see why the painting is so successful and has been so oft-published. It is dramatic, sexy, and it suggests high adventure. Today, fans and collectors hunt down this painting in its many manifestations on eBay and Amazon.

In other notes: Croft, the leader of the criminals, is portrayed by veteran actor

Roy Thinnes, famed for his starring role in the 1960s TV series *The Invaders*. Actor Dan O'Herlihy, who guest stars as Dr. Ravishol, also starred in *RoboCop* and its first sequel, *RoboCop 2*.

Intentional or not, there are echoes of this episode's theme of using criminals to carry out a mission in the reimagined *Battlestar Galactica* storyline in which convicted terrorist Zarek (played by original *Galactica* star Richard Hatch) is introduced. The echoes are particularly loud in that series' two-part "Home" episode. Like that episode, the criminals are plotting to take over, the stakes are very high for the *Galactica* and its fleet, and viewers are unsure whether any or all of the criminals will turn against the Galacticans.

And, finally, just another sad note about poor science. The fleet is "herded" toward a planet. Space being incredibly vast and, of course, 3-D, it's hard to envision how a Cylon force could herd the *Galactica*'s fleet somewhere specific unless it had a massive number of basestars surrounding the fleet, in which case it could have easily attacked and finished off the humans. Looks more like the writers were thinking in two-dimensional terms of a fleet of ships on an ocean.

The Magnificent Warriors

Writer: Glen A. Larson. **Director:** Chris Nyby, Jr. **Airdate:** November 12, 1978.

The Cylons destroy most of the *Galactica* fleet's food stores, so Adama decides to try trading with humans on some planets the fleet is approaching. However, to get the power energizer needed to trade for the food, Adama must woo Siress Belloby, an old flame of his.

When they land on the planet to bargain for food, they find that the locals are living in fear of the pig-like Borays. Starbuck finds himself tricked into serving as the local town's sheriff. It's a luckless role—and one that doesn't usually last long. It's also a role he must put into play for real when the Borays kidnap Siress Belloby, who had accompanied her faux beau Adama to the planet. Sheriff Starbuck manages to win Belloby back from the kidnappers, in return for passing along the sheriff's badge to one of their leaders.

Starbuck: You're contradicting yourself. If it's impossible to resign, and half the people in town have held the office—
Bogan: Not the half that's still alive.
Starbuck: Beg pardon?

Notes: Basically another Western episode, "The Magnificent Warriors" is made a bit more palatable by giving Adama an opportunity to get off the battlestar and engage in some light comedy.

The actor Barry Nelson portrays Bogan, the not-quite-upfront leader of the agricultural settlement of Serenity. Nelson will be forever known as the very first person to appear as James Bond onscreen. He was Bond in a 1954 TV production of *Casino Royale*.

The Young Lords

Writers: Don Bellisario, Frank Lupo, and Paul Playdon. **Director:** Don Bellisario. **Airdate:** November 19, 1978.

So much for the expert pilots aboard the *Galactica*. "The Young Lords" sees Starbuck crash land on the planet Trillion (or Attila, depending on who you're listening to), where he is able to avoid a Cylon patrol with the help of a band of kids. The children plan to trade Starbuck to the Cylons in return for their father, who is being held captive. However, Starbuck convinces them instead to raid the garrison and free their father.

As things go badly for the local Cylons, their leader, Specter, convinces Baltar to let him flee the planet, leaving Starbuck's ragtag, fugitive fleet of kids to take it over.

Specter: We have had our problems.
Baltar: Problems?
Specter: This planet is so wet, half our garrison is down with rust.

Notes: Yes, it's another crash-on-a-planet episode; it can be hard to keep them straight.

In fact, sometimes you can't keep them straight. You don't need to be a nitpicker to be surprised that the cover of Berkley Books' 1980 novelization of this episode features a painting of a marooned Apollo, not Starbuck. The novel also has quite a few differences from the televised episode (such as telepathic unicorns, for one), so it's a treat for *Galactica* fans. Often, I am disappointed when I read a movie or television show's novelization, only to find it's pretty much a line-by-line regurgitation of the production I've already seen. The *Galactica* novels have enough tantalizing differences and additions to make them well worth your time. They provide good background and really deepen your involvement in the storyline and characters. (A fine non-*Galactica* example of this is David Gerrold's novelization of the premiere episode of *Star Trek: The Next Generation*, "Encounter at Farpoint.") Search for them in your local used bookstore, or on Amazon, eBay, and other online markets.

In actor news, Bruce Glover, who portrays Megan, is the father of actor Crispin Glover. The Cylon garrison leader, Specter (a Lucifer-like Cylon), is played by Felix Silla, who was also in Twiki's suit in Glen Larson's other SF series, *Buck Rogers in the 25th Century*.

And, finally, make of this what you will: A young woman named Miri introduces Starbuck to her siblings, who make up a young rebel fighting force in the absence of their father, Megan. In "Miri," a first season episode of the original *Star Trek*, a girl by that name is James Kirk's connection to a band of young people running roughshod in the absence of adults.

Lesson learned: Never name your daughter Miri.

The Living Legend (Parts I and II)

Writer: Glen A. Larson. **Director:** Vince Edwards. **Airdates:** November 26, 1978 & December 3, 1978.

Apollo and Starbuck, while on patrol in their vipers, discover the battlestar *Pegasus*, thought to have been destroyed with the other battlestars in the Cylon ambush. They are met by *Pegasus* vipers, one of which is piloted by the Colonial warrior Sheba, daughter of the *Pegasus*' commander.

Sheba: You will maintain silence until we land aboard the battlestar *Pegasus*.
Apollo: *Pegasus*? That's just not possible.
Starbuck: Apollo—do you know whose ship that was?
Apollo: Cain, the greatest military commander who ever lived. He was my idol.
Sheba: Your idol will order you blasted out of the sky if you don't shut off your transmitters. In case you clowns don't know it, we are right in the middle of a quadrant controlled by Cylons.
Apollo [*spotting the* Pegasus *up ahead*]: Oh my lord, it isn't a dream, and we're not dead. It is the *Pegasus*.
Sheba [*bewildered*]: They won't shut up.

When the *Pegasus* joins up with the *Galactica*'s fleet, its leader, Commander Cain, urges Adama to join him in striking at the Cylons. Cain has something else he wants to pursue: his past relationship with a certain socialator named Cassiopeia.

Adama is more cautious about going after the Cylons, as the leader of a fleet of civilian ships must be. The fleet is short on fuel, so instead of attacking the Cylons on the planet Gamoray, as Cain desires, they agree to Adama's plant to raid nearby Cylon fuel tankers. But Cain sabotages the attack as a way of asserting his will, and Adama removes Cain from command of the *Pegasus*, commandeering its fuel for the fleet. The two battlestars' crews are at loggerheads until Baltar shows up with a Cylon attack. Cain, restored to his command, helps route the surprised Cylons, who were not expecting to see two battlestars.

With the Cylons seen off for the moment, Adama and Cain mend their relationship enough to attack Gamoray and get the needed fuel supplies. A commando team of Apollo, Starbuck, Sheba, and Bojay (another *Pegasus* warrior) land on Gamoray, along with medtech Cassiopeia, and destroy the Cylon command center. The vipers then attack Gamoray and the fleet loads up the fuel it needs.

Cain keeps pushing his luck, though, throwing his battlestar into the thick of the action. His ship suffers damage in one such attack, and the injured, including his daughter, Sheba, are taken to the *Galactica*. Cain then attacks two of Baltar's three basestars after Apollo and Starbuck knock out the Cylon ships' cannons, and in the ensuing battle, which results in the destruction of the two basestars, the *Galactica*'s fleet is unable to tell if the *Pegasus*, too, was destroyed. Sheba, Bojay, and some other *Pegasus* survivors now find themselves part of the *Galactica*'s crew.

Notes: The story of "The Living Legend," in which the *Galactica* discovers that it is not the only surviving battlestar after all and teams up with the *Pegasus* and her tough-as-nails leader Cain, not only makes up one of the best storylines in the classic *Battlestar Galactica*, but it was one of the best storylines in the reimagined *Galactica* a quarter century later.

In the Syfy version, the story plays out over many episodes, beginning with "Pegasus" (see chapter three). In both versions, Cain is more hardcore-military than Adama and pushes the *Galactica*'s leader to be more aggressive in attacking the Cylons. Though the original Cain, portrayed by legend Lloyd Bridges, was arrogant, he was not the fanatic that was the new Cain, portrayed by Michelle Forbes, who had dispatched her human civilian fleet of survivors in order to be better able to wage warfare.

In the Department of Vague Rumors and Wishful Thinking, fan sites have reported that Glen Larson planned to bring back Lloyd Bridges' Cain and the *Pegasus* in the never-filmed second season of *Battlestar Galactica*.

Fire in Space

Writers: Jim Carlson, Terrence McDonnell. **Director:** Chris Nyby, Jr. **Airdate:** December 17, 1978.

A kamikaze attack by Cylon raiders leaves the *Galactica* in flames, some crew members trapped, and Commander Adama in critical condition. Muffit finally earns his keep by bringing oxygen masks to the trapped crew, which includes Boxey, Boomer, and Athena. After a failed attempt to put out the flames by having vipers shoot Boronton at them, Starbuck and Apollo blow a hole in the hull of the battlestar to extinguish the fire, and Adama gets fixed up by the doc.

Boomer: Boxey, it looks like I mashed your mushies.

Notes: There are science fiction lies that might grate on people but that we accept in much of our SF entertainment. Sounds in space, for example. We know we wouldn't really be able to hear a viper or the *Enterprise* fly past us in space, because there is no sound in space. We let it go, accepting it as no more a violation of the rules of the universe than background music in a scene.

But there are some things that just go over the line. To quote the great *Friends* philosopher Joey Tribbiani: "You're so far past the line that you can't even see the line! The line is a *dot* to you!" And thus it is with this episode.

Fire.

In space.

Unless you believe there was a force field around the fires seen raging on the *Galactica*'s landing bay, which had been set alight by one of those kamikaze Cylons, or that some sort of liquid-ish material is shot out of vipers (how?) (and why doesn't it freeze in space?), then you have to smack your forehead at the scenes with the fire somehow burning in the airless realm of space.

Then there's the plot idea to blow open the hull to let out the air, thus extinguishing the flames. The writers act as if having oxygen masks is key to the survival of the humans stuck in the section that's about to have all of its air super-sucked into the frozen, airless void of space. But they would have needed to have had an extremely short-lived opening to space to prevent the humans from freezing or exploding or whatever happens to you from the lack of pressure. Neither is conducive to long life. They could have gotten away with this story device if a door on the side of the ship had been flipped open and slammed shut, but it's hard to believe an explosive blast in the hull was able to be sealed in time to prevent mass death.

And, as other writers have pointed out, the vipers that shoot Boronton, a water-like substance, through their modified laser cannons are in the realm of pure fantasy. In the 2.7 degrees Kelvin temperature of deep space, the liquid would freeze long before it got to the *Galactica*. Whatever miracle solution Boronton is supposed to be with a *really* low freezing point, it's unbelievable that that point is below 2.7 Kelvin. That might be the weakest example of writing in the whole script, because shooting ice at the raging fire would not be a totally useless thing to do and could have been written into the script. But they decided to go with liquid Boronton. In space.

The destruction on the *Galactica* is a mix of tired standard disaster footage mixed with some great special effects. (Watching the bridge fall apart after a raider rams it is impressive, in particular seeing the bridge's giant viewscreen shatter.)

If the bad writing doesn't bother you, then enjoy the episode. If it does bother you, then relax; the situation is not so bad, because "Fire in Space" is sandwiched between "The Living Legend" and "War of the Gods," two of the best stories of the entire series.

War of the Gods (Parts I and II)

Writer: Glen A. Larson. **Director:** Dan Haller. **Airdates:** January 14, 1979 & January 21, 1979.

A viper patrol including Bojay is confronted by zooming balls of light; eventually, a massive lightship appears and captures or otherwise takes in the warriors. Upon learning that the patrol has gone missing, Adama dispatches Apollo, Sheba, and Starbuck to search for them. The trio finds a planet and investigates a large impact crater on its surface, where they find the wreckage of a ship and one lone, unharmed, rather creepy survivor.

The survivor, the mysterious Count Iblis, tells them the ship was destroyed by some unnamed beings. Back among the fleet, Iblis has a powerful influence upon Sheba and others, and he lets them know that he is aware of their flight from their Cylon enemies.

Iblis takes credit for the sudden growth of food on the Agro ships. Faced by a curious Quorum of Twelve, he suggests they give him three tests. They oblige: First, bring them Baltar; second, plot a course to Earth; and the third, well, they haven't thought of a third.

Part I of "War of the Gods" ends with the arrival of Baltar, who has also witnessed the lightships and wants to see if the Galacticans can help him against them. Unmoved, the Quorum promptly throws Baltar in prison. Meanwhile, Iblis expands his influence throughout the humans' fleet. But Adama believes Iblis is just using mind tricks to impress people; he believes Iblis and the lightship beings are merely advanced beings, not gods or angels.

When the mysterious balls of light once again swarm around the *Galactica*, the vipers try to chase them, but Boomer is taken by the giant lightship. Apollo, Starbuck, and Sheba travel back to the planet for a look at the wreckage of the ship. When Iblis appears, he kills Apollo and is unhurt by Starbuck's laser weapon. Turning into a Satan-like creature, he promises to return.

On their way back to the *Galactica*, Starbuck and Sheba's shuttle—carrying Apollo's lifeless body—is intercepted by the lightship. Taken aboard, the beings resurrect Apollo, saying it was not his time to die. The three Galacticans then return to the fleet, complete with a "gift" from the lightship beings: Knowledge of Earth's location.

Starbuck: I don't know who you are, but whatever you want from me, you can have.
Lightship alien: We want nothing from you.
Starbuck: Then why are you doing all this?
Lightship alien: Because we fight a common foe—the forces of darkness and evil throughout the stars.

Notes: It should be no surprise that the writer of this two-part episode was Glen Larson, who was very much influenced by ancient-astronaut and other extraterrestrial mythology.

The lightship and the mysterious beings aboard it will reappear before the end of this series. In the episode "Experiment in Terra," also written by Larson, the beings play a role in helping guide the events of an Earth-like planet. That makes it tempting to consider what Larson might have done with the lightship storyline if the show had been picked up for a second season. The placement of these two episodes in the second half of the first season do lead one to guess that the lightship would have been back for more in Year Two.

Kirk Alyn plays the role of a Gemonese man; Alyn of course is forever famous for starring as Superman in early serials. The evil Count Iblis is portrayed by Patrick Macnee, who not only had starred in *The Avengers* but provides the voice for the Imperious Leader and narrates the opening of the series ("There are those who believe . . ."). In "War of the Gods," when Baltar meets Count Iblis, he says he recognizes the voice as that of the Imperious Leader. Was that an in-joke? Was it an indication that the Cylon empire was led by the Galactican equivalent of the devil? Probably only a second season of *Battlestar Galactica* would have made that clear.

The Man with Nine Lives

Writer: Don Bellisario. **Director:** Rod Holcomb. **Airdate:** January 28, 1979.

A con man named Chameleon is being pursued by a group of tough Borellian Nomen. Chameleon manages to get to the pleasure ship *Rising Star*, where he intrigues Starbuck with the possibility that he is the pilot's father. Boomer and Apollo intervene to prevent the Nomen from capturing Chameleon, who in turn secures a trip to the *Galactica* under Starbuck's protection; there, he will be genetically tested to see if he's related to Starbuck.

But the Nomen aren't put off their blood trail that easily. They join a pilot training program so they, too, can get onto the battlestar. Once there, they trick a crewmember so they can get access to the rest of the ship and continue their hunt for Chameleon.

The Borellians find their prey, but they are outwitted—and killed—by the old con man. When Chameleon learns from the blood tests that he is, indeed, Starbuck's father, he urges Cassiopeia to keep it secret from Starbuck; he doesn't want to lose the friendship he built up with the young pilot.

Starbuck: I can't wait until we get to that gambling deck. I got a new system that can't lose.
Apollo: Can't lose?
Starbuck: Nope.
Apollo: The gaming chancery on Pinius.
Starbuck: That's not fair.
Apollo: I didn't think so either—especially since I lost a secton's pay betting your last system.
Starbuck: Yeah, I—I know what went wrong.
Apollo: So do I! I lost a secton's pay.

Notes: Chameleon is portrayed by dancing and acting legend Fred Astaire. Though his role here is primarily acting with little dancing, it is the final time he dances on screen. The resolution of this storyline leaves open the possibility of Chameleon's return in a future season, presumably to explore more deeply the father-son relationship with Starbuck.

Murder on the Rising Star

Writers: Don Bellisario, James Carlson, Terrence McDonnell, Michael Sloan. **Director:** Rod Holcomb. **Airdate:** February 18, 1979.

Apollo and Boomer step in to act as legal defenders for their pal Starbuck after he is accused of murdering a rival following a game of Triad. Starbuck's weapon is matched to the killing, but he refuses a plea deal and seeks a trial.

His defense team uncovers a network of blackmail connected to Baltar (himself now a prisoner of the *Galactica*—see "War of the Gods"). Apollo and Boomer trick the real killer, Karibdis, into coming out of hiding and making sure Starbuck's tribunal hears the evidence.

Baltar: Think about it, Apollo. There's more than one prisoner on this barge who'd love to have Lieutenant Starbuck here. He won't live long enough to reach his cell!

Notes: Genre fans are likely to recognize Brock Peters, who portrays Solon in this episode. Peters' screen credits include two *Star Trek* movies (*The Voyage Home* and *The Undiscovered Country*, portraying Fleet Admiral Cartwright), *Deep Space Nine* (as the father of Benjamin Sisko), the classic dystopian film *Soylent Green* (as Hatcher), and he lent his voice to the public radio adaptation of *Star Wars* (as Darth Vader).

This episode also sees the return of Triad, the sorta-basketball court game that first showed up a few episodes earlier. "To lure women [viewers], a basketballish game called Triad was invented," Tom Shales wrote in 1979. "It is played by handsome young men wearing slingshots for shorts." The reimagined *Galactica* might have gone further with its viper pilots showering and dressing in the locker room, but the original Triad scenes were a 1970s way to watch fit young men wearing little more than helmets, padded underwear, and harness vests right out of a gay party-gear store. For what it's worth, the reimagined series renamed the Pyramid card game as Triad, and it introduced a basketball-baseball-football mashup sport called Pyramid, as played by Samuel Anders.

Greetings from Earth

Writer: Glen A. Larson. **Director:** Ahmer Lateaf. **Airdate:** February 25, 1979.

Cruising through space with its occupants in deep sleep, a small ship is intercepted by Apollo and Starbuck and brought aboard the *Galactica*. Inside the ship are four children and two adults, a man and woman. Fleeing their home planet because of the evil Eastern Alliance, they were heading toward the planet Paradeen.

The humans of the fleet are excited about references to "Terra," another name for Earth, and the Quorum of Twelve badgers Adama into letting them control the situation. The small ship and its occupants are returned to space on their original course, and Apollo, Starbuck, and Cassiopeia go along to learn what they can. On the planet Paradeen, they find the home that has been prepared for the ship's inhabitants; unfortunately, they also find two bumbling, comedic robots named Hector and Vector.

Starbuck goes off to investigate a deserted nearby city and becomes trapped there for no other reason than to add some danger to the plot and pad the running time. Meanwhile, an Eastern Alliance ship arrives, having tracked the vipers that accompanied the sleeper ship, and they take some of the family hostage. With the help—what's in a word?—of the robots and the kids, Starbuck is found and rescued, and he and Apollo manage to free the family from the Eastern Alliance troops, who are then brought to the *Galactica*.

Vector: You all right?
Apollo: I'm just trying to conserve air. You don't know how lucky you are.
Vector: Yeah, well, I may not suffocate, but I could rust myself to death. Or we may all get lost down here. These chambers go on forever and ever and ever!
Apollo: You're a lot of laughs, Vector.

Notes: The bait-and-switch of having a planet get up the Galacticans' hopes because it is named Terra—which they know to be another name for the legendary planet Earth—is echoed in the SyFy *Battlestar Galactica*. Toward the end of the series, in "Revelations" and "Sometimes a Great Notion," they discover Earth, only to find it a burned-out hulk that had been populated by a previous iteration of humanoid Cylons. They go on to find another planet in the final episode, which turns out to be the planet Earth we all know and love and defile. But a print ad for 1979's "Greetings from Earth" is headlined "The *Galactica* encounters people from planet Earth!" even though, of course, the people were pointedly *not* from planet Earth.

"Greetings from Earth" originally aired as a two-hour special episode. Three of Glen Larson's children and Lorne Greene's daughters guest star in it. Robots Hector and Vector, as annoying as they are to watch, were portrayed by two aging Vaudeville performers, Bobby Van and Ray Bolger. Knowing that might make watching their painful slapstick routines a bit more bearable, but they bring the proceedings dangerously close to making this the "Spock's Brain" of *Battlestar Galactica*.

Baltar's Escape

Writer: Don Bellisario. **Director:** Rick Kolbe. **Airdate:** March 11, 1979.

The Quorum of Twelve reasserts its authority over the fleet, leaving Adama feeling pressured to step down. The civilian government is particularly interested in negotiating with the newly discovered Eastern Alliance.

Meanwhile, Baltar takes the opportunity to escape from the prison barge with the help of the Borellian Nomen (remember them from "The Man With Nine Lives"?). Along with the Eastern Alliance officers, they head to the *Galactica* in an attempt to take it over. When they arrive, the Colonial warriors have been told to stay in their barracks by the Quorum, whose members await the shuttle's arrival.

With Baltar trying to get Adama to return his Cylon raider to him, the Galacticans buy some time so Dr. Wilker can tinker with the robotic Cylon centurions (originally captured along with Baltar) to help them thwart Baltar's escape.

Baltar: Is it a bargain?
Maga, a Nomen: Your record to date does not exactly inspire confidence.
Baltar: I, uh—I had incompetent followers.
Maga: We do not follow, Baltar.

Notes: This is a reprise of the military-civilian clash and commentary from the premiere "Saga of a Star World" episode. In both cases, the civilian leadership in the form of the Quorum tries to sideline the military leadership in the form of Commander Adama. Also in both cases, the Quorum is shown to be dangerously ignorant and eager to have peace at all costs, leading to disaster or near disaster.

John Kenneth Muir, in his 1998 book *An Analytical Guide to Television's Battlestar Galactica* (recommended for an in-depth, intelligent, and at times controversial look at the series), makes more of this military–Quorum conflict. A bit too much, in my view, especially his claim that Adama's rule is fascist. Authoritarian, maybe, but "fascism" is a specific type of authoritarian rule that doesn't fit the military rule that Adama conducts. For one thing, there is no cult of personality around Adama, and the nonmilitary part of the fleet appears to be anything but regimented. But that terminological hyperbole aside, Muir is correct in pointing out the clear ideological through-line in the series about the incompetence of nonmilitary leadership, at least in times of existential threat, which is what the fleet faces. Others might argue that moments of existential threat are exactly those times when the military is called upon to exercise supreme authority—not forever, but until the crisis passes.

In the SyFy *Battlestar Galactica* series, the military (Commander and later Admiral William Adama) and civilian leadership (President Laura Roslin) have a rivalry that is much more virulent and raw, and it runs through much of the series, though it's particularly strong in the first couple years, with mutinies and marshal law. Adama and Roslin eventually achieve a working peace. In fact, Adama and Roslin literally end up in bed together. In the more chaste 1979 episode "Baltar's Escape," Adama ends up arm-in-arm with Siress Tinia of the Quorum.

Experiment in Terra

Writer: Glen A. Larson. **Director:** Rod Holcomb. **Airdate:** March 18, 1979.

Apollo and Starbuck follow the Eastern Alliance spaceship that has escaped from the *Galactica*'s fleet and headed back to Terra. Their mission is interrupted by the lightship, whose crew wants the Galacticans' help stopping an apocalyptic war centered on Terra. Apollo, dressed in monochrome white, is made to appear like Charlie Watts, an astronaut from Terra, and is sent down to that planet to find a way to stop the war.

On Terra, he meets Charlie's girlfriend Brenda, who reports him to the Western Nationalists (the enemy of the Eastern Alliance), and Apollo/Charlie is arrested. Starbuck lands on the planet and is drawn into the lightship's plans for Apollo. The Western Nationalist president is trying to strike a deal with the Eastern Alliance to stop the war, but amid great discord within the government, the war flares up and only the *Galactica* can stop the destruction of both sides. As a parting gift, the lightship crew inform Apollo that the *Galactica* is on the right course for finding Earth.

General: The Eastern Alliance has launched—
Terran president: Launched what?
General: Everything they have.
President: Er, that's . . . that's not possible. I—I have this treaty. They've signed it!
Maxwell: Well, frame it—but hurry.

Notes: The role of Brenda is played by Melody Anderson, who would hit the bigtime on the big screen as Dale Arden in Dino De Laurentiis' 1980 camp film version of *Flash Gordon*.

Also, some sources say that the role played by Apollo here was originally written for Dirk Benedict's Starbuck, but was given to Apollo over concerns that Benedict was being given more choice jobs than Richard Hatch.

And for a non-*Galactica*-based military-civilian naiveté conflict, see this episode. Its recurrence does underscore what was likely the view of Larson and others who argue for strong defenses. Adama does not want to wage war; he is not conquering any of the planets the fleet encounters. Being strong enough to fight off the Cylons if they attack means he can protect the human fleet; it does not mean he wants to commit genocide against the Cylon empire. That would be saved for the reimagined *Galactica*, which clearly had its sympathies on the other side of the topic from the Larson version of the show—that might say more about how its writers view people who believe in a strong defense than it says about people who believe in a strong defense.

Take the Celestra

Writer: Jim Carlson, Terrence McDonnell. **Director:** Dan Haller. **Airdate:** April 1, 1979.

Commander Kronus of the civilian fleet vessel *Celestra* is honored with the Distinguished Service Medallion during an impressive ceremony; he is also given overall command of three of the "industry" ships in the fleet. But things go downhill for him after that. A power struggle on the *Celestra* draws in Starbuck and Apollo, who come aboard in an attempt to resurrect Starbuck's relationship with a former girlfriend, Aurora. Charka, the *Celestra*'s brutal second-in-command who thought incorrectly that he would get command after Kronus' ceremony, leads a revolt against the tough Kronus, who must put his life on the line to save the ship before Charka and his compatriots can be brought to justice.

Cassiopeia: A relationship based on possession isn't for me. I—I don't want to own Starbuck, or anyone else, for that matter. If what he and I have together is worth anything at all, we're gonna—we're gonna survive all this.

Notes: Starbuck, despite being seriously attached to Cassiopeia (and coming into conflict with the legendary Commander Cain over her), and apparently having left Athena behind, is still on the prowl for another woman. Nice guy.

We get some background information in this episode about how ships in the fleet stay together, apparently through the use of a homing beacon. It plays a role here when the *Celestra* goes "dark" to avoid being located during the mutiny.

Paul Fix, who portrays Kronus, also served aboard the U.S.S. *Enterprise* for the second *Star Trek* pilot as Dr. Piper. He was replaced by DeForest Kelley's Dr. Leonard McCoy, who became the immortal Bones.

The Hand of God

Writer: Glen A. Larson. **Director:** Rod Holcomb. **Airdate:** April 29, 1979.

Apollo shows his friends Sheba, Starbuck, and Cassiopeia his escape, or maybe it's his man cave: an observatory on the *Galactica* where he goes to contemplate and observe the universe.

Meanwhile, the *Galactica* spots a Cylon basestar and Adama uncharacteristically decides to risk a surprise attack on the ship. He sends Apollo and Starbuck on a mission in Baltar's captured Cylon raider to infiltrate the basestar, incapacitate its scanners, and prepare the way for the battlestar's assault. But in a firefight with Cylons on the basestar, Apollo loses the transmitter that would alert the fleet that their raider was friendly. Only some last minute fancy flying saves their lives after the successful attack on the basestar.

The price Adama must pay for the information that enabled the attack is to free Baltar, stranding him on a habitable planet.

Sheba: Where in heaven's name are we?
Apollo: As high as you can get on the *Galactica*. We're directly over the main thrusters. It's a great spot to get away from everyone to think.

Starbuck: A cozy little place like this could be used for more than just thinking.

Notes: Larson is back as the writer for this final episode of the series, and he revisits the theme of Earth, though only in the framing scenes. The reception of a video of the NASA moon landing tells us that in the series' reality, Earth does exist as we know it, and that if (in the second or third season?) the fleet arrives there, it would be in our present or in our future.

Unfortunately, bad decisions by ABC and an abysmal budget would see that most of that sentence comes true in *Galactica 1980*. After that, when *Battlestar Galactica* would again be resurrected, it would not be a continuation but a complete reimagining.

CHAPTER TWO

Galactica 1980

This is admittedly for completists only. I can't very well include episode guides here to the original and the reimagined *Battlestar Galactica* without including this quirky short-lived version, no matter how far it strayed from what came before and what came after in terms of presentation, storylines, and quality. Well, it might also be of interest to those of us who occasionally want to wallow in painful childhood memories.

Galactica 1980 is the infamous bastard child of the *Galactica* canon. I call it a "bastard" not to be crude but to be fairly accurate; it is a child disowned by even its father. Shortly after ABC canceled *Battlestar Galactica*, the network apparently realized it had let go of something of value and announced it was bringing back the ragtag fleet as a TV movie. Naturally, it wanted to do it on the cheap. Instead of the grand space opera of the original series, the 1980 version would mostly take place on Earth, with only a few returning characters and the addition or recasting of a few more. Gone completely were the theological mysteries, the unexplained phenomena, and the sense of thousands of years of exciting history behind the storyline; all of that was replaced with a sort of *Incredible Hulk* with vipers, in which Bill Bixby's character is substituted by a couple of Colonial warriors and a human sidekick, and supplemented with a bunch of annoying Colonial kids.

Still, network wisdom being what it is, plans for a TV movie morphed into a weekly series.

Predictably, this poor-man's *Galactica* was panned by reviewers. Author Isaac Asimov, who had been mentioned as a science advisor to a second year of *Battlestar Galactica* that never happened, must have been thanking his lucky stars he didn't sign up for this turkey. Author John Kenneth Muir, in *An Analytical Guide to Television's Battlestar Galactica*, writes that the revamped series "is not a 'guilty pleasure.' There is nothing remotely pleasurable about the series at all. It is like watching a train wreck or a plane crash."

Perhaps *Starlog*'s editor, Howard Zimmerman, got to the core of it when he wrote a harsh editorial after the *Galactica 1980* premiere. Amid a short essay of overall opprobrium, he asked why, if the Galacticans can now travel through time, they didn't just go all the way back to before the Cylons destroyed the Twelve Colonies and create a better result? "Why don't they use Doctor Z's time machine to change the course of their previous war with the Cylons? Couldn't they go back and warn the still-intact Colonial fleet of the coming treachery and set a trap for the evil Cylons?"

Zimmerman had other criticisms of the time travel abuse in the storytelling (more on that in the episode guide below), but once you've revealed a fundamental flaw in the series basis, why go on? If Adama and his crew have the ability to completely change their situation, why don't they? There can be reasons, but tell us the reasons, even if they're paper-thin. Instead, the show continued as if the audience would never wonder about that; however, sooner or later even the young ones would, because the early plan was to have the show be a series of visits to different time periods in Earth's past. It revealed that *Galactica 1980*, just like far too often in the original series, was being written by people who didn't understand the tropes they were playing with and seemingly wasn't being story-edited by anyone who cared about the show's integrity.

And hats off to the Wikipedia contributor who wrote, "The premise of setting the series 30 years after the original series created a plot hole in that the original series ended with a video transmission being picked up by the *Galactica* from the Apollo moon landing, meaning that the original series would have to have taken place sometime after 1969 by Earth's calendar. A thirty-year journey would mean that the Colonial fleet could not have possibly reached Earth until the turn of the 21st century rather than in 1980."

And that's just the show's problems with time and time travel. The budget restrictions clearly hurt the quality of the presentation. The majority of the episodes were far worse than the worst episode of the original *Battlestar* series. A band of annoying 1970s-era TV kids; baseball; evil corporations; Galacticans as farmers. Grand space opera this was not.

In short, it was a show that retained and expanded upon every shortcoming of the original series but kept none of its strengths.

THE BLAME GAME

The network caused arguably most of the problems. Just as we saw how it had rushed the original series into production and messed with the premise to its detriment, ABC rushed *Galactica 1980* into an even quicker series run, and gave it an early evening airtime that saddled it with being a milquetoast child-friendly series. The result was disaster carried out in front of millions of Americans.

Robyn Douglass, who portrayed Jamie on *Galactica 1980*, said she was cast in the series without ever seeing a script or even knowing what the show was; she only found out later from her agent that she got the job and it was for *Battlestar Galacti-*

ca. Only, of course, it was a different *Battlestar Galactica*.

In her charming and candid 2020 audio CD *Messages for the Future: The Galactica 1980 Memoirs*, Douglass described the various Galactican uniforms she was given to wear for the first episode: "One of the times I was in wardrobe, it had Anne Lockhart's name in the uniform I was going to put on. They had to change . . . the length of it. I thought, 'Oh, how odd, why aren't all these people that were on the original show back on our show?' I don't think anyone wanted to tell me, but I thought 'Wow, I'm in Anne Lockhart's costume. I hope this is okay with her.'"

In *Starlog* 34 (May 1980), Douglass told interviewer Karen E. Willson about the very rushed schedule for the series. "I did the first scene with safety pins in my back, and the guys—Kent [McCord] and Barry [Van Dyke]—their pants were ripping out at the seams. It's hard. Kent was cast Friday night and started shooting Saturday."

Yes. It was hard for the audience, too. As a young viewer who had loved the original series, I watched each episode. I had eagerly awaited the premiere of the "Galactica Discovers Earth" TV movie. But it is very strange when a fan of a show is watching a clearly incompetently assembled zombie version of a beloved series, and the fan is silently mentally urging the show not to fail. Yes, as a 12-year-old I knew this show was not just bad but was insultingly so—it was thrown out onto a national network TV schedule as if science fiction viewers would accept anything.

And we almost did.

I watched every episode. In modern parlance, I should write that I hate-watched every episode. Every minute of every episode I was prepared to forgive the preceding nonsense; I kept hoping it would start to get better, that the silliness would stop, that the previous series' space opera drama would return. And instead I watched *The Bad News Bears from Caprica*.

Oh, and they had flying motorcycles. Because *CHiPs*.

UNLOVED, UNMOURNED

Creator Glen Larson later agreed the series was terrible. The stars were disappointed in it (though Kent McCord would redeem himself in science fiction circles two decades later with his recurring role as John Crichton's father in the excellent series *Farscape*). Fans tried to forget about it. Later attempts to revive *Galactica* in film or television form all ignored it, and it now holds as much relevance to the *Galactica* canon as Luke-Jabba slash fan fiction has to the *Star Wars* films.

In total, *Galactica 1980* lasted for only six episodes for a total of 10 hours of pain inflicted upon the SF community. It was mourned by almost no one, and to this day upon recitations of the curses heaped on the show, it is almost unheard of for defenders to speak up in social media. It did not get a long-lasting memorial of fans as did *Star Trek* or *Space: 1999* or the original *Battlestar Galactica*. Instead, *Galactica 1980* was treated like the ancient Romans dealt with a particularly hated tyrant or criminal, being dragged through the streets of the city and thrown into the Tiber.

So, with that loving introduction, let us dive into the dumpster fire that was *Galactica 1980.*

Creator and Executive Producer: Glen A. Larson
Broadcaster: ABC
Studio: Universal; Glen A Larson Productions
Producers: David O'Connell, Frank Lupo, and Jeff Freilich
Art Director: Sherman Loudermilk
Composers: Stu Phillips and John Andrew Tartaglia
Special Effects Unit: Universal Hartland
Special Effects Supervisors: David M. Garber and Wayne Smith
Story Editors: Chris Bunch, Allan Cole, and Robert W. Gilmer
Troy: Kent McCord
Dillon: Barry Van Dyke
Jamie Hamilton: Robyn Douglass
Adama: Lorne Greene
Dr. Zee: Robbie Rise ("Galactica Discovers Earth"), James Patrick Stuart (rest of series)
Boomer: Herb Jefferson Jr.

Galactica Discovers Earth (Parts I, II and III)

Writer: Glen A. Larson. **Director:** Sidney Hayers. **Airdates:** January 27, 1980, February 3, 1980, & February 10, 1980.

Three decades after the destruction of the Twelve Colonies (unless you understand time and space better than this spinoff's writers and producers), the *Galactica* and its fleet finally arrive at Earth. Unfortunately, it's the Earth of 1980, bad hairstyles and all. Worst of all is that the Cylons still dog the fleet, so Commander Adama leads the fleet off in another direction to prevent the Cylons from discovering the unprepared humans.

Earth has the galactic equivalent of third-world technological capabilities, so the Galacticans come up with a plan to help nudge the planet's scientists to develop more quickly so they can help the Colonial survivors fend off the Cylons.

Two Colonial Warriors head up the plan to reach out to Earth scientists. They are Troy, the adopted son of the missing Apollo who used to be known as Boxey, and his friend Dillon. They are befriended by an American journalist named Jamie, and together the three of them end up chasing a member of the fleet's ruling council, Xaviar. Xaviar has used Dr. Zee's time machine (don't get me started) to go back to Nazi Germany to try to jump start technological advance by helping the Nazis.

They manage to stop Xaviar from boosting the Nazis' V-2 rocket efforts (even though in real life the Nazis *did* successfully develop the V-2 and launched 3,000 of them at Allied cities and both the United States and the Soviets used captured Nazi V-2 technology to build their own such missiles after the war, but nevermind), but the renegade Galactican escapes to the 17th century.

Dillon: You must have us confused with somebody else. My name's not Turkey, and neither is his.

Notes: As noted in the introduction to this chapter, this series kicks off with numerous fundamental problems that never get fixed.

Oh, let's get just a bit into the time travel mess, because it's so morally godawful here. Back in Nazi-era 1944, Troy and Dillon—who are not supposed to interfere—nonetheless do so when they see Nazis loading some Jews into a train for transport to you-know-where and you-know-what. They interfere by rescuing one young Jewish girl. They're literally advanced spacemen; why didn't they rescue the entire damned train of Jewish prisoners? Or, again, as time travelers, you know, why not travel back enough to prevent the Holocaust altogether, something that Jamie, said to be an expert on the time period, would have known about? It's hard to believe the Colonial Warriors, after seeing almost their entire civilization wiped out by Cylons, would have had any compunction about a laser blast into a pre-World War II Adolf Hitler. But really changing history in any sensible or moral way would have necessitated a higher budget for the altered-1980 scenes for the rest of the series, so let's just skip that.

The Dr. Zee character (portrayed first by Robbie Rist and then by James Patrick Stuart) was reportedly introduced to help teach the anticipated young audience lessons from a "peer." Well, as a viewer who was right in between the ages of Rist and Stuart, I hated the character then, and still do. The problem wasn't the actors; it was the very idea of the character; someone who the actual wise leader of the humans—Adama—had to consult as if he were an intern instead of the man who had saved the remnants of the Twelve Colonies. It's a sad sign of how little network decision makers understand their audiences. My heroes as a young child weren't other young children; young children are, well, stupid, and I knew it then. My TV heroes were Alan Alda's Hawkeye Pierce, Gary Sandy's Andy Travis, Mary Tyler Moore's Mary Richards, and Richard Hatch's Apollo. The only thing that makes the Dr. Zee character interesting and even slightly palatable is what we learn about him in the final episode of this series (see below).

Ohwaitohwaitohwait: This time travel thingie . . . : Why not just go back to shortly before Xaviar departed and confine him to quarters or prison? That would be a really budget-friendly resolution.

Or they could hide from the Cylons by taking the entire fleet back in time a couple centuries.

But they wanted the drama of historical adventure; I can understand that. But why Nazi Germany? Why not travel back to Industrial Revolution-era England? 1960s America? Wilhelmine Germany? Or any other time in history when technology was growing by leaps and bounds? Keep the Roman Empire from falling? Stop the Chinese Empire from its periodic times of troubles? Or wait, have maximum effect and go back to the ancient "Egyptians or the Toltecs or the Mayans"—remember them?—and really super-charge the hell out of human technology?

(Reviewer's head explodes.)

The Super Scouts (Parts I and II)

Writer: Glen A. Larson. **Director:** Vince Edwards, Sigmund Neufeld, Jr. **Airdate:** March 16, 1980 and March 23, 1980.

Dr. Zee tells Adama that there's a problem with the children: They need to get out of space and onto terra firma or else. It will have to be done secretly to avoid a military conflagration on Earth, because of the backwardness of people there and the prevalence of lawn darts or something.

There's a surprisingly small number of children in the *Galactica* fleet, at least judging by the 137 of them who are on the freighter *Delphi* that is used as a school ship. Troy and Dillon are teaching some of the kids on the ship when it is attacked by Cylons. The two warriors manage to get all of the kids off the ship before its destruction, but they themselves end up with 12 students on a shuttle that is forced to land on Earth to avoid the Cylons. There, they pose as scoutmasters and the kids as their scout troop.

Investigating reports of a UFO, Air Force Colonel Sydell begins to look into the case of these extraterrestrial visitors. The kids have a more immediate problem, though: despite exhibiting some special powers (such as being able to jump really high), they are becoming sick from water polluted by a chemical factory run by John Stockton.

Dr. Zee comes to Earth to get the kids all fixed up; while there, he gives Stockton a vision of what the end results will be of his pollution' and corruptin': the death of his own son. In true after-school-special form, he promises to be a better business person in the future.

Stockton: How do you do, Your Honor? Um, Majesty . . . Eminence. Eminence. Um, I only work there. I'm not really responsible.
Adama: We are all responsible.
Stockton: We are?
Adama: Yes. We have lips so that we may speak. We have eyes so that we may see. Does it not follow, ironically, that there must be some purpose for the brain?

Notes: If one child on the original series was good, a dozen in the sequel series will be 12 times as good, right? Turns out the answer is "no."

Here's another negative about this episode: The *Delphi*'s troubles begin when it has engine trouble and, er, stops dead in space. Now, everyone who wasn't sleeping in junior high science class knows that Newton's First Law of Motion declares that a body in motion at a constant velocity will remain in motion in the same direction unless acted upon by an outside force. The *Delphi* is in space, so there is no outside force to act against it—no wind resistance, no bugs piling up on the ship's forward windshield deflector, no friction of tires against the road. Therefore, the engines are not needed to keep it going, only for accelerating it up to the maximum desired speed. If their engines cut out, the ship would keep going at its last attained speed, no engines or fuel needed. It would keep going until an "outside force" acted upon it, such as thrusters on the front of the ship firing or the freighter running into a star.

The reason this is an unforgivable error is because it is so basic and so unnecessary (and on a show with an educational content mandate, no less!). It would have taken the writer less than five minutes to come up with another, better, non-scientifically impossible reason for the ship to stop. Not even necessarily a good reason, just not the terrible one they used. Here—I'll try it. Off the top of my head, without pre-planning, I'll come up with several alternative reasons (go ahead and time me). The ship stops intentionally, because there's some unnamed engine trouble that requires a halt, shutdown, and restart. Or the captain notices some problem on the ship and the only way to track down the problem is to stop the ship and do a full inspection. Or the forward thrusters misfire, causing the ship to slow to a stop. See, they don't even need to explain what the unnamed problem or trouble is; they just don't have to explain that it is something that's impossible according to the laws of physics. Easy peasy.

Of note to trivia fans is that *Galactica 1980* is replaced with *Battlestar Galactica* as the series title at the beginning of this episode and will continue through the rest of the series. No one is fooled.

Of note to *Galactica 1980* sufferers: Cheer up! You're now officially 50 percent through this 10-hour-long series.

Spaceball

Writer: Frank Lupo, Jeff Freilich, and Glen A. Larson. **Director:** Barry Crane. **Airdate:** March 30, 1980.

Dillon and Troy learn that Xaviar (played by Richard Lynch in the pilot movie and here by Jeremy Brett) has returned to 1980. A Colonial warrior named Nash gives them a ship and instructions on how and when to capture Xaviar. But Nash actually is Xaviar, just disguised as Nash so he can get rid of Dillon and Troy for a while.

Jamie is tasked with babysitting the Galactican kids and decides to park them at a baseball camp that she's writing about. Nash shows up and claims he's been tasked with watching over the children, but his real plan is to hold the kids hostage. Nash/

Xaviar contacts Adama and tells him he'll release his prisoners if he will be left alone on Earth.

The Galactican kids are drafted to play for the Polecats, the team of the down-on-its luck Casey's Baseball Park, which is a camp for underprivileged children. But they are forced to try to lose the game so they don't show off their extraterrestrial strength, irritating the head of Casey's Baseball Park in the process, because he needs to win the game to ensure future funding for his camp. However, Jamie changes her instructions to the kids when she realizes that if they do win the game, they will be surrounded by people congratulating them, and thus they'll thwart Xaviar's plan to kidnap them.

Troy and Dillon manage to arrive in time to scare off Xaviar, who escapes.

Jamie: Now listen, I want you to promise me you won't do anything to betray who you really are.
Wellington: Which means we have to perform as complete muscular disasters. . .
Jamie: That's right. Now go out there and lose.

Notes: In 1976, Paramount released *The Bad News Bears*, a movie starring Walter Matthau and Tatum O'Neal, he as the alcoholic coach of a misfit little league team (the aforementioned Bears) and she as his star pitcher. The movie became a hit, earning more than four times its budget at the box office. It spawned the 1977 sequel *The Bad News Bears in Breaking Training*, 1978's *The Bad News Bears Go to Japan*, a two-season CBS series from 1979–1980, and much later a 2005 remake.

The best excuse for making the urchins from the *Galactica*'s fleet a baseball team is that the writers were consciously trying to rip off the success of the *Bears* movies. The worst excuse would be that they actually thought it was a smart thing to do. This episode cemented the positioning of this series as a children's program, one that would grate on the teeth of adults looking for good drama or even decent melodrama.

Also, Adama's log entry tells us that the *Galactica* is leading the Cylons away from the planet Earth. However, a stranded viper is said to be within the gravity well of Earth but will eventually circle around to within the *Galactica*'s reach. So which is it? The *Galactica* is far away or it's just beyond Earth and the Moon?

The Night the Cylons Landed (Parts I and II)

Writer: Glen A. Larson. **Director:** Sigmund Neufeld, Jr., Barry Crane. **Airdate:** April 13, 1980 and April 20, 1980.

Troy and Dillon head out to meet what they think is a ship from the *Galactica*'s fleet that has crashed on Earth, but it turns out to be a Cylon. They must track down two Cylons and prevent them from using a local radio tower to transmit a message to the Cylon forces in space. The human-like Cylon, Andromus, and the

Centurion, unimaginatively named Centuri, are picked up by a couple traveling to a Halloween party.

The two Colonial warriors fly across the country to reach the crash site, and they prevent an airplane hijacking in the process. But they are dogged after they reach the East Coast by police who think they are drug runners. They didn't hijack a plane, but they did steal a police car, which they ditch in the water to elude pursuing police.

Troy and Dillon arrive too late at the crash site to catch the Cylons, but they track them down to the roof of the radio station. A firefight ensues and the Cylons are shot, dropping into a trash bin far below.

Centuri: You were speaking of danger.
Arnie: Danger? No, I, uh . . . [*looks at Norman*]. Did you say anything about danger?
Norman: No. Uh, well, I, uh, I said that it was dangerous—I mean the meatballs. I mean, you take one, and, uh, you have to take another. And they just grow on you.

Notes: Such a pickle the Galacticans get themselves into. If only they had a time machine or something to go back and avoid it altogether.

As has been noted in many other places, this is the first introduction of a human-like Cylon, a concept that would be a major part of (well, perhaps the whole point of) the reimagined *Battlestar Galactica* on Syfy.

As for the Cylon plan to use a radio transmitter to send a signal to their compatriots in space, again, just how far away is the Cylon force? If Adama didn't lead his fleet far away, then he's criminally negligent. Radio waves travel at the speed of light, which would mean their message would shoot out into space at about 186,000 miles per second (or about 300,000 kilometers per second).

Wolfman Jack, a radio personality who was quite famous at the time, appears as himself in this episode. The Wolfman had also played himself in George Lucas's seminal film *American Graffiti*, and he profited handsomely over the years due to that film's enduring success.

A couple compliments: This show was a bit of a high point for the series, even acknowledging the low barrier to the competition. There was some actual laugh-out-loud humor in it, and it was nice to see the kids largely ditched for the story. And kudos to the special effects team for the new, advanced Cylon fighter ship in this episode. We don't get a lot of new special effects in *Galactica 1980*, but when we do, they're welcome. Now if only the Cylons in the new fighter didn't have English-language readouts on their instruments.

And, finally: Larson reportedly had a lot of trouble with ABC censors over this episode, including the censor—er, network standards and practices executive—thinking that "meatballs" was some slang sexual innuendo. In retaliation, Larson added numerous additional meatball references into the two-part episode. I think it's clear my overall negative attitude toward *Galactica 1980* and its writing and production; but I've got to love Larson for that.

Space Croppers

Writer: Robert L. McCullough. **Director:** Daniel Haller. **Airdate:** April 27, 1980.

Upon orders of the Cylon Imperious Leader, a Cylon attack wipes out two of the fleet's agricultural ships, forcing Adama to look toward Earth as a source of food, because it's nearby and because the show's budget won't let them build new ships or visit other planets. Naturally, Troy and Dillon are dispatched to make it happen. They team up with a struggling Latino farmer, Alonzo, whose crops are being hurt by a nearby white farmer, Steadman. To overcome Steadman's actions, the Galacticans apply some fast-grow techniques.

Despite various efforts by Steadman to make Alonzo fail and to get the Galacticans to abandon him, his efforts are thwarted. When he steals Alonzo's water supply, Dr. Zee makes it rain. When he convinces Dillon to ride a wild horse (named Satan, because subtlety is so 1979), the Colonial warrior is able to subdue the animal.

After Steadman observes some of the Galacticans' extraterrestrial technological feats in action, he fails to get members of the local farmer's association—of which he is the head—to intervene. He also tries and fails to get the local law enforcement to intervene.

Alonzo's crops are saved, and he is joined by the first band of permanent Galactican colonists.

Imperious Leader: I'm growing impatient waiting for the Galactican fleet to lead us to the last outpost of humanity. Launch a full-scale attack on their agricultural ships. We must destroy their food supply, thereby forcing them to lead us to Earth.

Notes: A month ago, the fleet's school ship was destroyed; now two agro ships are blown up.

I'll admit, when I was going back over these old programs and I saw the wild horse-riding incident, which seemed so out of place to me, my first thought was that they were trying to ride the coattails of *Urban Cowboy*, in which John Travolta's Bud Davis rides a mechanical bull. That set off a fad of mechanical bull riding in bars that lasted for years. Might even still be going on in isolated Southern locales. So was *Galactica* doing another *Bad News Bears*-type homage? Turns out—nope; *Urban Cowboy* was released about five weeks after this episode aired.

Dennis Haysbert provides the voice of the Imperious Leader in this episode, instead of the original series' Patrick Macnee. Then again, we've been led at various times to think that a succession of Imperious Leaders takes place, so it's not necessarily just a cheap budget cut move. But probably so.

The Return of Starbuck

Writer: Glen A. Larson. **Director:** Ron Satlof. **Airdate:** May 4, 1980.

Dr. Zee tells Adama that he has been having strange dreams. Teenage boys being what they are, Adama probably wants to avoid this conversation at all costs, but when Dr. Zee says it involves a Colonial warrior named Starbuck, Adama's interest perks up. He asks Dr. Zee to tell him about the dream.

About 10 years earlier, Starbuck and Boomer get into a battle with Cylons, and Starbuck's viper is hit and crashlands on a nearby planet, as does one of the Cylon raiders. Boomer pleads with Adama to send a rescue party to get Starbuck, but Adama says the fleet is so desperate to escape the Cylons' relentless pursuit that it can't stop, even for someone they all loved.

Starbuck survives the crash landing on what turns out to be a wasteland planet, the type of studio backlot place you'd expect to find Captain Kirk battling a Gorn. Starbuck promptly names the planet after himself, and sets out to investigate the crashed Cylon craft. The Cylons inside appear to be inoperative, and Starbuck uses parts of the ship to build a shelter for himself. He uses parts of the three Cylons to build and activate one complete Cylon, whom he dubs Cy. He and Cy spend lots of time talking to each other and evolving from enemies to frenemies to friends, until one day the Cylon ventures out and comes back carrying a woman. The woman, Angela, is also pregnant, and she tells Starbuck the child is his spiritual offspring, which is just what every experienced Casanova most dreads hearing. But she's not planning to stick around and collect child support; she has Starbuck and Cy build an escape ship for her and the child, which they do out of the wreckage of their ships, and Angela and the child blast off into space.

Then a trio of Cylon centurions lands. They come to the site of Starbuck's shelter, but Cy destroys two of them and Starbuck shoots the third. Unfortunately, Cy is hit and effectively "killed" in the process. Starbuck is left marooned on the planet.

Back on the *Galactica*, Adama tells Dr. Zee that the events in his dream were real, and that the "spiritual child" of Starbuck and Angela is none other than Dr. Zee himself.

Starbuck: Cy, this isn't funny. This is a living, breathing human being.
Cy: Yes. I feel I have already compromised everything I believe in. What's helping one more human going to matter more or less?
Starbuck: Cy, this is more than a woman.
Cy: I'm sorry if you are displeased. There wasn't much of a selection.
Starbuck: Cy, this woman is with child.
Cy: Child?
Starbuck: Small human. She's going to bear another human life.
Cy: I am rapidly being surrounded.

Notes: Though a bit ragged around the edges at times (low budget and quick writing are still in evidence), this is by far the best episode of this very short-lived series. It not only is a return to the space opera of the original series, it brings back one of the most popular characters from that show. And though the damaged-centurion bit has been done before (see Red-Eye in "The Lost Warrior"), this *Enemy Mine*-type story is at least a sound framework for a cost-conscious tale. It succeeds in bringing back Starbuck, leaving his ultimate status unclear (thus leaving him open for another subsequent return), tying him to the current *1980* continuity story, but keeping him out of the *1980* action—so we don't have to watch his character slum it by teaching children to look both ways before crossing the road.

And Dirk Benedict (and Glen Larson, the writer) deliver the goods. If you are going to have an episode that relies overwhelmingly on one character talking, Starbuck's the one you want. He has the humor and friendliness and wryness that make what could otherwise be a boring hour turn into an hour spent with a friend.

Alas, *Galactica 1980*'s cancellation was announced a week before this episode even aired, so it was a bittersweet victory for the show. The very quality of this program also served to highlight the low quality of the episodes that preceded it, as well as the incredibly uneven stories (We're a time travel show! We're an after-school special show! We're a traveling savior show!). If there is anything good I can say about *Galactica 1980*, it is that this episode showed that despite all that went before it, the show's creative team was still capable of mounting an effective production, and maybe, just maybe—without the ABC-created problems of insufficient production time, story interference, $1.98-per-episode budget, and ridiculous kid-friendly time slot—*Galactica 1980* could have been a decent franchise continuation.

In a 1997 email interview, *Galactica 1980* story editor Allan Cole told John Larocque about "The Return of Starbuck": "Basically, GL [Glen Larson] was tired and pissed off. This was never the show he wanted to do. And he and Dirk Benedict were always pretty tight. He talked Dirk into coming back to do one last episode. Which was basically a two-man radio play. Personally, I think it was the only decent episode in the series and showed what GL could have done if they had let him alone."

I hope in all of my criticisms in this chapter, I have been clear that I am faulting the finished product and the circumstances under which it was assembled. I am not attacking the people who wrote, acted, produced, directed, designed, built, costumed, and in other jobs played a role in assembling each episode of *Galactica 1980*. I don't think anyone sets out to make a bad show (or movie or book); if anything, my heart goes out to people who really put their energy into a show that never seriously had a chance of success in the first place. For some of them, this was their big break to work on a network television show. It wasn't their fault that ABC insisted on an impossible schedule.

To make the airdates, the production ended up shooting two shows simultaneously, starting "Super Scouts" while still filming the previous episode. It got confusing to know which script they were filming in which scene, according to Douglass. While they were deeper in the series, she noticed changes coming in hours before you do the scene, "sometimes minutes before you do the scene," she said in her audio memoirs. Each revised script page would have a different color, as is traditional in productions, and at one point, they had 40 different colored pages, with changes coming almost every half hour: "That's not typically a good sign."

She says that shooting episodes simultaneously, with equipment breaking down, and cost overruns all helped lead to the show's cancelation.

To make ABC's actions even more idiotic, let's remember that this was 1980. There was an expanding cable TV industry and a smattering of independent television stations across the country, but for the most part, the three big networks were the ball game. There were no streaming video services, and home video players were in their infancy. So ABC, CBS, and NBC were kings of the hill, emperors of televisionland. Networks had high expectations for how many viewers a program could lure, and it therefore was in the networks' definite interests to air programs that would be popular and long-lived. Therefore, performing network malpractice on *Galactica 1980* is dumber than dumb. But even after all that ABC had done to ensure that *Galactica 1980* was a debacle, it could still have salvaged it if they had renewed the show for a second season, moved it an hour later and to a less important viewing day, and watched what "GL" was able to do with a summer of production, better planning, and no need to be educational for the little kids among the viewing public.

I think the audience would have been there, and *Galactica 1980* (presumably just officially renamed *Battlestar Galactica* for future years) would have been remembered as a rocky beginning for a new show and not as a laughable fiasco that put the franchise into the freezer for two decades.

CHAPTER THREE

Battlestar Galactica 2003–2009

This has all happened before, and it will happen again. The Cylons were created by man. They rebelled. Then they vanished. Forty years later they came back. They evolved. 50,298 human survivors hunted by the Cylons. Eleven models are known. One was sacrificed.

The first time it happened, science fiction television was synonymous with short-lived series, bug-eyed monsters, and ultra-cheap budgets. *Battlestar Galactica* only changed part of that.

In the months before and immediately after *Battlestar Galactica* premiered on ABC TV in late 1978, it was the talk of the country. It appeared on the covers of such non-SF magazines as *Newsweek*, *People*, and *Rona Barrett's Hollywood Super Special*; it was featured in a big preview in the high-brow *Smithsonian* magazine; and there was high-profile coverage in *US*, *Tiger Beat*, and even men's magazine *Saga*.

Galactica's main selling point was that it offered a *Star Wars* experience on TV (*Newsweek* even called it "Son of *Star Wars*"). Endless reports hyped the special effects by John Dykstra, the SFX wizard behind the first *Star Wars* film. The show debuted to spectacular ratings, and though its ratings did fall a bit from its premiere, the show was still reportedly in the top 20 when it was canceled by ABC at the end of the season in favor of less expensive fare.

The show did not rate well with critics, and over time, though its fan base continued, the conclusion of many critics was that a great opportunity for quality televised science fiction had been squandered. Insiders of the program argued that the show had originally been intended as a number of spectacular miniseries, not an ongoing weekly series. When ABC changed its mind at the last minute and ordered up a weekly series, the producers scrambled to stretch the budget for the shows and to come up with enough scripts. The result was an uneven series, as you've read in chapter one of this book—with ambitious, epic entries such as "The Living Legend" or "War of the Gods" alternating with under-powered episodes such as "Fire in

Space" or "Greetings from Earth."

After the even shorter-lived sequel series *Galactica 1980* and the release of the series repackaged into two-hour television movies, *Galactica* lay dormant.

Flash forward to the new century, when fans were treated to the confusion of dueling attempts to bring the show back to life. Original series star Richard Hatch was pushing his own planned revival that would have taken up the original storyline two decades later. At the same time, series creator Glen A. Larson was attempting to put together a theatrical version of the show. A third option was being pursued by director Bryan Singer and the Sci Fi Channel (now Syfy) to revamp the concept for a new series. When Singer left that project, veteran *Star Trek* writer Ronald D. Moore and writer/producer David Eick took over and came up with a complete overhaul of the concepts, characters, and storylines. This would be neither a continuation nor a remake of the 1978 series; instead, it would take the basic story and characters from the original but come up with an entirely new approach. New actors, new designs, new mythology, and—as we'll see in the episode guide—new political ideologies would characterize the Moore-Eick series.

ANTICIPATION AND PAYOFF

Whereas the first series was met with tremendous anticipation and media hype, much of the reporting on the new series leading up to its debut was concerned with trepidation among fans about the new producers' vision. Just how much would it deviate from the original?

The result was the 2003 *Battlestar Galactica* miniseries. There had been a great deal of resistance to the reimagining of the show, from fans and from people involved in the original series, including star Richard Hatch. When details emerged about the changes in store, the internet underwent a convulsive reaction. (And yes, I'd love to have seen how the internet would have treated *Galactica 1980*. Kids can be brutal.) Starbuck and Boomer were going to be female characters. Colonel Tigh was a drunk. There would be no lasers. The show would not necessarily follow the storyline of the original series. There was no 1,000-year war between man and Cylons. And so on.

But minds changed pretty quickly when the miniseries aired. It performed well enough to spawn a new series, which lasted until 2009 on Syfy. Unlike the original Glen Larson series, this new version was a critical as well as a ratings success. Everyone from *Time* magazine to *TV Guide* to Harlan Ellison heaped praise on it; you can probably still find the online video of Ellison introducing Moore to a convention crowd with his trademark outspokenness, calling the original series the worst TV show ever but the new *Galactica* one of the best. Hyperbolic perhaps in both directions, but as a sign of how well the Ronald Moore *Galactica* was received, it is appropriate.

As we'll see in the episode guide, the relaunched show was a good drama. Period.

Science fiction or otherwise, it ranks among the best shows on television at the time, and should be included in any discussion about all-time great American television dramas.

In the course of its run on SyFy, the show accomplished something few science fiction TV shows can do. Like *Star Trek: The Next Generation*, the new *Battlestar Galactica* brought in an audience of people who normally wouldn't watch a television show about spaceships, interplanetary travel, and mythology. It helped the muggle public change its view of science fiction to a more positive, adult one. It would also spawn short-lived spinoffs.

It's just like a prophecy from the priestesses of Kobol: History repeats itself. This has all happened before, and it will happen again.

Based on concepts, characters, and stories created by: Glen A. Larson
Broadcaster: Sci Fi Channel (later Syfy)
Studio: Universal
Developed by: Ronald D. Moore
Producers: David Eick, Ronald D. Moore
Opening Theme by: Richard Gibbs
Composer: Bear McCreary
Commander/Admiral William Adama: Edward James Olmos
President Roslin: Mary McDonnell
Lee "Apollo" Adama: Jamie Bamber
Kara "Starbuck" Thrace: Katee Sackhoff
Sharon "Boomer" Valerii: Grace Park
Gaius Baltar: James Callis
Colonel Tigh: Michael Hogan
Number Six: Tricia Helfer
Chief Tyrol: Aaron Douglas
Karl "Helo" Agathon: Tahmoh Penikett
Felix Gaeta: Alessandro Juliani
Samuel Anders: Michael Trucco
Anastasia Dualla: Kandyse McClure
Billy Keikeya: Paul Campbell
Cally Henderson Tyrol: Nicki Clyne

Battlestar Galactica: The Miniseries

Writer: Ronald D. Moore. **Director:** Michael Rymer. **Airdate:** December 8, 2003.

No one said robots can't plan. In the 40 years that have passed since the Cylon Wars, the robots have used their time efficiently. For example, they have developed new human-appearing models. Then—*quelle surprise!*—the Cylons carry out a nuclear attack on the Twelve Colonies, thanks to their successful infiltration of the humans' defense networks (itself the product of Dr. Gaius Baltar's seduction by a humanoid Cylon). Humanity is nearly wiped out, with the old battlestar *Galactica*—on the eve of its mothballing—rallying the survivors and escaping from the now Cylon-controlled 12 home worlds.

Only about 50,000 humans are rescued by the *Galactica* and its makeshift fleet of ships. So many of the humans' leaders have been killed that Laura Roslin, the secretary of education, is made the civilian president, setting her up for an often-tense relationship with the military, now led by the *Galactica*'s commander, Adama. This film shows us not only Roslin's rocky start as president and her uncertain hold over her "constituents" and the military, but it gives us an early look at the toughness underneath the education secretary's cover. She has to make the decision to abandon the humans who are on ships that do not have faster-than-light capabilities and can therefore not escape the Cylon attacks.

After a dangerous trip to a weapons depot, where Adama finally learns about the new human-form Cylon models, the "ragtag fleet" heads for Adama's announced goal: Finding the legendary lost planet Earth.

Adama: You're right. There's no Earth—it's all a legend.
Roslin: Then why?
Adama: Because it's not enough to just live. You have to have something to live for. Let it be Earth.
Roslin: They'll never forgive you.
Adama: Maybe. But in the meantime I've given all of us a fighting chance to survive. And isn't that what you said was the most important thing—the survival of the human race?

Notes: The events of this miniseries will be revisited numerous times in the course of the series proper and its TV movie spinoffs. In those flashbacks, we learn more about Roslin's personal and political situations. We also will find out more about Baltar's seduction by Number Six and how it led to the Cylon attacks.

On a technical note, the attack on the human colonies is so jarring that it appears to permanently knock cameras off-kilter, making it impossible for the producer to hold an image of a spaceship steady for more than 1 second.

SEASON ONE

33

Writer: Ronald D. Moore. **Director:** Michael Rymer. **Airdate:** January 14, 2005.

The Cylons are attacking the *Galactica*'s fleet every 33 seconds, causing the fleet to jump repeatedly to avoid being caught. The sleep-deprived crew is showing the strain of the constant tension and jumps, when they detect a link between the Cylon attacks and a civilian ship in the fleet. Adama and Roslin must struggle with the decision of whether to destroy the ship and its human civilian crew.

Number Six: Procreation is one of God's commandments.
Baltar: Really? Well, I'm sure some day if you're a good Cylon, he'll reward you with a lovely little walking toaster of your very own.

Notes: Whereas the original *Galactica* series stumbled with its initial non-mythology episodes (in which Starbuck or Apollo got marooned on a planet-of-the-week), this series has a real banger of a first stand-alone episode—tense, dramatic, and it even gets to the heart of both series' dilemma: how do you deal with a storyline that is essentially about one relentless villain (the Cylons, en masse) chasing a group of humans? This episode shows that it can be done in a way that tells us a lot about the incredible danger of the Cylons and the ability of the humans to handle ruthless decisions if needed.

Water

Writer: Ronald D. Moore. **Director:** Marita Grabiak. **Airdate:** January 14, 2005.

The majority of the *Galactica*'s water reserves are destroyed in an explosion, and Chief Tyrol and Boomer try to keep secret some evidence implicating Boomer (who doesn't yet know she's a Cylon herself, but she did wake up with some explosives, and her clothes soaking wet). She later redeems herself—sort of—by discovering a moon with available water.

With the *Galactica* leadership alerted to Cylons in human form in the fleet, Baltar is put in charge of creating a test to determine if someone is a Cylon. Captain Apollo becomes President Roslin's military advisor, setting up a simmering conflict with the captain's father, Commander Adama.

Adama [to *Roslin*]: I'm not going to be your policeman. There's a reason why you separate military and the police. One fights the enemy of the state. The other serves and protects the people. When the military becomes both, then the enemies of the state tend to become the people.

Notes: This is really an episode about Boomer, the *Galactica* version of whom is realizing she might be a Cylon and isn't sure if she is giving in to her programming or is fighting it (spoiler alert: in the end, she saves the fleet by fighting her programming and finding the water on a moon). But we are also seeing the version of Boomer back on Caprica, who saves Helo. So the seed is planted in our minds about what exactly a Cylon is (can one be a Cylon and fight one's programming?) and why there are multiple versions of Cylons, some of whom just might be collaborating with the humans the Cylons tried to wipe out.

Bastille Day

Writer: Toni Graphia. **Director:** Allan Kroeker. **Airdate:** January 21, 2005.

Following up on the events of "Water," the *Galactica*'s leaders try to come up with a plan for getting the water from the moon to refill the fleet's stores. Apollo suggests using prison labor, which President Roslin allows—if the prisoners agree to work in return for a reduction of their sentences. But the prisoners, under the leadership of a convicted terrorist named Zarek, reject the plan and instead take Apollo hostage. When Commander Adama sends in Starbuck with a commando team, it's up to Apollo to come up with a compromise that prevents a bloodbath and the ensuing political upheaval it would cause.

Baltar: Lieutenant Thrace—good to see you!
Starbuck: Good to see you, too.
Baltar: Really?
Starbuck: No!

Notes: Give yourself points if you heard an echo—in this business, we call it an homage, dearie—of the original series' prisoners-on-an-ice-planet episode "Gun on Ice Planet Zero."

A different type of homage here involves Zarek, who is played by veteran actor Richard Hatch, who of course starred as Apollo in the 1978 *Galactica* series. There's even a neat scene between Hatch's Zarek and Jamie Bamber's Lee Adama discussing Lee's call sign "Apollo." Before the announcement of the Ronald Moore *Galactica* remake, Hatch had vied with the show's creator, Glen A. Larson, to develop rival new versions of the original series, and Hatch even self-funded a short demo film of his intended production, which would carry on the storyline of the 1978 version. (Hatch's demo film, *Battlestar Galactica: The Second Coming*, was shown to enthusiastic science fiction convention audiences, but it didn't move the studios to support his vision. You can find clips from that 30-minute production online.) Hatch was reportedly none too thrilled with the plans to reimagine the series, though he eventually changed his mind and joined the team with the recurring character of Zarek.

My personal Richard Hatch story: One day in the year 2000, while I was living in New York—tech journalist by day, independent science fiction columnist at night—I covered a relatively small science fiction convention in Manhattan. I only had time to cover a small portion of it, such as a fascinating discussion between former writers and stars of *Space: 1999*. Before I left for the day, I ducked into the bathroom, and just before I exited that space, in came a breathless Richard Hatch, who was due to give a presentation in a few minutes. He was wearing sweat pants and a t-shirt, and he zipped into a stall to change into more presentable clothes for his program. Such was my brush with glory.

It is, of course, better that I never got a chance to actually talk to him during that moment. I left, knowing he was busy and in a hurry (and in a place one doesn't generally want to have extended conversations with strangers). Because, even though I was an adult, I would have probably been reduced to something of the 10-year-old I was when I first watched Hatch as he portrayed the handsome and heroic and upright Captain Apollo battling Cylons on the original *Battlestar Galactica*.

One of the twin sides of fame is that people think they know you when they have only seen you on television or the movie screen or have absorbed your works in some way. Even after meeting you, they don't know you; they have only spent a few minutes in your presence. What you are really like only comes through over protracted periods of time, tested under many circumstances. So it was particularly bittersweet for me to learn that my childhood hero-crush was reportedly every bit the good guy I had imagined he was, back when I dreamed of wearing a *Galactica* battle jacket and flying vipers.

"This one hurts," David Gerrold wrote on his Facebook page following the news of Hatch's death February 7, 2017. "Richard was one of the nicest guys in the industry. He had a generous spirit and he cared about everything he was involved with."

Born in 1945 in California, Hatch had a number of notable roles before landing aboard the *Galactica* in 1978. He was a regular for a season on *The Streets of San Francisco*, he played a recurring role on *Mary Hartman, Mary Hartman*, and he had a two-year stint on the soap *All My Children*. But it was *Galactica* that would be his calling card for the remaining four decades of his life, even though the show only lasted one season; he wisely did not appear in the short-lived sequel series *Galactica 1980*. Along the way, he co-wrote a series of enjoyable and well-received *Galactica* novels.

In the end, Hatch was felled by pancreatic cancer, and he passed away at the age of 71. Following news of Hatch's death, Ronald Moore tweeted, "Richard Hatch was a good man, a gracious man, and a consummate professional. His passing is a heavy blow to the entire BSG family."

So say we all.

Act of Contrition

Writers: Bradley Thompson, David Weddle. **Director:** Rod Hardy. **Airdate:** January 28, 2005.

President Roslin gets bad news about her cancer and is essentially told by the doctor that her best chance is prayer. The *Galactica*'s Dr. Cottle, by the way, has all of the warm bedside manner of Roy Cohn.

Meanwhile, Starbuck is forced to train new fighter pilots following the deaths of 13 pilots in an on-ship accident. Her duties are made more difficult by the memories the training is reviving in her: She had given Zak Adama, Commander Adama's younger son, a passing grade in flight training despite his lack of readiness. His subsequent death is something for which she feels guilty, and when Commander Adama gets the story out of her, he also clearly blames her. After Starbuck and her new recruits are attacked by a bunch of Cylon raiders, she takes on the last remaining Cylon herself, only to end up spinning out of control—along with the damaged raider—to destination unknown.

Dr. Cottle: You are obviously an intelligent, well-educated young woman. Would you mind explaining to me why you waited five years in between breast exams?
Roslin: Yes, I would mind. It's none of your business. I was busy.

Notes: In the original *Battlestar Galactica* movie from 1978, Zak is "Zac" and was played by Australian actor and singer Rick Springfield. In that show, he was the first human killed in the Cylon sneak attack, dying just short of the Colonial fleet. However, he was not the lover of Starbuck (except, perhaps, in some slash fan fiction), as he is in the reimagined *Galactica*. The reimagined Zak is played by Tobias Mehler, a young Canadian actor.

You Can't Go Home Again

Writer: Carla Robinson. **Director:** Sergio Mimica-Gezzan. **Airdate:** February 4, 2005.

As much as Commander Adama might have been surprised and angered by Kara "Starbuck" Thrace's admission in the previous episode about her possible connection to Zak's death, he pulls out the stops to rescue Starbuck from wherever she might have ended up after the Cylon dogfight in "Act of Contrition." Meanwhile, Starbuck is stranded on an alien planet and locates the Cylon ship she damaged in a dogfight. She learns how to control it and is able to rejoin the fleet after making her newly acquired Cylon raider recognizable as a "friend" to the *Galactica*.

And back on Caprica, Helo and Sharon—the Cylon Boomer double—have found a safe hideaway, but after Helo gets into a fight with some patrolling Cylons, he can't find Sharon.

Roslin: Skip the formalities. You both know why I'm here.
Adama: Termination of a pilot's rescue mission is a military decision.
Roslin: That's a bunch of crap. It's not military; it's personal. Neither of you can let go of Kara Thrace because she's your last link to Zak.
Apollo: You don't know anything about my brother.
Roslin: Don't even begin, Captain. You've lost perspective. . . . Under normal circumstances, it would just be sad that the two of you can't come to terms with Zak's death. In this situation, you are putting your pilots at risk, and you're exposing the entire fleet to possible attack every moment we stay here.
Adama: We've been at risk of an attack since day one. Cylons won't be missing their

patrol for at least one more day.

Notes: Sure, the original Starbuck also ended up stranded on a planet after a dogfight ("The Return of Starbuck" in *Galactica 1980*). He, too, managed to find the crashed Cylon ship he had fought with in space. He also used the Cylon ship for his own purposes. But the similarities end there. While he reconstituted and befriended a Cylon centurion, the Kara Thrace Starbuck crawls into the gooey insides of the Cylon raider pilot and flies its ship back to the fleet. Because in this new *Galactica*, the raider pilots are basically bio-organisms that are part of (are the same as?) their raider fighter ships.

Croatian-born Sergio Mimica-Gezzan, who helmed this episode, is a second-generation director whose work also includes *Heroes*, *Halo: Nightfall*, and *Terminator: The Sarah Connor Chronicles*, among other productions.

Litmus

Writer: Jeff Vlaming. **Director:** Rod Hardy. **Airdate:** February 11, 2005.

After an attempted assassination of the *Galactica*'s commander, Adama and President Roslin decide it is time to let the rest of the fleet know the little secret that Cylons can pass in human form. At the same time, they begin an inquest into the breaches of security—an investigation that eventually comes to criticize Adama himself before he calls an end to it. The personal impacts of the security problems come to a head when Chief Tyrol breaks off his relationship with Boomer, refusing to protect her any more at the cost of defending the crew under his command.

Back on Caprica, Helo's devotion to Sharon is tested—by Sharon and other Cylons.

Adama: These proceedings are closed. You'll be transported back to your ships and we appreciate your help.
Board leader: This is an independent board. You have no power to close our inquiries.
Adama: This is a witch-hunt. I will not have it aboard my ship.

Notes: The *Galactica*'s cigarette-smoking medical man, Dr. Cottle, is played by the late Donnelly Rhodes, a Canadian-born actor with a lot of credits, both genre and non. Of particular note to Harlan Ellison fans is that he guest-starred in "The Implant People" episode of the Ellison-based (and Ellison-disowned) 1970s SF TV series *The Starlost*.

Six Degrees of Separation

Writer: Michael Angeli. **Director**: Robert M. Young. **Airdate:** February 18, 2005.

What would make the vain Gaius Baltar pray to the Cylon god? Baltar stands accused of being a traitor to the Twelve Colonies, and his accuser is no less than Number Six herself in flesh-and-blood human form. Normally appearing only in his mind, courtesy of an implanted chip, she now is visible to everyone and she appears bent on making Baltar's life a misery. She presents evidence of Baltar's complicity, and the doctor is thrown into prison while Gaeta studies the evidence. And so, Baltar prays.

Meanwhile, Starbuck slowly recovers from her injuries incurred in recent episodes.

Adama: No pain, no gain. No cliché left unturned, as Kara Thrace returns to the world of the walking. Can she do it or will she fall on her ass?
Starbuck: I swear to the Gods that I'm going to beat the crap out of both of you as soon as I get better. . . [*She tries to move.*] No, I can't.
Adama: Yes, you can. You did it.
Starbuck: No, I can't. I can't. I can't.
Dr. Cottle: You're not going to get better lying on your back.
Starbuck: Oh, frak off.
Adama: We'll just take a break for five minutes.
Starbuck: I don't want to do it again. I want a pill. Now—please.
Dr. Cottle: Sorry, but we're weaning you off the magic pills starting today. Besides, I need them for myself.

Notes: Shelly Godfrey is the name of the Number Six version who appears and accuses Baltar of treachery. Thus begins an ever-more-complex mystery about the Cylon models, what the hell they're up to, and why they seem to be working at cross purposes. I'm not sure all of the storylines eventually match up, or—more likely—that even most intrepid viewers understood how all of the storylines matched up. But it makes for mind-smacking storytelling.

Flesh and Bone

Writer: Toni Graphia. **Director:** Brad Turner. **Airdate:** February 25, 2005.

Leoben Conoy, a Cylon in human form, appears in President Roslin's dream, and a copy of Leoben then appears on a ship in the fleet. Under interrogation, he says a nuclear weapon is hidden on one of the ships, and Starbuck is told to use any means necessary—read: torture—to get him to give them the location of the nuke.

President Roslin stops the torture, but she ultimately decides he is a liar and too dangerous to keep alive, and she orders him expelled into space. Whoosh.

Leoben Conoy: I see love that bonds everything together.
Starbuck: You don't know the meaning of the word.
Conoy: I know that God loved you more than anything. And how did you repay

His divine love? With sin, evil. So God created the Cylons.
Starbuck: The gods did not create you! We did! It was a stupid and fracked-up decision, and we are paying for it.

Notes: This episode gives us more insight into the Cylon religion, which is focused on a single god, rather than the bucket-o'-gods the humans revere. The robots' religion is explained to us in drips throughout the course of the series, leaving us at times unsure if Number Six is just toying with Baltar when she talks to him about the one god and uses language we would recognize as Christian or at least monotheistic. In the end, it is Starbuck who prays for the Cylon Leoben after he is killed.

And if you haven't gotten the message yet, here it is: Laura Roslin is tough. Don't mess with her.

Tigh Me Up, Tigh Me Down

Writer: Jeff Vlaming. **Director:** Edward James Olmos. **Airdate:** March 4, 2005.

Tigh's estranged wife Ellen appears and immediately starts sowing distrust between Adama and Tigh (and pretty much everyone else). Meanwhile, Roslin, acting on a whispered message from the Cylon Leoben in "Flesh and Bone," suspects Adama is a Cylon and has Baltar secretly test the commander using his new Cylon-detection system.

Battlestar Galactica did not have much humor in it, but when it did, it was done beautifully. Edward James Olmos does double duty this episode, portraying the commander and directing the show. His good work comes to a head during a scene late in the episode when many plot threads all collide. The mixture of tension, humor, and secrets revealed is played perfectly by the actors, and it's difficult to take your eyes off the scene as it unfolds:

Baltar: I have started and stopped the [Cylon detection] test twice already now, so I am running a little behind.
Apollo and Adama: Twice?!
Roslin: My fault. Long story.
Adama: Your fault?
Baltar: Yes, I probably shouldn't have mentioned that.
Roslin: No, you probably shouldn't have.
Adama: Did you tell him to stop Ellen's test?
Roslin: Yes, I did.
Adama: Why?
Roslin: Well, I had some concerns.
Adama: About what?
Roslin: In all honesty, I think it's fair to say that your behavior recently has been . . . odd.

Adama: *My* behavior? What do you think—I'm a Cylon? *Me*?

Well, yes, she did think that. The accusations and revelations go on and on, with Ellen and Tigh joining the conversation, adding another layer of lies and conflict. A truly delicious scene.

Notes: This is one of the best episodes of the entire series. Though I appreciate the humor very much, it's even better because it was all done in perfect culmination of plot threads that have been woven through previous episodes, with each revelation playing off what we already know about each character's personality, problems, fears, alliances, and sense of power. Genius.

The Hand of God

Writers: Bradley Thompson, David Weddle. **Director:** Jeff Woolnough. **Airdate:** March 11, 2005.

The religious overtones of the series deepen in this episode, in which President Roslin sees a vision of snakes and is told by a priestess of a Pythian prophecy that the humans will be led to their new home—by a dying leader. Consider that a good-news, bad-news situation for Roslin, who is battling terminal cancer. Meanwhile, Baltar is led by Number Six to believe that God is directing him when he gives advice that helps select a target on a Cylon asteroid.

The fleet, dangerously low on fuel, discovers an asteroid rich with tylium but also chock full of Cylons mining that tylium for their own fuel. Starbuck helps craft a sneaky plan to trick the Cylons into leaving the base relatively unprotected, and Apollo learns to think like Starbuck in the execution of the plan, which succeeds in replenishing the fleet's supply of fuel.

Adama: There are no reserve vipers. Everything is on the board already. Now we play for all the marbles. Starbuck—it's your plan.
Starbuck: Mr. Gaeta, will you please tell Dee to get on the scrambler and inform Apollo the back door is open?
Felix Gaeta: Aye, Lieutenant. Dee, please send a scrambler to Captain Apollo. Message reads "The back door is open."

Notes: "The Hand of God" was also the title of the final episode of the original *Battlestar Galactica* TV series, airing in April 1979. There are other similarities besides the title, though they might be coincidental. Fuel is not the driving motivation in 1979, but still the fleet discovers a Cylon outpost and, weary of always running from their enemies, decides to attack the Cylon baseship. Starbuck and Apollo lead the daring attack, and key help is provided by none other than Baltar, who gives advice about how to destroy the ship in return for his freedom.

The title of the episode is from a comment by Apollo (Richard Hatch) in the original episode, who is showing his friends an observation dome with a 365-degree view of space: "It's like riding in the hand of god; at least that's the way I like to think of it." That episode, written and directed by Donald Bellisario (who is, among other things, the creator of *NCIS*), ends with Starbuck and Apollo leaving the observation dome just before the receiver in the dome gets a video transmission of the Apollo moon landing.

Colonial Day

Writer: Carla Robinson. **Director:** Jonas Pate. **Airdate:** March 18, 2005.

It's political shenanigans and drama as only a dying ember of humanity on a fleet going nowhere can provide. Colonial Day is the annual celebration of the Twelve Colonies' foundation, and this year, President Roslin re-establishes the Quorum of Twelve to help lead the remainder of humanity.

What should provide a new spark of hope and normalcy for the fleet turns into a threat to Roslin. Zarek, the former terrorist introduced in "Bastille Day," is nominated as one of the Quorum members and suggests an election be held for the position of vice president—for which he is also nominated. To counter Zarek's growing popularity, Roslin teams up with Baltar, who wins the vice presidential spot. Zarek warns Roslin that he'll try for higher office again, specifically for her presidency at the next election.

Adama: Politics—as exciting as war, definitely as dangerous.
Roslin: Though in war you only get killed once. In politics it can happen over and over.

Notes: There is an interesting parallel to the Quorum of Twelve in the original *Galactica* series. In both series, the council is supposed to perpetuate the humans' ancient government traditions and preserve some sense of civilian normalcy, but the council frequently is filled with troublesome characters and power-hungry individuals who make life difficult for Adama (and Roslin in the new series). Neither series presented a full-throated defense of the republican form of government. Though Roslin is the civilian leader and is therefore overall leader of the humans except in military decisions, her conflicts with the Quorum are basically the same as Adama faced in the 1978–79 series: Its members keep interfering in her ability to govern or rule as she sees fit.

Kobol's Last Gleaming (Part I and II)

Writer: David Eick. **Director:** Michael Rymer. **Airdates:** March 25 & April 1, 2005.

What to make of a program that includes Starbuck and Baltar having sex, the discovery of mankind's birthplace, insurrection in the fleet, betrayal of family and duty, a secret mission to Caprica, and an assassination attempt? It's the season-ending two-parter that seems designed to leave viewers reeling, with minds full of questions and implications throughout the summer until the next season starts.

The fleet thinks it might have discovered the planet Kobol, the legendary place where humanity originated. Roslin, reacting to a series of visions she has been having, sends Starbuck back to Caprica in the Cylon raider she had captured earlier, in search of the Arrow of Apollo, which Roslin believes will help them discover the path to Earth.

Adama orders the arrest of Roslin for sending Starbuck to Earth without his orders. After Apollo supports Roslin, he ends up in prison with her. Meanwhile, Boomer is growing increasingly suicidal, learning from Baltar that she might in fact be a Cylon.

On Caprica, Starbuck discovers Helo and a copy of the Boomer Cylon and learns that the Cylon is carrying Helo's baby. But in the fleet, the other Boomer finally succumbs to her Cylon programming by shooting Commander Adama.

Number Six: It's time to do your part and realize your destiny.
Baltar: Which is what exactly?
Number Six: You are the guardian and protector of the new generation of God's children. The first member of our family will be with us soon, Gaius. It's time to make your choice.
Baltar: But I don't understand what you're talking about. Really, I don't understand.

Notes: At least one source reports that an early idea for the script came from producer Ronald Moore, who wanted to end the episode on Kobol with the appearance of a character played by Dirk Benedict—the original Starbuck, remember—who would announce, "Hi. I'm God." Moore was eventually talked out of it.

SEASON TWO

Scattered

Writers: David Weddle, Bradley Thompson. **Director:** Michael Rymer. **Airdate:** July 15, 2005.

We have known from the outset that Col. Tigh is of questionable stability, having already learned about his alcoholism and troubled history in the Colonial fleet until Adama took him under his wing. Now, with Adama in sick bay trying to recover from Boomer's assassination attempt, Tigh is in charge, and his decision making at this critical time in the fleet's history might be making things worse.

The *Galactica* is separated from the rest of the fleet as the result of a mixup during a jump. Tigh makes the decision to network the ship's computers—against Adama's strict orders—to speed up the attempt to find the rest of the fleet. During an ensuing battle with Cylons, Felix Gaeta's firewalls are quickly broken down by Cylon attempts to hack the now-networked systems, and a raider crash lands on the *Galactica.*

Back on Caprica, Boomer steals Starbuck's raider (which, to be fair, she had stolen from the Cylons).

Starbuck: She's right, huh? Sharon the Cylon is right? Let's all just listen to Sharon the Cylon! Do whatever she says. Because that's a good idea!

Notes: This episode really highlights how much the reimagined series' Col. Tigh deviated from the straight-arrow Tigh of the 1978 series. It's another sign that this is a more adult version of the space opera tale. And, again, that's not necessarily Glen Larson's fault with the original series; it was the network that insisted on scheduling that series early in the evening. It might be a good parlor game to imagine how that show and its characters—including but not just Cassiopeia—would have been better if it had been allowed to go for a bit more adult audience.

Valley of Darkness

Writers: David Weddle, Bradley Thompson. **Director:** Michael Rymer. **Airdate:** July 22, 2005.

Things go from bad to worse for the fleet in general and for Tigh specifically. The Cylons attack on two fronts: Centurions survived the crash landing on the hangar deck in "Scattered," and they are fighting to take over the *Galactica*; meanwhile, a Cylon computer virus is coursing through the battlestar's computers as a result of Tigh's decision to network the system.

Apollo and Roslin, stuck in the brig when Tigh accused them of mutiny, are trying to get out so they can defend the fleet and restore democratic rule. Down on Kobol, a stranded landing party is trying to establish itself despite injuries and inadequate supplies as a result of their crash landing. One of the party, Chief Tyrol, must decide whether to end the life of a grievously wounded comrade.

Helo: Sharon said—Cylon Sharon said they had troops picking up bodies, transporting them to mass incinerators.
Starbuck: Your girlfriend's from a lovely family. Good people. Great values!

Notes: Have you caught your breath? It is common for a series that ends one season with a cliffhanger to resolve the cliffhanger at the beginning of the next season, and then go into cruising mode. Instead, Moore and his team kept the pedal to the metal here at the beginning of the second season, in which things not only don't let up, they if anything get more tense and dangerous. In fact, it will be another four episodes before the humans stop flying apart and begin to mend the wounds created or exacerbated in recent weeks.

Fragged

Writers: Dawn Prestwich, Nicole Yorkin. **Director:** Sergio Mimica-Gezzan. **Airdate:** July 25, 2009.

Did we say things went from bad to worse in the last episode? Well, they hadn't hit bottom yet. Tigh is egged on by Ellen to declare a state of martial law, but he has overstepped his mark, bringing President Roslin and the Quorum closer together. Roslin, with the help of her cancer medication, shares with the Quorum the prophecy that someone—oh, say, a cancer-stricken leader like her—will lead humanity to Kobol.

On Kobol, Chief Tyrol and Crashdown, the senior officer, confront each other over dueling plans to attack a small detachment of Cylons on the planet who pose a risk to any rescue team from the *Galactica*. When Crashdown threatens to kill Cally, who is too traumatized to follow his orders, Tyrol nearly kills Crashdown—but he is beaten to the punch (or the bullet, in this case) by Baltar, who kills the man. When they are rescued by a shuttle, the team doesn't report the fragging, instead telling others that Crashdown fell in battle.

Baltar: This is insane. I've never fired a gun in my life!
Selix: I haven't fired a weapon since basic [training].
Baltar: You?
Cally: I only joined up to pay for dental school!

Notes: Part of the interest in watching Tigh mess up his chance at ultimate command is that he is not an entirely unsympathetic figure. He genuinely is trying his hardest, and he is trying to do what he thinks will hold together the fleet and save humanity. But he is undercut by his own flawed judgment and alcoholism, and by the terrible influence of his wife, Ellen.

Resistance

Writer: Toni Graphia. **Director:** Allan Kroeker. **Airdate:** August 5, 2005.

It seems that the battlestar's brig is nothing more than a hotel. Everyone apparently gets to spend some time in there, and much of this episode centers on the brig—leaving it, being in it, or going to it. Apollo and Zarek help Roslin escape from prison, but Tyrol is thrown into the brig after he returns to the *Galactica* and is accused of working with Adama's attempted assassin, the Cylon Boomer. While Boomer is being led through the *Galactica* on her way to a new jail cell, she is shot and killed by Cally.

On other fronts, ships in the fleet are refusing to provide supplies to the battlestar as a way of protesting martial law, so Tigh—Mr. Never-back-down—attempts to use commandos to take the supplies from the recalcitrant ships. What could go wrong?

Tigh: Four civilian dead. How the frak could this have happened?
Dr. Cottle: What did you expect, genius? You put a pilot in charge of crowd control.

Notes: Seriously. Tigh is not a good top commander. Case closed.

The Farm

Writer: Carla Robinson. **Director:** Rod Hardy. **Airdate:** August 12, 2005.

At long last, Adama has recovered sufficiently to resume command, but he finds a huge mess to clean up. Mutiny. The fleet split in its loyalty between the *Galactica*'s military command and the civilian leadership of President Roslin, who is on the lam. Roslin sends out a message telling her supporters to join her on a visit to Kobol to look for the location of Earth, and one-third of the fleet goes with her.

On Caprica, Starbuck is hospitalized after a Cylon battle. She learns that the Cylons have been conducting experiments on humans so they can learn how to reproduce like them, but they haven't had success. She finds one of the women from Anders' human resistance group connected to a machine in a roomful of other women, and she destroys the machine. After escaping from the hospital with the help of Boomer, who uses the Cylon raider she took from Starbuck a while ago, the two of them take Helo and head back to the *Galactica*.

Number Six: Is that regret I hear in your voice, Simon?
Simon: If it is, it certainly is none of your concern.

Notes: I'll admit, this episode always felt strange to me, as if it didn't really fit in with the other *Galactica* episodes before or after it. While it is a showcase for Katee Sackhoff's acting, the whole attempt to harvest babies from unwilling human women is a side trip into horror and away from science fiction. However, in the overarching mystery of this show and the drip-drip-drip reveal of its secrets of the Cylon plans and Cylon beliefs, this show plays an important role by communicating the Cylon inability to biologically reproduce. They need humans to do that.

Home (Parts I and II)

Writers: David Eick, Ronald D. Moore. **Directors:** Sergio Mimica-Gezzan, Jeff Woolnough. **Airdate:** August 19, 2005, and August 26, 2005.

The high-tension plotlines of the season so far all come together and establish a new equilibrium in this episode, which also pushes forward the Earth mythology subplot.

With the fleet split between Roslin's followers around Kobol and Adama's followers further out in space, and with the commander nursing hurt feelings of betrayal by his son Apollo, the *Galactica*'s leader will have to decide if and how to bring the humans all back together again. He is eventually convinced to reunite with the breakaway faction, and the remaining fleet jumps to Kobol.

Apollo's on the bad side of someone else, too: Zarek. The former terrorist plans to end Lee Adama's life. Zarek attempts to enlist Sharon—the Boomer Cylon version that returned from Caprica with Helo and Starbuck aboard the raider. She has saved her own skin from Roslin's wrath by promising to lead the landing party to the Tomb of Athena; she later saves Apollo's skin by taking out Zarek's accomplices.

When Adama and his *Galactica* team catch up with Roslin's landing party, he completes the reunion of the fleet, but he also has to overcome the surprise of seeing another Boomer, his attempted assassin. She tells him she is different from the Boomer who shot him; she's rewarded by not being killed, but she is taken prisoner.

They find the tomb and enter it. When the Arrow of Apollo is placed in the bow of a statue, Adama, Apollo (our Lee Adama, not the Apollo of Arrow fame, of course), Roslin, and Starbuck are instantly transported from the old stone cave-like tomb to a nighttime meadow, surrounded by stone pillars with the constellations visible on them. The constellations help them identify the location of Earth.

Apollo: Where are we?
Roslin: I don't know. The Tomb of Athena, I think.
Adama: I thought we were already in the Tomb?
Starbuck: I think that was the lobby.

Notes: There are a number of echoes in "Home" of a two-part episode of the original *Battlestar Galactica*, "Lost Planet of the Gods," in which the Galacticans find Kobol and try to glean the secret of the location of the Thirteenth Tribe: Earth. "Lost Planet of the Gods" was the second installment of that series, deepening the Egyptian mythology connections to the series' story of human history on Earth.

As with "Lost Planet of the Gods," the humans in "Home" and the preceding Kobol episodes find that Kobol is not exactly what they imagined it would be.

Final Cut

Writer: Mark Verheiden. **Director:** Robert M. Young. **Airdate:** September 9, 2005.

A fight between Galactican troops and civilians forces Adama and Roslin to look for ways to ease the tensions and distrust within the fleet, so they bring aboard the battlestar a reporter named D'Anna Biers. Looking to explain the *Galactica* to the rest of the fleet, the journalist uncovers such uncomfortable secrets as the pregnant Cylon in the brig (Boomer, fresh from Kobol) and a plan to kill Col. Tigh. Though her eventual documentary is complimentary to Adama and his military, we learn that she is just another Cylon model and that her compatriots back among the Cylons on Caprica have big plans for Boomer's Cylon-human hybrid baby.

Tigh: This is a military vessel—we have rumors for every occasion.

Notes: The reporter Biers is played by New Zealand actress Lucy Lawless, the star of the long-running syndicated fantasy series *Xena: Princess Warrior*.

Flight of the Phoenix

Writers: Bradley Thompson, David Weddle. **Director:** Michael Nankin. **Airdate:** September 16, 2005.

Boomer begins to work her way out of the web of hatred and suspicion that many people in the fleet, including Commander Adama, feel for her. As a Cylon "logic bomb," a computer virus, threatens the *Galactica*, it is Boomer who not only helps defeat the virus but who arranges for a little cyber-payback when she transmits a virus of her own to cripple the Cylon ships that have jumped into the fleet to attack what they expected would be an undefended humanity.

In the background, Chief Tyrol and others decide to build a brand new viper, the blackbird (though they name it *Laura* in honor of President Roslin). Faced with a shortage of spare parts with which to construct the new fighter ship, they use carbon composites, which gives it stealth capabilities for avoiding detection.

Gaeta: Sir, I'm running every diagnostic we've got. Checking each line of code could take days.
Tigh: I am not interested in excuses. Fix it.
Gaeta: It's not an excuse, sir! It's a fracking fact!

Notes: Remember in the original series, "The Long Patrol" also involved a newly created viper called *Starchaser*, though that one was hobbled by an annoyingly flirtatious computer named C.O.R.A., and it was never again heard from for the rest of the series. Both *Laura* and *Starchaser* lack weapons due to design necessities, though the blackbird will be modified with a bomb for a special mission later this season.

The actor who portrays the pilot known as Hot Dog is Bodie Olmos, the son of series star Edward James Olmos.

Pegasus

Writer: Anne Cofell Saunders. **Director:** Michael Rymer. **Airdate:** September 23, 2005.

Among the best *Galactica* episodes, "Pegasus" introduces us to the *Pegasus*, another battlestar that everyone had believed to have been destroyed in the attacks on the colonies. Its appearance gives the fleet new hope, but it quickly becomes clear that the *Pegasus*' Admiral Cain is going to come to loggerheads with Commander

Adama and President Roslin.

On board the *Pegasus*, a Cylon prisoner has been tortured, and when Cain orders the same for Boomer, Tyrol and Helo rescue her, in the process accidentally killing the *Pegasus*' interrogator who was trying to rape her. For these actions, Cain sentences Helo and Tyrol to death. Adama is determined to stop the sentences from being carried out, and the two battlestars prepare to battle one another.

Baltar [*to the Cylon prisoner on Pegasus*]: My name is Gaius Baltar, and I am here to help you.

Notes: The tale of the *Pegasus* is, of course, a re-imagining of one of the better episodes of the original *Galactica* of the 1970s, "The Living Legend." In that episode, Cain (a commander and not an admiral) is portrayed by Lloyd Bridges. *Pegasus* was rumored to be a likely candidate to return for another go-around with the *Galactica* if that series had been picked up for a second season; it was also rumored to be the basis of a new film if Glen A. Larson had been successful in his late 1990s/early 2000s attempt to resurrect the franchise.

Like the Lloyd Bridges version, Cain and Adama take up similar positions in "Pegasus." Cain is the hard-charging warrior hell-bent on attacking Cylons at all costs and running her ship with iron discipline; Adama is no weakling, but he is more humane and carries the burden of protecting a fleet of civilians.

Resurrection Ship (Parts I and II)

Writers: Michael Rymer, Ronald D. Moore, Anne Cofell Saunders. **Director:** Michael Rymer. **Airdate:** January 6, 2006, and January 13, 2006.

Both battlestars have launched their vipers as the struggle between Adama and Cain escalates, but the attack is called off when an unexpected ship appears. When the *Galactica* CIC realizes that the inter-human firefight was prevented by the appearance of Starbuck in the blackbird, Tigh mutters, "Another one of her crazy-ass stunts. Thank the gods!"

Starbuck's private mission to the Cylon outpost that Cain wants to attack has resulted in closeup photos of two basestars and a giant odd ship they haven't seen before. Baltar finds out from Gina, the Cylon prisoner who has been tortured aboard the *Pegasus*, that the strange vessel is a resurrection ship, where Cylons are given new bodies after their old bodies have been killed.

Roslin, Adama, and Cain meet in Roslin's office, and the president manages to get the two military leaders to work together to destroy the Cylon ships. Following that testy confrontation, there is one of the greatest scenes of the entire series, in which Roslin and Adama sit alone and calm in the president's office:

Roslin: I'm afraid this can only end one way. We've gotta kill her.

Adama: What the hell are you talking about?
Roslin: Like she said, let's cut through it. The two of you were willing to go to war today. Do you think she's going to step down from that? She's going to bide her time and hit you the first chance she gets. That's a given. I hate to lay this on you, Bill, but she is dangerous, and the only thing you can do is hit her before she hits you.
Adama: I'm not an assassin.
Roslin: No. You are not an assassin. You are a Colonial officer who has taken an oath to protect this fleet. What do you think that she is going to do with this civilian fleet once she has eliminated you? You know I'm right. You just don't want to face it.
Adama [*getting up to leave*]: So, we're all going mad.

Tigh and other Galacticans learn from their *Pegasus* counterparts that Cain's ship used to have a civilian fleet of its own, but she stripped the ships for parts for her battlestar, press-ganged the valuable civilians into her military, and murdered the families of any civilians who refused to serve. Adama asks Starbuck to assassinate Cain after the resurrection ship is destroyed, and Cain sends a group of soldiers to the *Galactica* to do the same thing to Adama. But after the successful mission to the resurrection ship, it is Gina—who was helped in her escape from the brig by Baltar—who surprises Cain in her quarters and shoots her dead.

Notes: Now that his command includes two battlestars, Adama is promoted to the rank of admiral by President Roslin. No science fiction fan can hear that title without also hearing Ricardo Montalbán's voice: "Ad-mir-al Kirk?"

But even more impressive that his promotion is the conversation between Adama and Roslin excerpted above. The little-respected secretary of education who accidentally became president after the Cylon holocaust shows once again she's made out of steel, and is able to contemplate and put into action ruthless measures if she deems them necessary.

In the November 2007 *Galactica* TV movie *Razor*, we learn that Cain and Gina had been in a relationship, but when Cain learned that Gina was a humanoid Cylon, Gina was thrown into the brig and brutalized by *Pegasus*' crew.

Epiphanies

Writer: Joel Anderson Thompson. **Director:** Rod Hardy. **Airdate:** January 20, 2006.

Things are looking dire. The Cylon Gina, freed from her *Pegasus* cell, takes a leadership position with Demand Peace, a group urging a negotiated settlement with the Cylons. The group conducts acts of sabotage and terrorism to get its way, and its members are given a nuclear warhead by Vice President Baltar after he falls out of favor with Roslin.

President Roslin orders Boomer's unborn baby to be killed because she fears it is a threat to the human fleet, but when Baltar discovers incredible healing properties in the baby's blood cells, Roslin is given a new lease on life, as is the baby.

Helo: Does she know?
Adama: Not yet.
Helo: Then I should be the one to tell her. If that's all, sir.
Adama: Helo, I don't expect you to agree to the decision, but I need you to accept it.
Helo: We're talking about my child, sir. Part of me. But I guess it's easier to kill when you call it a Cylon.

Notes: Here is the flip side of Roslin's toughness. I think most people could see the logic behind her decision in the earlier episode to take out Cain; it was a brutal measure, but justified because of the danger to the *Galactica*'s civilian fleet. But the decision to kill the baby of Boomer and Helo is based on more speculative fears, and it frankly feels like a weak attempt to build up tension leading to what is the real point of this episode's revelations, which is the healing power of the hybrid human/Cylon baby (and thus a bit of a reprieve in Roslin's cancer fight).

Black Market

Writer: Mark Verheiden. **Director:** James Head. **Airdate:** January 27, 2006.

With the help of the Cylon baby's blood cells, Roslin is getting better. And Apollo is still getting over injuries he received during the attack on the resurrection ship. He is put in charge of investigating the murder of Jack Fisk, who took over command of the *Pegasus* after Admiral Cain's murder. Apollo learns that Fisk (and others, possibly including Baltar and the former terrorist Zarek) are involved in a big black market operation. After Zarek saves his life and points him in the direction of the black market's leader, Apollo finds that the illegal trading operation is much darker than he had thought.

Phelan [*to Apollo*]: You're not gonna shoot. You're not like me. You're not gonna [*Apollo shoots him*] . . . uuuhh.

Notes: Yep, not too long ago, in "Home," Zarek was ready to kill Apollo, and here he saves his life. Let any serial story go long enough on television, and everyone will switch sides multiple times.

This episode received a lot of criticism as one of the series' weakest or worse so far. I don't know if I'd go that far, but it is a rather muddled message and seems focused mainly on showing the seamy underside of the post-holocaust humans' society. But hey, if you want to see Apollo visit a prostitute, this is your show.

Scar

Writers: Bradley Thompson, David Weddle. **Director:** Michael Nankin. **Airdate:**

February 3, 2006.

Just like the humanoid Cylons, Cylon raiders are sentient beings filled with gooey insides, as we learned in "You Can't Go Home Again." One raider that has been killed in battle and resurrected numerous times, becoming more vengeful each time, is called Scar for the mark on its front. Starbuck and another viper pilot, Louanne Katraine (known as Kat) vie for the privilege and the glory of destroying Scar, who has been eliminating a lot of vipers. But first Starbuck must deal with the demons of her unresolved feelings for Anders. When Scar is finally destroyed, it is because Starbuck makes a particularly unusual decision.

Starbuck: You know the president says that we're saving humanity for a bright, shiny future—on Earth. That you and I are never gonna see. We're not, because we go out over and over again until someday, some metal motherfrakker is gonna catch us on a bad day and just blow us away.
Apollo: Bright, shiny futures are overrated anyway.
Starbuck: That is why we gotta get what we can. Right now.

Notes: "Scar" is a fairly simple, self-contained story that, though it provides some depth to Starbuck's relationship with Anders, is largely free of the sturm und drang of the overall storyline of the series.

Sacrifice

Writer: Anne Cofell Saunders. **Director:** Rey Villalobos. **Airdate:** February 10, 2006.

Apollo, apparently now eschewing ladies of the evening, is on a date with Anastasia Dualla aboard the *Cloud 9* ship when a group of gunmen take them and others hostage. They are demanding that Admiral Adama turn over the Cylon Boomer (aka Sharon), but Adama refuses.

Roslin and Adama struggle to formulate a response to the hostage situation that won't blow the lid off the already volatile situation in the fleet, with terrorists demanding peace with the Cylons and news of the existence of a pregnant Cylon (Boomer again) causing suspicion. When Adama tricks the hostage-takers by sending them the body of the murdered Boomer (the one who had shot Adama), the situation ends with bloodshed in the bar.

Tigh: What if Sharon has been playing us all, plotting our destruction with every passing day? What if the terrorists are right?
Roslin: This isn't about Sharon. It's about something much bigger than that. It's about the long-term survival of the fleet. It's about the way we conduct ourselves in all of this.

Notes: A hostage situation seems like one of those stories that is unavoidable for any series that lasts very long. The plot is pretty much already there for the writer (the setup, the hostages are taken, much gnashing and threatening by the hostage-takers, and then the peaceful or violent resolution), so it's just a matter of what window dressing one puts on it. This one includes the exit of Billy Keikeya, the personal assistant to President Roslin. He is killed while defending Dee. Billy was played by Paul Campbell, who soon starred in the short-lived revival of *Knight Rider*, which was another revival of another Glen A. Larson-created series.

The Captain's Hand

Writer: Jeff Vlaming. **Director:** Sergio Mimica-Gezzan. **Airdate:** February 17, 2006.

Lee Adama, like his admiral father, gets a promotion. Major Adama (Apollo) now serves on the *Pegasus*, working with its Commander Garner. But when Garner recklessly jumps the *Pegasus* to the location of a supposed human distress signal, the battlestar comes under attack by several Cylon basestars. Garner, the ship's former chief engineer, dies while successfully fixing the ship's FTL drive. Apollo repels the Cylon attack and returns the ship safely to the fleet. As a result, he gets yet another promotion: Commander of the *Pegasus*.

The fleet is also preparing for elections, and the hot-button issue of abortion plays a central role in the campaign after President Roslin reverses her earlier support for abortion and bans it, agreeing with Admiral Adama that the human race needs all the babies it can get. But naturally it gets messy when Roslin gives a pregnant teen-age girl asylum from her family, and Vice President Baltar—nursing a grudge since he discovered that Roslin never trusted him—latches onto the issue and announces that he is a candidate to replace Roslin as president.

Apollo: I know why I was mad at you, Kara.
Starbuck: A simple "thank you" would've been sufficient.
Apollo: 'Cause you are doing what you always did: Buck authority, and get away with it. . . . When I showed up on *Pegasus*, there you were, doing it all over again. I don't know, it pissed me off. Doesn't make a lot of sense, does it?
Starbuck: You should hear the way my brain works sometimes. Are we okay?
Apollo: You have a brain?

Notes: Of all the issues that science fiction series get into, abortion is generally not one. Perhaps it is assumed that in a more advanced society, unwanted pregnancies will be easier to avoid. But in this episode, Roslin changes her public position on abortion based on both political calculations and pragmatic reasons (in the latter case, acceding to the need to perpetuate the dying human race, which Baltar pre-dicts will go extinct within two decades). But Roslin also provides protection to a girl who wants an abortion, so the president gets to have her cake and eat it, too (as do, presumably, the writers, who don't really have to present in-depth a position unpopular with their neighbors and many among their audience). It's a disappointing dodge.

Downloaded

Writers: Bradley Thompson, David Weddle. **Director:** Jeff Woolnough. **Airdate:** February 24, 2006.

Turnabout is fair play, perhaps. Just as Baltar has visions of Number Six, it turns out that a copy of Number Six has visions of Baltar.

On Caprica, downloaded Cylons Number Six and Boomer are coming to terms with life on Caprica after their last assignments, and they are starting to change their views of humans. When a terrorist attack by Anders' resistance fighters traps another Cylon, Number Three (the Lucy Lawless model), Number Six and Boomer agree to try to change the way Cylons think of humans.

On *Galactica*, the Cylon Boomer (who used to be on Caprica; yes, it is probably supposed to be confusing) gives birth to her child with Helo. Roslin initiates a plan to pretend the child died, and instead they secretly give the baby to a human mother to raise.

Baltar: What are you suggesting?
Roslin: I'm not suggesting anything, doctor. If I want to throw a baby out an airlock, I'll do it.

Notes: Both storylines in this script emphasize the meaning of humanity. Are they better than the "toasters"? And some of the Cylons themselves are beginning to question whether they are better than the humans, or if the humans are better than they've been given credit for being. As we'll see, the final episode of the entire series basically makes all of that into one big mind-you-know-what.

Lay Down Your Burdens (Parts I and II)

Writers: Anne Cofell-Saunders, Ronald D. Moore, Mark Verheiden. **Director:** Michael Rymer. **Airdates:** March 3, 2006, and March 10, 2006.

When an FTL jump goes wrong, a raptor pilot discovers a planet that supports life and is hidden inside a nebula, offering the alluring prospect of a new home for the humans. Baltar and Zarek seize on the new planet as an issue that will help defeat Roslin in the presidential election. Roslin, however, argues that the fleet should only make a resupply stop at the planet, fearing that it is not as hidden from the Cylons as many people believe.

Starbuck leads a rescue team to bring back the survivors on Caprica. She and Anders become involved again, and Apollo and Dualla deepen their relationship. In the process, Apollo and Starbuck become estranged from each other.

However, it is the election that has the biggest impact here. Roslin's re-election is rigged to give her a victory, but Adama forces her to acknowledge Baltar as the true winner of the campaign, despite her claims that the vice president is a Cylon collaborator. Once in office, President Baltar orders the colonization of New Caprica, as they have dubbed the newly discovered planet.

The episode then shifts ahead in time one year, with the fleet in orbit around the now-colonized planet, Anders and Starbuck have married, and Roslin has returned to teaching. But when the Cylons show up in force, the Adamas jump the battlestars away from the planet, unable to protect the humans. After Baltar capitulates, the Cylons take over New Caprica unopposed.

Zarek: Things are gonna turn around. You'll see.
Baltar: What is that—*advice*? Well, thank you for your keen insight, your astounding political acumen. You know, I'm so assured right now, Tom, I'm just going to sit right back and wait for the hand of God to reach down and change my political fortunes!

Notes: Bridging the time between this season two-ending episode and the beginning of season three is a ten-part web-only series of short videos called *Battlestar Galactica: The Resistance*. Each episode is between a minute and a half and four minutes long; the entire web series totals about 27 minutes. They tell tales of life on New Caprica under Cylon control and the guerrilla warfare carried out by the humans.

SEASON THREE

Occupation

Writer: Ronald D. Moore. **Director:** Sergio Mimica-Gezzan. **Airdate:** October 6, 2006.

It is four months since the Cylons occupied the planet. Col. Tigh is leading the resistance against the occupation, working with Anders, Chief Tyrol, and others to disrupt Cylon operations wherever and whenever possible, often violently.

Off in space, Adama and Apollo, leaders of the *Galactica* and *Pegasus* respectively, disagree about how to deal with the situation. Eventually, contact is made with the resistance forces on the planet, thanks to some double-agenting work by Felix Gaeta, Adama's former bridge officer who is now working closely with President Baltar.

Cavil: Send a message that the gloves are coming off. The insurgency stops now, or else we'll start reducing the human population to a . . . more manageable size. I don't know, say less than a thousand.
Boomer: We need to stop being butchers!

Number Six: The entire point of coming here was to start a new way of life, to push past the conflict that separated us from humans for so long.
Cavil: And what has it gotten us? It's not like they welcomed us with, with—oh, frak it, never mind. You're all living in a fantasy world. Consider the irony in that! Delusional machines! What's the universe gonna come up with next?

Notes: Real-life politics played a major role in a number of episodes, plots, and subplots of *Battlestar Galactica*, sometimes obviously and sometimes subtly. "Occupation" is one of the most political episodes in the series' run, and its commentary on the American-led occupation of Iraq, the terrorist suicide bombings, and resistance activities is about as thinly veiled as can be. As to whether the writers and producers were actually taking a side in the real-life political matters or were "just raising questions," I don't claim to know. But as the series goes on, and the Cylon-human interactions get muddier (not to mention that more and more of the humans turn out to be Cylons, that some humans who are Cylons are very anti-Cylon humans, and that some humanoid Cylons start to sympathize with the humans), it becomes more difficult to take the stories' depictions of human errors and atrocities as a commentary on humanity, current real-life or fictional Twelve Colonies-ish.

Precipice

Writer: Ronald D. Moore. **Director:** Sergio Mimica-Gezzan. **Airdate:** October 6, 2006.

The Cylons try to win over Starbuck, giving her a baby they tell her she bore when she was in the creepy "The Farm" episode near the beginning of season two. The Cylons are trying to track down the perpetrators of a devastating suicide bombing that took place in "Occupation," and they are following twin paths: Trying to win over more collaborators and trying to harshly punish perpetrators. Ellen Tigh is forced to tell the Cylons about the location of the next resistance planning meeting in an attempt to save her husband's life.

Back on the *Galactica*, Sharon Boomer finally is released from her imprisonment and is made a Colonial officer by Adama. He then sends her to New Caprica to make contact with the resistance there.

Zarek: Laura, that election last year—you tried to steal it, didn't you?
Roslin: Yes, Tom, I did.
Zarek: Ah—I wish you'd gone through with it.
Roslin: Me too.

Notes: Ellen Tigh is such a great surprise in this whole series. When she was introduced, she appeared as if she would be a one-episode throwaway character. Yeah, sure, she survived the holocaust and is now back for her husband, right. Then we learn more about her tempestuous but real bond with her husband, Colonel Saul Tigh. And (as we'll witness in the next two episodes) things turn tragic, but we'll see much more of her, as she turns out to be (I told you this book was full of spoilers aplenty) not just a Cylon but a Cylon who has, with her husband, played a pivotal role in Cylon-human history for millennia. Now *that*'s a long-lasting relationship.

Exodus (Parts I and II)

Writers: Bradley Thompson, David Weddle. **Director:** Felix Enriquez Alcala. **Airdate:** October 13, 2006, and October 20, 2006.

The humans' plans for escaping the Cylon occupation on New Caprica all come together in "Exodus." Tyrol and his resistance fighters manage to save a couple hundred humans who were about to be massacred by the Cylons. Boomer lets the resistance leaders in on Admiral Adama's plans for the evacuation of the planet; she also is told by Cylons that Hera, the baby she had with Helo, is still alive. In another revelation of a hot-button secret, Tigh learns that his wife had shared resistance information with the Cylons, and he reluctantly kills her with a poisoned drink in retaliation. When the Cylons decide to destroy the settlement on New Caprica with a nuclear bomb, President Baltar must decide if he is going to escape with the toasters or help the humans.

When the *Galactica* jumps into the atmosphere, launching fighters to attack the Cylons on the planet, it sustains damage in the unusual maneuver. Jumping back to a higher orbit, it is taken on by four Cylon basestars. The old ship's skin (so to speak) is saved when the *Pegasus* jumps into the battle, despite Adama's orders to Apollo. Commander Apollo sends the *Pegasus* on a suicide collision course that takes out two of the basestars and lets the humans get away.

Adama: I guess you didn't understand my orders.
Apollo: I never could read your handwriting.

Notes: These are very momentous episodes—the human fleet reuniting, the heroic loss of the *Pegasus*, the escape from New Caprica. Strange, then, that they received some of the series' lowest viewer ratings. Might Americans have been tired of the Iraqi war, both the real one and the fictionalized versions of it?

And this is all set against the socio-political explorations of—wait, Colonel Tigh killed his wife?—wartime morality, and the situational morality of existence when confronted by existential—*Ellen Tigh is dead*? And she kinda knew she was drinking poison, right?!?—ancient philosophers and theologians disagree about the ethics of using deadly violence to confront evil when it is presented as—SAUL KILLED ELLEN?

What a couple of episodes!

Collaborators

Writer: Mark Verheiden. **Director:** Michael Rymer. **Airdate:** October 27, 2006.

Tom Zarek, who became president following Baltar's escape with the Cylons, authorizes a secret group called the Circle to be judge, jury, and executioner of suspected collaborators. The punishment is expulsion out an airlock. When Felix Gaeta is brought before the group, he must try to prove that he was feeding the resistance leaders secret Cylon information during the occupation.

The one collaborator the Circle might most have liked to judge, Dr. Gaius Baltar, is beyond their reach—with a council of Cylons voting on the life of their prisoner.

Zarek, who is smart enough to know that he won't be accepted as president by many in the fleet, arranges with Laura Roslin to re-create the Quorum of Twelve, nominate her as his successor, and then he will become her vice president.

Tigh: Long as you're here, maybe you can help me out. I'm missing something. I lost it in detention. Since you're so buddy-buddy with the Cylons, maybe you know where it is. How about it? Do you know where my eye is?

Notes: Let's just take a moment to consider Gaius Baltar, the fictional reincarnation of John Colicos' Baltar from the original series. Then he had been a rather typical sneering baddie, issuing orders to his Cylon minions to attack the *Galactica* hither and yon. That Baltar only began to become interesting when he was made vulnerable, delivering himself to the *Galactica* and being imprisoned.

But this new Baltar has little in common with his predecessor. Not intentionally a traitor, he is instead a brilliant but weak man who seems always to be five minutes away from a debilitating panic if others discover just how complicit/criminal/craven/weak/confused he really is at any one moment. Actor James Callis makes him such a mix of cravenness, comedy, genius, and (rarely) morality that he deserves a hearty "Well done, sir."

Torn

Writer: Anne Cofell Saunders. **Director:** Jean de Segonzac. **Airdate:** November 3, 2006.

Boomer—or Sharon—is hailed as a hero for her work with the escape from the Cylons, and she is rewarded with a new flight handle, Athena. Elsewhere on the *Galactica*, though, things are not so full of harmony. Adama gets so fed up with complaining by Tigh and Starbuck that he reads them the riot act, leading Tigh to quit his post.

Baltar manages to uncover some secrets of the Cylons when a basestar's crew becomes infected with some strange virus. Baltar discovers an unidentified box that the Cylons say originated with the 13th colony.

Adama: You're full of bile, hatred—and I know it has something to do with Ellen. I'm sorry for that. And if you need time, Saul, you take all the time you want, but I gotta run a ship. And the last thing I need is a one-eyed drunk sitting down here, sowing discontent and disobedience. So I'll tell you once again, Saul, you can pick up that weapon and kill me. Or you can get your ass back into your quarters and not leave 'til you act like the man I've known for the past 30 years.
Tigh: That man doesn't exist any more, Bill. And you won't be seeing me again.

Notes: In the 1978–79 *Battlestar Galactica*, Athena was the name of Commander Adama's daughter, portrayed by Maren Jensen. In that series, Athena was a part of the *Galactica*'s bridge crew and she was Cassiopeia's rival for the fleeting affections of the male Starbuck. In some of the non-TV media from that series (such as the novelizations), Athena also had been a viper pilot.

A Measure of Salvation

Writer: Michael Angeli. **Director:** Bill Eagles. **Airdate:** November 10, 2006.

The *Galactica* discovers a Cylon basestar and its crew, most of whom are dead. Taking the few survivors away with them, the humans concoct a plan to kill the surviving Cylons within reach of a resurrection ship, which would result in them being downloaded—presumably with the virus that killed their compatriots. Adama and Roslin argue over the plan, with the president making the final decision. But Helo steps in to prevent a genocide of the Cylons.

Baltar: I'm a scientist. And as a scientist, I believe that if God exists our knowledge of him is imperfect. Why? Because the stories and myths we have are the products of men, the passage of time. That religion in practice is based on a theory, impossible to prove. Yet you bestow it with absolutes like, "There is no such thing as coincidence."
Number Three: It's called faith.
Baltar: Absolute belief in God's will means there's a reason for everything. Everything! And yet you can't help ask yourself how God can allow death and destruction and then despise yourself for asking. But the truth is, if we knew God's will, we'd all be Gods, wouldn't we? I can see it in your eyes, D'Anna. You're frustrated. You're conflicted. Let me help you. Let me help you change. Find a way to reconcile your faith with fact. Find a way toward a rational universe.

Notes: The humans have a chance here to deal a debilitating blow to the Cylons, spreading a deadly virus through their resurrection ship. But Helo, apparently wanting the show to continue past episode seven of season three, thwarts the plan, and Adama and Roslin let the matter drop. Over in *Star Trek: The Next Generation*-land, they, too, once had a chance to try to infect all of the Borg with a virus. As Dr. Crusher tells Captain Picard, "I just think we should be clear about that. We're talking about annihilating an entire race."

That's an interesting similarity, against very different backgrounds. *Star Trek: TNG* was set in a successful future of technological and social development that was largely a safe place threatened from time to time by adversaries or just plain old misunderstandings. But the Borg were a new kind of threat (and one that energized that series). Compare that to *Battlestar Galactica* (original and reimagined), which is about complete collapses of human civilization, with the human race literally confronting its annihilation at the hands of an enemy that had an explicit plan to wipe out the human race. Does the same morality apply?

Hero

Writer: David Eick. **Director:** Michael Rymer. **Airdate:** November 17, 2006.

When a crew member of Adama's previous ship shows up in a stolen Cylon raider, the admiral is pleased to see his old friend, Novacek. But Adama also grows rueful, remembering that it was he—Adama—who had actually shot down Novacek's ship while they were on a secret mission to spy on the Cylons a year before the attack on the Colonies. Novacek was subsequently imprisoned by the Cylons for three years before he was able to steal a raider and escape. He had thought all this time that he had been captured after being shot down by a Cylon, but when he learns the truth, he wants revenge.

Tigh: I hear you got a medal.
Adama: Yeah. They're handing them out for anything these days. Good behavior. Attendance. Plays well with others.

Notes: This is a pretty standard plot, one that—with a few details changed—could have been an episode of the original *Galactica* series (or any of the *Trek* series, *Buck Rogers in the 25th Century*, *Babylon 5*—you get the point).

Unfinished Business

Writer: Michael Taylor. **Director:** Robert M. Young. **Airdate:** December 1, 2006.

An Adama-sanctioned boxing tournament is taking place aboard the battlestar, serving as an outlet for the crew's built-up tensions, especially those resulting from the disastrous attempt to colonize New Caprica. Rank holds no privilege in the ring, and Tyrol gets to deck Admiral Adama with gusto. But the big matchup is between old friends Apollo and Starbuck, who have a lot to work through—not the least of which is the matter of their respective spouses.

Adama: When you step on this deck, you be ready to fight, or you dishonor the reason why we're here. Now remember this: When you fight a man, he's not your friend. Same goes when you lead men. I forgot that once. I let you get too close, all of you. I dropped my guard. I gave some of you breaks, let some of you go before the fight was really over. I let this crew and this family disband, and we paid the price in lives. That can't happen again.

Notes: There are a couple directors named Robert Young, but the Robert M. Young who directed this episode has notably used *Galactica* star Edward James Olmos in eight of his movies, and he produced *American Me*, the 1992 directorial debut of Olmos (who would, of course, go on to direct a number of well-received *Galactica* episodes himself). The official *edwardjamesolmos.com* website has an entire page devoted to Robert M. Young and Young's involvement with Olmos Productions. (In fact, even putting Young aside, Olmos' website is a worthy visit, for it will remind you or inform you for the first time of Olmos' accomplishments and the many ways he tries to make the world a better place.)

The Passage

Writer: Jane Espenson. **Director:** Michael Nankin. **Airdate:** December 8, 2006.

In desperate need of food supplies, the fleet must reach a planet rich in food on the other side of a nebula. The nebula is too large to go around or jump through using FTL drives. Instead, ships must be escorted through by shielded raptors. But it's a dangerous exercise, and it particularly tests the skills of pilot Kat.

On the basestar, Baltar tries to find out if he is a Cylon, one of the remaining five with secret identities.

Adama: I hear they're still eating paper. Is that true?
Tigh: No. Paper shortage!

Notes: The echoes of original *Galactica* plots in past episodes dealing with the planet Kobol and *Pegasus* were too obvious to have been accidental. But sharp-eyed—or bored—viewers of "The Passage" might note a resemblance to a subplot in "Saga of a Star World," the first *Battlestar Galactica* movie in 1978, in which Apollo, Boomer, and Starbuck must guide the fleet through a nebula; they fly shielded vipers on a risky mission to shoot up Cylon space mines blocking the way. This echo of an idea from the previous series was likely unintentional. Nebulae are, after all, irresistible to science fiction characters. Just ask Khan Noonien Singh.
Oh, wait, you can't—he's dead.

The Eye of Jupiter

Writer: Mark Verheiden. **Director:** Michael Rymer. **Airdate:** December 15, 2006.

On the planet where the fleet has gone to gather food, the humans discover the mythical Eye of Jupiter in the Temple of Five. Cylon basestars jump into orbit around the planet, and Baltar tells the *Galactica* that they need to talk. Baltar and the Cylons say they want the Eye of Jupiter and will leave the humans alone if they are allowed to have it. Adama refuses and threatens to nuke the Temple of Five if the Cylons try to take the Eye. With Starbuck's raptor shot down by a Cylon and the local star about to go supernova, the basestars and the *Galactica* gear up for battle.

Athena learns from another Boomer-model Cylon that her child Hera is indeed alive on the Cylon basestar, not dead as Roslin had led her to believe.

Starbuck: Can I make a suggestion you won't like?
Apollo: Do you make any other kind?

Notes: Once again showing that the new *Galactica* takes its ancient cues from Greek myths as opposed to the Egyptian myths of the 1978–79 series, this episode really lays the foundation for the endgame of the Moore-Eick series. We see the beginning of the teamup between humans and a Cylon faction.

Rapture

Writers: Bradley Thompson, David Weddle. **Director:** Michael Rymer. **Airdate:** January 21, 2007.

As the humans and Cylons skirmish on the planet's surface, the toasters come up the winners, gaining control of the Temple of Five. As the sun starts to go supernova, everyone flees the system, jumping away just as the star lets loose its fury. As people exit their shuttles in the *Galactica*'s hangar deck, Helo is reunited with Athena, who escaped with her baby thanks to help from a Number Six model, who is also aboard the shuttle. And Baltar is aboard another shuttlecraft, having been captured by Tyrol on the planet. He goes into the brig.

Gaeta: Safeties disabled. Warheads are armed.
Adama: XO, please input your firing code.
Tigh: These nukes will obliterate anything or anyone within 20 clicks of the Temple.
Adama: I know.

Notes: Inside the Temple of Five, the humans see an image that reminds Helo of a painting in Starbuck's Caprica apartment. Asked why she painted it, she professes ignorance and says she just liked it.

This episode lays out a lot of such breadcrumbs that will be picked up through the remainder of the series, including the vision of five mysterious cloaked figures in the temple. Now who could they be?

Taking a Break from All Your Worries

Writer: Michael Taylor. **Director:** Edward James Olmos. **Airdate:** January 28, 2007.

Baltar is interrogated aboard the *Galactica*. The humans try everything from threatened execution to drugging their prisoner in an attempt to get him to tell them secrets about the Cylons. Baltar demands a trial, his right as a citizen of the Twelve Colonies. Gaeta is sent in to try to get him to talk, and Baltar whispers something to Gaeta that leads the younger man to stab Baltar in the neck.

Elsewhere, Starbuck and Apollo's marriages to Anders and Dualla, respectively, are disintegrating.

Baltar: She—Caprica-Six—she chose me. Chose me over all men. Chosen to be seduced, taken by the hand. Guided between the light and the dark. But is she an angel, or is she a demon? Is she imaginary, or is she real? Is she my own voice, or the voice—

Notes: In "The Face of the Enemy," a series of webisodes for *Battlestar Galactica*'s fourth season, Baltar's whispered words to Gaeta are revealed: Baltar accused Gaeta of being a double agent during the Cylon occupation of New Caprica.

And yes, this episode's title is a line from the theme song to the 1982–1993 sitcom *Cheers*.

The Woman King

Writer: Michael Angeli. **Director:** Michael Rymer. **Airdate:** February 11, 2007.

While Roslin and Zarek try to come up with a plan to hold the trial of Baltar without introducing more chaos into the fleet, the *Galactica* has hundreds of sick Sagittarons aboard, quarantined in an unused hangar bay. They are being treated by Dr. Robert, but many of them are refusing treatment, accusing the doctor of atrocities against them back on New Caprica. It's up to Helo to try to convince Adama and Tigh that something is wrong, but they dismiss his complaints and let Robert continue his work with the Sagittarons.

Helo finds evidence that 90 percent of Roberts' patience on New Caprica died; things get personal when Dee asks Roberts for some medical attention.

Dr. Cottle: What the hell happened to "do no harm," doctor?
Dr. Robert: Look, I intervened because someone has to make the tough choices. But it doesn't matter, it doesn't matter because—look at 'em—they're going to destroy themselves anyway. Look at them out there. They're like worms crawling on a hot rock. Remember what you used to say, Saul? "Aside from a Cylon, is there anything that you hate more than a Sagittaron?"
Tigh: I'll tell you what I hate, Mike. Being wrong. Captain Agathon?
Helo: Sir?
Tigh: Arrest this son of a bitch. Gag him if you have to.
Helo: My pleasure, sir.

Notes: There's an odd pleasure in having Dr. Cottle and Colonel Tigh ride to the rescue at the end. These are two of the more untrustworthy and uninspiring characters among the *Galactica*'s officer corps, but they do the right thing here, and it is fun to see their harsh comments and judgments turned against a genuine villain instead of fellow protagonists.

Dr. Robert is portrayed by Bruce Davison, whose genre credits include appearances in *Willard* (the 1971 and 2003 versions), *Ben*, *Tales of the Darkside*, *The Lathe of Heaven*, *Star Trek: Enterprise*, *Knight Rider*, *X-Men* and *X2*.

A Day in the Life

Writer: Mark Verheiden. **Director:** Rod Hardy. **Airdate:** February 18, 2007.

Adama is coming to terms with how his devotion to work had led to the dissolution of his marriage, and he finds himself paying more attention to his relationship with his son, Apollo. Roslin and Adama agree that Apollo should lead an effort to organize Baltar's upcoming trial, but Apollo turns down the request.

Chief Tyrol and Cally, another married couple juggling work and family pressures, are stuck in an airlock that has a leak, and the *Galactica* crew decides to use a risky rescue by opening the outside door and capturing them in a raptor.

Apollo: A kick in the butt is worth a thousand words.

Notes: The scenes with Tyrol and Cally in the airlock add tension to what is otherwise a quiet, character-driven episode. Though it gives us a view inside their marriage, the producers might have been better off tacking that onto a different episode and letting this one just run with the less-dramatic but more rewarding character development of the rest of the story. The characters and actors of the series were strong enough to carry an hour-long tale without having to manufacture a life-and-death struggle.

Dirty Hands

Writers: Jane Espenson, Anne Cofell. **Director:** Wayne Rose. **Airdate:** February 25, 2007.

Strike! Workers in some of the fleet's grungier jobs are protesting not only the unrelenting labor of their positions, but the fact that many of them have been doing the same jobs their parents did. The conflict is fueled by a secretly written book by the imprisoned Baltar, which argues that the old aristocracy of the Colonies is being continued in the fleet, with certain tribes getting the high-quality white collar jobs while others get stuck in dangerous blue collar jobs.

Chief Tyrol is sent to find a way to get the workers back in line, but he eventually agrees with their side of the argument, and he leads a strike that threatens to bring a ruthless response from Adama. Can the fleet avoid an all-out social civil war?

Baltar: Oh, yes, I left Aerilon after my eighteenth birthday. I turned my back on my family, my heritage, all of them. Of course it doesn't matter, though—they're all dead now.

Notes: A little taste of "The Cloud Minders" here, though it is pretty clear from both iterations of *Battlestar Galactica* that it helps to be related to or close friends with the Adamas if you want a position of power on the battlestar. In the end, Roslin and Tyrol manage to back away from the abyss and find ways to get the overlooked people a chance to become trained for jobs they have been traditionally excluded from holding. The episode ends with one such lucky deck crewmember, Seelix, who is promoted and assigned to train as a pilot, under the watchful/tough/unique eye of Starbuck.

Maelstrom

Writers: Bradley Thompson, David Weddle. **Director:** Michael Nankin. **Airdate:** March 4, 2007.

Starbuck is struggling to come to terms with strange dreams she has been having regarding the Eye of Jupiter (remember the Temple of Five and Starbuck's painting from "Rapture"?), so she goes to see Yolanda Brenn, an oracle. Brenn already knows about her dreams and connects it to a message from Starbuck's mother. We later learn more about Starbuck's troubled relationship with her mother, who was also a soldier in the first Cylon War. Her mother seems to be telling her something about embracing death.

On a patrol flight around a gas giant planet and later on the *Galactica*, Starbuck continues having visions about the Eye of Jupiter, and her senior officers begin to wonder if she's mentally stable. On a subsequent mission, the Galacticans are shocked when Starbuck's viper is destroyed.

Starbuck: So you don't think I'm nuts?
Apollo: I didn't say that. You're a raving lunatic. As demented and deranged as the first day I met you.

Notes: And like that, Starbuck is gone. This episode is worth a repeat viewing. When do you think Starbuck died? In the earlier flight? She thinks her viper sustained damage from bullet impacts, but Tyrol says that's not the case. She also sees a younger version of herself in her viper cockpit. Is she going crazy, or was she already dead? Or was she seeing visions courtesy of her mother, who had died of cancer? And will this be like so many other TV series deaths, and in the next episode Starbuck will return?

The Son also Rises

Writer: Michael Angeli. **Director:** Robert Young. **Airdate:** March 11, 2007.

Starbuck does not return.

Baltar's lawyer is killed by a terrorist bomb as preparation for the trial gets into high gear. His new attorney, Romo Lampkin, is a former protege of Apollo's lawyer grandfather. Lamkin, whose eccentricities include a penchant for kleptomania, agrees to the assignment even though he himself becomes the target of the anti-Baltar bomber.

Through clues found in the quirky lawyer's possession, Apollo tracks down the person who has been setting the bombs. The bomber admits his guilt, but says he'll keep doing it if he's able, until Baltar is dead.

Lampkin: Everybody has demons. Them, Baltar, you, me. Even the machines. The law is just a way of exorcising them. That's what your father's father told me. You want to know why I hated him? Because he was right.
Apollo: So you hated him because he was right, and I hated the law because it was wrong. Because of what—of what it put him through. I mean, he defended the worst of the worst. I remember reading about him. The outrage. Helping murderers go free. What I don't understand is why he put himself through all that abuse.
Lampkin: You think he gave a flying frak?

Notes: A good episode, but like "A Day in the Life," this would have been just as strong or even stronger if the bombing element had been left out. The real drama in this story is the tension between the older and younger generations of the Adama family. The question of justice and defending the accused—and the guilty—is the core of the story here, so it didn't need the amped-up bombing subplot.

Crossroads (Parts I and II)

Writers: Michael Taylor, Mark Verheiden. **Director:** Michael Rymer. **Airdates:** March 18, 2007, and March 25, 2007.

As Baltar's long-awaited trial finally gets underway, it's visions galore, as Roslin and Athena share a dream, and Tigh and Anders both hear music that is audible to no one else.

Strange as Baltar's attorney, Lamkin, is, he is successful at getting the trial moving in his client's favor, especially by discrediting key prosecution witnesses such as Tigh and Roslin. When the trial ends with Baltar's acquittal, the fleet's leaders must move on, despite increasing visions by Roslin and others.

The musical tune leads four Galacticans to get together and realize that they are Cylons.

Speaking of which, four Cylon basestars suddenly appear, heading toward the

Galactica. And as the fleet prepares for battle with the enemy, Apollo discovers an unexpected ship: It's Starbuck, who announces that she has found Earth.

Starbuck: Hi, Lee.
Apollo: Kara?
Starbuck: Don't freak out; it really is me. It's going to be okay. I've been to Earth. I know where it is. And I'm going to take us there.

Notes: Just when you're thinking, "This is a surprisingly low-key episode with which to end a season of a series that delights in high-drama season cliffhangers," along comes the stinger. Boom! In other words, a lot happens in this two-part season-ending episode. We finally learn the identities of four of the Final Five Cylons and we get the return of Starbuck, but we are left with new questions about her: Is she a Cylon? Is she dead? Did she ever die or was she just lost?

The lead-up to the production of the earlier episode "Maelstrom," in which Starbuck's viper is destroyed, included an attempt by the producers to keep that plot point secret even from the rest of the cast and crew. But, according to the *Los Angeles Times*, the secret became un-secret during the episode's production.

TV MOVIE

Razor

Writer: Michael Taylor. **Director:** Felix Enriquez Alcala. **Airdate:** November 24, 2007.

Jumping between events that happened to William Adama and Helena Cain in battles with the Cylons when they were younger, and events on the *Pegasus* when Apollo commanded it following Cain's murder, "Razor" gives us a lot of backstory on how Cain came to be the person she is and how she runs her ship. We learn of her relationship with Gina, who turns out to be a humanoid Cylon and ends up in the brig, where she will be beaten and violated by the *Pegasus*' crew. In the "present," Apollo leads the ship on a mission to retrieve a science team that has been abducted by the Cylons, who are using them for experiments.

Adama: Any ruffled feathers?
Apollo: Well, she and Kara don't exactly get along.
Adama: I'd like to sell tickets to that dance.

Notes: This special TV movie aired before the beginning of the fourth season of the series, and could be considered to constitute the first two of 22 episodes in that final season. With Gina and Cain being shown to have had a relationship, the producers introduced the topic of homosexuality into *Battlestar Galactica* for the first time. It wouldn't be the last time.

SEASON FOUR

He That Believeth in Me

Writers: Bradley Thompson, David Weddle. **Director:** Michael Rymer. **Airdate:** April 4, 2008.

Baltar is beginning to build a following as some sort of a spiritual leader in the fleet. He seemingly cures a sick child, praying that God should take his—Baltar's—life instead of the child's. But Starbuck is being met with disbelief and distrust upon her return. She claims to know where Earth is and warns that the Eye of Jupiter should not be the focus of their searching; she soon comes to loggerheads with President Roslin. And the four recently revealed Cylons—Anders, Foster, Tigh, and Tyrol—worry that they will harm the fleet as they continue to perform their regular jobs.

Number Six: Yesterday you were facing execution; today you're free. Why the long face?
Baltar: Oh, gee, I don't know. From president of the Colonies to this—king of fools. Probably best to be hated by everyone than loved by this lot, doomed to live out the rest of my life in this looney bin.

Notes: More than a year after the *oh my God what does this mean* ending to season three, season four arrives.

"He That Believeth in Me" was nominated for two Emmy awards, winning the Emmy for Outstanding Special Visual Effects for a Series.

The title is a quote from the Christian Bible: John 11: 25–26: "I am the resurrection and the life; he who believes in me, though he die, yet shall he live, and whoever lives and believes in me shall never die. Do you believe this?" Well, do you?

And—oh, hey, does anyone remember the original series episode "War of the Gods," in which Apollo is killed and then brought back to life by the lightship? Or, again apropos of "War of the Gods," how Count Iblis was becoming popular among the fleet's people as a messiah figure?

Six of One

Writer: Michael Angeli. **Director:** Anthony Hemingway. **Airdate:** April 11, 2008.

Starbuck holds President Roslin at gunpoint in a disagreement about the direction to planet Earth. When security officers show up, Starbuck is arrested and thrown into the brig. She loses her sense of the direction to Earth when the fleet makes another FTL jump. Eventually, Adama relents and gives her a ship and some colleagues to use to locate Earth.

There's a different kind of dissension taking place among the Cylons, who are voting on whether to use raiders to destroy the fleet, even though it contains the Final Five humanoid Cylons. The Numbers One, Four, and Five Cylons vote to change the brains of the centurions so they don't recognize that the Final Five are in the fleet and can then be used to attack it. The Numbers Two, Six, and Eight oppose the plan. But their disagreement turns to murder when one of the Cylons—a Number Six—alters the Centurions by removing an artificial limit on their higher brain functions, enabling them to make their own decisions—and they use that freedom to kill the humanoid Cylons in the room who had voted to lobotomize them.

Starbuck: So you think I'm right?
Adama: Maybe. Maybe not. But I know she is—the president. She's been right all along. I'm tired of losing. I'm tired of turning away from the things that I want to believe in. And I believe you when you say that you'll die before you stop trying. And I won't lose you again. Now go. Find a way to Earth.

Notes: The beginning of the program shows the Twelve Colonies have only 39,676 survivors left. Of greater interest is the outbreak of open, violent rebellion among the Cylons; it has been long-brewing, and it makes possible the eventual teaming up of some Cylons with that dwindling remnant of humanity from the Twelve Colonies.

Also of note in this episode is that Lee Adama formally retires from the military, soon to take a position on the Quorum of Twelve. It would probably have had more impact if he didn't bounce around from position to position all through the series—CAG, advisor to the president, commander of a battlestar, acting president, vice president. Ultimately, this move seems less like he's assuming his destiny and more like he's taking on his latest temp job.

The Ties that Bind

Writer: Michael Taylor. **Director:** Michael Nankin. **Airdate:** April 18, 2008.

Civil war is breaking out among the Cylons, as different factions struggle over what to do about the Final Five. While Starbuck and her little crew on their mission are having no luck finding Earth and tensions among them begin to increase, Apollo is busy establishing himself in his new career as a politician. He is the delegate for Caprica to the Quorum of Twelve. Tom Zarek warns Apollo about Roslin's and Adama's secretive ways of governing.

And the ties that bind Tyrol and Cally finally break; she thinks he is having an affair, but she learns instead that her husband is a Cylon. She is stopped from killing herself and her child by Tory Foster, one of the Final Five, who saves the child but shoots Cally into space.

Adama: Well, sometimes a benevolent tyrant is exactly what you need.
Zarek: No. A tyrant craves power for its own sake. And all Laura wants is to save us all.

Notes: This episode's title, "The Ties that Bind," comes from a hymn written by a British theologian and pastor John Fawcett, "Blest Be the Tie that Binds." These religious echoes are of note as we keep going into the fourth season; interestingly, there are a lot of Christian allusions, despite the basically pre-Christian Greek religious structure of the Twelve Colonies. Were the writers and producers using this to indicate the growth of the monotheistic Cylon faith?

Escape Velocity

Writer: Jane Espenson. **Director:** Edward James Olmos. **Airdate:** April 25, 2008.

The religious content of *Battlestar Galactica* continues to grow apace as the series heads toward its denouement. Baltar's spiritual status rises, even as attempts to harm him and disrupt his activities continue. The opposition is made up of a sect of believers in the traditional pantheon of gods, while Baltar begins preaching a monotheistic gospel. Meanwhile, Apollo challenges President Roslin's manner of ruling by decree, and she tells Baltar that her impending death from cancer has made her more willing to act outside of the law; then she releases him from prison.

Roslin [***at the funeral for Cally***]**:** I like this service.
Adama: It's not for me, I'll tell you that.
Roslin: I know, but I want you to know what I like.

Notes: Baltar preaches about a kind of monotheistic god, instead of the multiple gods of the traditional Twelve Colonies sort. In real life, all three of the main monotheistic faiths on Earth—Christianity, Islam, and Judaism—posit the belief in a single god as an advance over the polytheism of pre-existing religions. In the reimagined *Battlestar Galactica* mythology, however, as we'll see in the final episode, these Cylons and humans on their long journey to Earth settle on our planet about 150,000 years ago and presumably interbreed with the primitive humans initially seen off in the distance. Because we have just witnessed for several seasons how similar the technology, behaviors and customs of the Twelve Colonies are to 20th century Earth, we have to assume that there was transmission of considerable information from those beleaguered colonists to the primitive humans. Yet, our own history shows us that polytheism was the predominant religious outlook for a long time before in particular Christianity and Islam spread so widely, all of which took place in roughly the past couple thousand years (five thousand if we go by Judaism's origins).

It is unclear whether the writers took that into consideration when they built their very intricate mythology for the series, or if they just painted themselves into a corner and said, essentially, "Screw it" when it came to matching all of that up with real life.

The Road Less Traveled

Writer: Mark Verheiden. **Director:** Michael Rymer. **Airdate:** May 2, 2008.

On the mission aboard the *Demetrius* to find Earth, Starbuck resists turning back despite having no luck so far in their search. Her team members pressure her to give up and return to the fleet even without success. But when a raider shows up, with a Leoben Conoy Cylon model aboard, the humans are told the Cylons can help. A protective Anders confronts Leoben, learning of the civil war among the Cylons; Leoben suggests the humans and Leoben's Cylon faction should team up together. Leoben tells Starbuck that it is her destiny to lead the humans forward. But when Starbuck orders the *Demetrius* to jump to the location of Leoben's basestar, her small crew mutinies.

Starbuck: Leoben?
Leoben Conoy: I'm here for you—to offer a truce between Cylon and human. And a chance to complete your journey.

Notes: First Helo and then Gaeta refuses to follow Starbuck's order to take the *Demetrius* to the basestar. We already know Helo is willing to take heat for doing what he thinks is right even if it goes against his commanders' wishes. But as we'll learn, Gaeta will come to demonstrate that mutinying is a bit of a Gaeta specialty.

Faith

Writer: Seamus Kevin Fahay. **Director:** Michael Nankin. **Airdate:** May 9, 2008.

When her crew refuses to take the *Demetrius* to the Cylon basestar, Starbuck takes a raptor instead; Athena and Anders join her. She finds a damaged basestar and Cylons unable to decide on a path forward. Starbuck and her team get control of the basestar and join up with the *Demetrius*. Back in the fleet, Roslin deals with the steadily growing attraction of Baltar's monotheistic message among the people.

Emily Kowalski: Oh, Laura. And the Lords of Kobol are *real*? Reigning from a metaphysical mountaintop in those silly outfits? Zeus? Handing out fates out of an urn like they were lottery tickets? "You're gonna work on a tylium ship. You're gonna be an admiral. Your family's gonna be evaporated in an attack on the Colonies, but you'll survive for three more years on a moldy compartment on a freighter 'til your body starts to eat itself up alive." Those are the gods that you worship? Capricious, vindictive—
Roslin: But they're not meant to be taken literally. They're metaphors, Emily.

Kowalski: I don't need metaphors. I need answers.

Notes: Emily Kowalski, a cancer patient, is portrayed by Nana Visitor, who starred in *Star Trek: Deep Space Nine* as Kira Nerys. Perhaps more intriguing is that this fictional cancer patient's name is shared by an actual oncologist—a doctor focusing on cancer—at the University of Maryland.

Guess What's Coming to Dinner?

Writer: Michael Angeli. **Director:** Wayne Rose. **Airdate:** May 16, 2008.

The unlikely alliance that will see the series through to its completion takes shape. Starbuck's team succeeds in getting the *Demetrius* and the Cylon basestar back to the fleet. The *Galactica* sends soldiers to take over the basestar, and the rest of the *Galactica*'s leaders learn about the civil war among the Cylons. Starbuck and Roslin try to unravel the mysterious dreams the president has been having. Of particular interest is a shared dream that Athena and Roslin have that takes place in an opera house. And Roslin and Adama agree to team up with their new Cylon compatriots in a mission to go to the "hub" where they can destroy the whole resurrection system of the Cylons, turning them into mortal beings unable to rebirth after being killed—and getting one of the Number Three models who supposedly holds the secret of the identities of the Final Five among the fleet.

The Cylon Natalie: Madam President, you asked for a reason to help us? Vengeance. You destroy the hub, the Cylons lose their ability to download. All of us.
Roslin: Why would you be willing to lose your ability to resurrect?
Natalie: We're rebels. We can't go back.

Notes: A lot of information is jammed down the viewers' throats in this and other episodes late in the series. While some of it is confusing—such as pretty much everything to do with the hybrid in the muck on the basestar, who spouts difficult to understand prophecies—some of it serves to clear up things considerably. The role of the resurrection ships we understood already; Cylons are destroyed, and *poof!* they're brought back to life in another body. But the destruction of the whole resurrection system cuts right to the core of the Cylon outlook; their superiority over humans and their inferiority regarding procreation. If the resurrection system is gone, then the Cylon rebels are correct that the remaining Cylons will have to team up with the humans—or die out, or somehow replicate the resurrection system. Wait, couldn't they just manufacture more of themselves the way the first humanoid Cylons were made?

Sine Qua Non

Writer: Michael Taylor. **Director:** Rod Hardy. **Airdate:** May 27, 2008.

Aboard the basestar, the hybrid has been "plugged in" again, and tells the ship to immediately jump—which it does, with Roslin and others aboard. Adama sends a scouting mission to try to track the basestar, but it finds a destroyed basestar instead. Believing that Roslin is lost, the Quorum searches for a new president, and signs point to Quorum member Apollo taking on the role; Lee becomes the acting president of the humans.

Accused of endangering the fleet with his search for Roslin, Adama puts Tigh in charge of the *Galactica* and heads out in a raptor in his own search.

Adama: I know that you've been spending a lotta time interrogating the Six, but now the brig guards tell me that every time you order them out, you turn off the cameras.
Tigh: I'm not torturing her, if that's what you're worried about.
Adama: I'm not. That I could almost understand. This I can't. Cottle tells me she's pregnant. What the frak have you been thinking, colonel?

Notes: Oh dear, Tigh's in charge again . . .

The Hub

Writer: Jane Espenson. **Director:** Paul Edwards. **Airdate:** June 6, 2008.

Baltar, one of the humans aboard the Cylon basestar with Roslin, tries to calm the hybrid, whom he believes to be in a state of panic as the ship jumps and jumps again toward the Cylon hub. During each jump, Roslin has visions, in which she meets with the dead priestess Elosha and sees visions of her fate. The other humans on the basestar decide to use the vipers they took with them to destroy the hub when they find it. Finally, the ship gets to the hub, and after a fierce battle, the vipers destroy the hub with nuclear weapons. When the victorious basestar returns to the *Galactica* fleet's last known coordinates, there is Admiral Adama in his raptor, awaiting his love: Roslin.

Adama: Missed you.
Roslin: Me too. I love you.
Adama: About time.

Notes: Sharp-eyed viewers have noted that in the starscapes of the past few episodes and continuing through to the end of the series there have been visible well-known constellations, implying that the ragtag fleet is getting closer to its goal of our home planet.

Never having had an eye for identifying constellations, I'll just take their word for it.

Revelations

Writers: Bradley Thompson, David Weddle. **Director:** Michael Rymer. **Airdate:** June 13, 2008.

The Cylon-human alliance is off to a rocky start as D'Anna Biers takes human hostages on the basestar in return for the Final Five Cylons in the fleet. But, in another example of why you shouldn't mess with Laura Roslin, who is one of the hostages, she orders Adama to destroy the basestar if the hostage negotiations fail. When one of the Final Five, Col. Tigh, finally reveals to Adama that he is a Cylon, the admiral has his old friend arrested. On the basestar and aboard the *Galactica*, the two sides play brinksmanship, threatening to kill hostages. Tigh had even offered himself as a sacrifice to call Biers' bluff (she wouldn't want one of the Final Five killed), but the Galacticans can't go through with it.

A possible resolution to the standoff pops up when Starbuck finds a signal (via her viper) that she believes comes from Earth. The Cylons and humans join up again for the trip to Earth, but when the landing party goes down to the planet's surface, they find nothing but the radioactive remains of a destroyed city.

Tory Foster [*after revealing that she is a Cylon*]: You had no idea, did you?
Roslin: No.
Foster: Might be worth pondering what else you've been wrong about.

Notes: Note that Starbuck, yet again, comes up with an out-of-left-field development that puts an end to a high-stakes conflict (see also "Resurrection Ship" and "Crossroads"). It might have been simply writerly coincidence; or it might have been a reflection of Starbuck's undefined status—dead? alive? angel? And, I'm probably making more of this than I should, but the episode titles include religion-weighty words, including *resurrection*, *revelations*, and even *crossroads*.

Also: Though this is the middle of the fourth season, it is still a bit of a cliffhanger, because the second half of the season is not aired by Sci-Fi (later Syfy) until six months later, presented as a fifth season.

SEASON FIVE

Sometimes a Great Notion

Writers: Bradley Thompson, David Weddle. **Director:** Michael Nankin. **Airdate:** January 16, 2009.

The Cylons and humans are struck by despair at finding the planet Earth a burned-out ruin. Even more surprising is that the remains of the bodies found on the planet turn out to be Cylon, not human. The landing party concludes that the planet was colonized by the Thirteenth Tribe, which was Cylon, not human, and was destroyed in a nuclear war 2,000 years ago. Anders, Tyrol, Tory, and Tigh all experience memories of their former Cylon selves on the planet and its destruction, and Tigh realizes that the Fifth of the Final Five Cylons was his wife, Ellen. When Starbuck tracks the source of the signal she received in "Revelations," it leads her to a crashed viper with her corpse in it.

Back in the fleet, Tigh and Adama reestablish their friendship and trust, and Adama decides to partner with the Cylons in finding a new home for the fleet.

Roslin: It's perfect. We traded one nuked civilization for another.

Notes: The planet, called Earth, will turn out to be the first of two planets with that name, as we'll find out in the final episodes when the human-Cylon joint fleet finds a planet to colonize and give it the name of Earth, which turns out to be the Earth we all know and love.

A Disquiet Follows My Soul

Writer: Ronald D. Moore. **Director:** Ronald D. Moore. **Airdate:** January 23, 2009.

Tigh and a Number Six model are having a baby, the first all-Cylon baby to be created, offering the Cylons a way of continuing without the resurrection technology that was destroyed in the attack on the Cylon hub. Meanwhile, acting President Tom Zarek argues with Apollo and Adama about the alliance with the Cylons, which he opposes strongly. When the Cylons offer their help in improving the fleet's jump capabilities in return for becoming citizens of the fleet, opposition to the alliance grows. Following the attempted secession from the fleet by a fuel ship, Gaeta and Zarek make a pact to try to change things more to their liking.

Adama: You know, there are days that I really hate this job.

Notes: This episode ends with a surprise scene of Adama and Roslin in bed together, a less surprising surprise than the famous *L.A. Law* episode that showed law firm head Leland McKenzie in bed with his longtime rival Rosalind Shays. There's no connection between these two shows other than the one reminded me of the other in this instance. But it's fun to note that Shays was portrayed brilliantly by Diana Muldaur, who of course played Dr. Katherine Pulaski during the second season of *Star Trek: The Next Generation*. But more on that in the next chapter.

The Oath

Writer: Mark Verheiden. **Director:** John Dahl. **Airdate:** January 30, 2009.

The long-simmering tensions in the fleet come to a boil in this story of score-settling, rebellion, and betrayal. Zarek is sprung from prison by Gaeta and takes over the president's ship, *Colonial One*; Gaeta lights the fuse of mutiny aboard the *Galactica* and succeeds in taking over the CIC. Adama, Roslin, and other loyalists flee and try to rally their supporters in the fleet, and Roslin and Baltar have a rapprochement of sorts, at long last.

Adama: I want you all to understand this! If you do this, there will be no forgiveness. No amnesty. This boy died honoring his uniform. You—you'll die with nothing.

Notes: A recurrent theme of *Battlestar Galactica* is that humanity is self-destructive (and I guess the same is shown to be true for Cylons, too). The hybrid fleet is nearing its long-sought goal of a new planet to settle, and yet it is tearing itself apart.

Blood on the Scales

Writer: Michael Angeli. **Director:** Wayne Rose. **Airdate:** February 6, 2009.

Zarek puts Admiral Adama on trial and condemns him to death. The former terrorist (and one-time acting president) goes all-out for the mutiny, ordering the murder of the Quorum of Twelve when its members refuse to join his side. On the battlestar, Starbuck and Apollo build up a counter-force to the mutineers, managing to save Adama before he could be executed, and also rescuing other prisoners.

Despite all of Zarek's actions, Gaeta understands that the rebellion is losing its steam, and he gives up when Adama's forces retake the CIC. For their role in the mutiny, Gaeta and Zarek are executed.

Gaeta: We had the truth on our side. Now . . . now . . .
Zarek: The truth is told by whoever is left standing.

Notes: Felix Gaeta, portrayed by Alessandro Juliani, had long been a seemingly loyal nerd on the bridge, but he ends up killed for his part in the mutiny. Gaeta is also the first male gay character on the show, something that was handled in a matter-of-fact way, which suited Juliani just fine. He told Marcel Damen on Galatica.tv in 2009, "I was worried that it would feel that it was kind of caked on. . . . [T]he way it was handled, the matter of factness of it, was actually very, very positive and tasteful. They didn't make a huge deal of it in the show, because it shouldn't be a huge deal. It would just be like anybody else. What put it in a strange context though for me was that Felix had never been seen . . . hooked up with anybody through the course of all seasons. . . . Whether he hooked up with a man, woman, or whoever, [fans] were going to be looking for it and make a big deal out of it. For more casual watchers of the show, then it could be interpreted as just a very illuminated way of looking at sexuality—a matter-of-fact [way] of looking at a same-sex relationship. So I was conflicted about it. In the end I conceded, and I think that it was handled well."

No Exit

Writer: Ryan Mottesheard. **Director:** Gwyneth Horder-Payton. **Airdate:** February

13, 2009.

Tigh and Adama consider what to do about the physical state of the battlestar *Galactica*, which is disintegrating and might not survive more jumps. Tyrol suggests using a Cylon solution to fix the fractures, but Adama rejects it and even insists that the repair crew be entirely human. The admiral only changes his mind when he sees the extent of the damage to his ship.

Meanwhile, Roslin and Apollo create a new Quorum to replace the one massacred by Zarek's mutineers.

Roslin: You are the right one, Lee—you have always been the right one. My only concern about you is that you're so hellbent on doing the right thing that you sometimes don't do the smart thing.
Apollo: Well, I'll try to be smarter and wronger.

Notes: In this episode, we learn more about the Final Five when Anders remembers their back stories. They were scientists on the Cylon Earth who were trying to recreate resurrection technology, which had been lost over time. They created a resurrection ship, and they were able to save themselves when Earth was destroyed in nuclear war. They then traveled in the ship to the Twelve Colonies to warn the humans there not to provoke a war with the Cylons, but they arrived too late. The Five's interaction with the Cylon Centurions that had been battling the humans leads to a mess of problems that explains much about how the entire *Galactica* series came to be.

In other words: OH MY GOD, THAT'S HUGE!

Deadlock

Writer: Jane Espenson. **Director:** Robert M. Young. **Airdate:** February 20, 2009.

The resurrected Ellen—the final Final Five Cylon—arrives on the *Galactica* and has a typically testy reunion with her eternal husband, Tigh. She is less than thrilled that Tigh has gotten a Number Six Cylon pregnant; but that pregnancy is leading other Cylons to suggest leaving the humans, because they no longer need them to procreate. Their plans become more complicated when Six suffers a miscarriage.

Elsewhere onboard, Baltar gets Adama's help in using his religious sect as an armed force to counter simmering tension among the civilian population. A religious militia—what could go wrong?

Roslin: Oh, my gods—it's Ellen Tigh.
Hot Dog: How many dead chicks are out there?

Notes: There's no situation that isn't frakked up enough that it can't be made worse by Ellen Tigh (and I write that as a compliment to the writers and the actor, Kate

Vernon). Even resurrected however many times, she retains the propensity to create chaos, and here she first hesitates and then agrees with the other two of the Final Five who vote to leave the human fleet. That of course changes when the miscarriage occurs, hinting that Cylon-on-Cylon coupling cannot (yet?) produce a viable offspring.

But even that drama might have happened because the pregnant Cylon—Caprica Six—had the miscarriage after she became upset by being told by Ellen that Ellen and Saul had had sex when she returned to the fleet. Oh, and Ellen brought Boomer—the resurrected version of the Cylon who had shot Adama—with her. Adama promptly throws Boomer into the brig.

Someone to Watch Over Me

Writers: Bradley Thompson, David Weddle. **Director:** Michael Nankin. **Airdate:** February 27, 2009.

Starbuck, feeling out of sorts after seeing her corpse in the viper on Earth and awaiting improvement in her husband Anders' health, heads to the bar where she befriends a fatherly piano player. The two of them collaborate on a song, and Starbuck remembers a song her father used to play for her. The song is the same one that Tigh, Tyrol, Foster, and Anders all heard in "Crossroads." Starbuck also realizes that a drawing that Hera had given her isn't what she thought it was—a starscape—but is the written form of the music in the song she just played.

Meanwhile, Boomer escapes from the *Galactica* brig by tricking Tyrol and Helo, kidnapping Hera, and attacking Athena.

Starbuck: The first one who sights a habitable rock will get this fine oral hygiene product. It is the last tube of Tauron toothpaste in the universe. Gods know most of you need it.

Notes: Part of the opening theme music from the 1978–79 *Battlestar Galactica* lives again, at least in some incidental music created by the piano player while he's trying to conjure up a melody for Starbuck.

Islanded in a Stream of Stars

Writer: Michael Taylor. **Director:** Edward James Olmos. **Airdate:** March 6, 2009.

Boomer brings Hera to the Colony, a Cylon base. Adama sends a heavy raider—a souped-up Cylon fighter—to try to find the Colony and bring back the baby. But is Boomer starting to connect with the child?

Baltar analyzes the dog tags that Starbuck brought back from her corpse on Earth and declares that the DNA matches Starbuck's. He publicly announces that Starbuck is an angel. Her husband, Anders, is moved into a hybrid tank like the one used on the Cylon basestars, and he begins to speak like a hybrid about past and future events, and he gains access to the *Galactica*'s systems. With the rapidly deteriorating state of the ship, Adama decides to strip the ship and abandon it. He and Tigh drink a tribute to their dying ship.

Ellen: You must understand what we were trying to do. We wanted to end the cycle of war between man and machine.
Tigh: That was a bust.
Ellen: Yes, we failed, but we have a second chance now: Hera. Without her, our children are going to die off one by one, just like they're dying right now in Cottle's sickbay.
Tigh: I had a child. He died.
Ellen: You're wrong, Saul. You have millions.

Notes: The mysterious matter of just what is Starbuck—lucky human? resurrected human? Cylon? angel? some other superhuman being?—continues. When Baltar dubs her an angel, Adama tells him to shut up, Starbuck slaps him, and later Starbuck places her own photo on the *Galactica* wall featuring pictures of the deceased.

Daybreak (Parts I and II)

Writer: Ronald D. Moore. **Director:** Michael Rymer. **Airdate:** March 13, 2009, and March 20, 2009.

The Galacticans decide on a plan to rescue Hera from her Cylon captors, and Admiral Adama offers an amnesty to everyone in the recent mutiny. A rescue team is put together, and the *Galactica* jumps to the Colony, which is located next to a black hole. Anders, who is still essentially connected to the battlestar's programming, is able to disable the other Cylon hybrids. The *Galactica* rams the Colony and Starbuck leads a commando team to find and rescue Hera. With the child back on board, the Galacticans still have to contend with Cylon boarding parties, and ultimately they must defeat Cavil, the leader of the Colony Cylons. But when the Final Five join together to transmit the knowledge Cavil demands for the resurrection technology, the situation heats up again as old secrets are revealed.

Starbuck uses the musical tune to guide her in setting new coordinates for the *Galactica* to jump to. The jump is successful, but the ship is damaged beyond repair, unable to jump further. It won't need to; it has jumped into our system, near the third planet. They call the rest of the fleet to join them, and they go down to Earth, where they see primitive humans. The emptied *Galactica* and the other ships in its fleet are sent into the sun to their destruction, and the Cylons give their Centurions their freedom and control of the basestar, in which the Centurions promptly leave. The new colonists give up their technology and they make up their own minds about where they want to settle on the peaceful planet. While Roslin and Adama select their new home, she finally passes away—finally fulfilling the prophecy about the terminally sick leader who would bring her people to a new home.

Boomer: We all make our choices. Today I made a choice. I think it's my last one.
Starbuck: All right, this is really touching. Now can we get the frak out of here?
Boomer: You should know that your raptor has been destroyed. You can't go back that way.
Athena: Yeah well, that is not the plan.
Starbuck: Can we not tell her the plan?
Athena: Right.

Notes: The series ends with this episode, the very last minutes of which jump ahead 150,000 years to our current time, with Baltar and Six walking the streets of New York City and discussing whether history will repeat itself or if enough has changed this time. It is a bittersweet ending for a series that was based in tragedy and never went far away from warfare, strife, genocide, murder, betrayal, terrorism, and dashed hopes. With Hera playing the role of "Eve" on the new planet, we are left to assume that the humans of today are all human-Cylon hybrids of one sort, a harmonious ending to the Cylon-human holocaust that set the series in motion.

So if we're all human-Cylons, does that mean we will repeat the mistakes that the series tells us have happened over and over, or that the merging of the two races/species/lifeforms has changed the trajectory?

The final population of survivors from the Twelve Colonies is said to be only 38,000.

TV MOVIE

The Plan

Writer: Jane Espenson. **Director:** Edward James Olmos. **DVD release date:** October 27, 2009.

The Cylon plan for dealing with the humans is unveiled through the retelling of many events earlier in the series, though this time with more input from the Cylon side. The Number One Cylons, the Cavil model, coordinate an all-or-nothing attack that turns out to be not quite all. From their initial plans to destroy the human race to the budding movement among the Cylons to recognize that the holocaust was in error, we learn both of the initial successes of the plan and the reasons it started to unravel.

Ellen: This has happened before. Oh gods—am I gonna die?
Cavil: No, your suffering isn't over yet. Not when you've got so much left to learn.
Ellen: What?!?

Notes: Take your pick as to whether this film is an exercise in retconning or a helpful dose of rich background info for the saga. Half a year after the end of the series comes this coda, which portrays the Cylon plans for the annihilation of mankind to be more on-the-fly than the series would have led you to believe. Whether intended this way or not, such a (re)interpretation would also reflect reality here on Earth. Over the decades, the popular view of, for example, Nazi Germany's plans in the Second World War have been that it was this juggernaut carried out at the whim of a well-oiled albeit murderous regime. But the more we have learned about the Nazi regime the more we have realized that it was a very ad hoc outfit. The Nazi government was a cesspool of in-fighting and inefficiency, a far cry from the stereotype of German efficiency. And its war plans, as awful as they were, were adjusted as the changing situation offered opportunities or as disasters presented themselves.

Similar grand plans by others could be similarly dissected, and not just having to do with genocidal wars. Franklin Roosevelt's New Deal had aims and goals, and a willingness to do whatever it took to get the economy moving again and to make it fairer; but the exact mix of federal agencies and government policies was left up to throwing spaghetti at the wall and seeing what would stick.

In addition to the two TV movies included in these pages, *Galactica* also presented occasional webisodes, such as those dealing with the occupation of New Caprica. "Razor Flashbacks" appeared in seven installments of about three minutes each in October and November 2007. They show a young William Adama in the first Cylon war as he discovers what the Cylons secretly have been working on in the background. "The Face of the Enemy" appeared in 10 installments of between three and six minutes in December 2008 and January 2009. The miniseries centers on Lt. Gaeta's increasing dislike of the alliance with the Cylons, and it also shows his past relationships with a Number Eight Cylon (the Boomer model) on New Caprica, who betrays him, and his current relationship with Lt. Louis Hoshi, a former officer on the *Pegasus*. Despite his romantic relationship with Gaeta, Hoshi does not support Gaeta's eventual mutiny.

SPINNING OFF: *CAPRICA* AND *BATTLESTAR GALACTICA: BLOOD & CHROME*

You quickly find that life is short but not cheap in the *Battlestar Galactica* universe.

After Ronald Moore's *Battlestar Galactica* went off the air in 2009, it was succeeded by the short-lived *Caprica*. Lasting just one 18-episode season, *Caprica* divided fans deeply. Some loved learning more about the era of the Cylons' creation, which the show took as its setting. Other fans bemoaned the lack of the space opera aspects that have been a key part of the previous *Galactica* iterations. Set 58 years before Moore's *Galactica*, *Caprica* was more political and corporate soap opera than space opera, focusing on a civilization at the height of its technological advancement and hubris, quite a difference from its predecessor series, which ended with its titular spaceship literally decaying away.

Critics were somewhat unsure of what to make of *Caprica*. Why not show life on the *Galactica* during the Cylon war? Or just life on *Galactica* before the Cylon war? *Caprica* was not my cup of tea, but it might well have been a welcome show for people who wanted more human-based, less hardware-filled SF.

Another attempt to spin off a series on Syfy was called *Battlestar Galactica: Blood & Chrome*. This *was* my cup of tea. It also centered on the Adama family, which seems to demonstrate a self-limiting vision on the part of the creators. *Caprica* featured Joseph Adama, father to Edward James Olmos' Commander/Admiral William Adama; *Chrome* centers on a young William Adama, played by 22-year old Luke Pasqualino, early in the First Cylon War. Syfy noted: "As the battle between humans and their creation, a sentient robotic race [Cylons], rages across the 12 colonial worlds, a brash rookie viper pilot enters the fray." Additional stars of the show included Ben Cotton (*Stargate Atlantis*) as Coker Fasjovik, Lili Bordán (*Two Days in the Smoke*) as Beka Kelly, John Pyper-Ferguson (*Caprica*, *Brothers & Sisters*) as Xander Toth, and Zak Santiago (*Alice*) as Armin Diaz.

Unlike with *Caprica* and the critically acclaimed *Battlestar Galactica*, Ronald D. Moore was not on board as *Chrome*'s creator. That role was filled by Michael Taylor and David Eick, both of whom were *Galactica* producers. "While maintaining the themes of politics, social propaganda, and the timeless question: What does it mean to be human?—*Blood & Chrome* will also return us to the authentic, relentless depiction of combat and the agony and ecstasy of human-Cylon war, which was the hallmark of *Battlestar Galactica*'s early seasons," said Eick.

PILOT CONTROVERSY

Blood & Chrome promised to reintroduce us to the space drama of the original series and to the first decade of the conflict with the Cylons. A two-hour pilot was produced in 2011 in Vancouver, British Columbia, directed by Jonas Pate and written by Taylor, Eick, Bradley Thompson, and David Weddle. It centers on the young pilot Adama, fresh out of the academy, newly assigned to the battlestar *Galactica* and given a mission of escorting a woman who has important information about the Cylons. In the words of the official Syfy press release: "The talented but hot-headed risk-taker [Adama] soon finds himself leading a dangerous top secret mission that, if successful, will turn the tide of the decade-long war in favor of the desperate fleet."

An unofficial preview video created with scenes from the pilot lit up fan circles in early 2012. It showed lots of quick-cut scenes of space battles, explosions, confrontations, and zooming spaceships, clearly indicating that the show was much more action-oriented than either of its predecessors. Reactions to the leaked "sizzle reel" were wildly enthusiastic; the words "frakking awesome" featured prominently in many online comments.

But in March 2012, Syfy announced that it was not going to air *Blood & Chrome* as a regular series but the show would end up as a web series. Mark Stern, Syfy's president of original content and the co-leader of Universal Cable Productions, said in a statement, "Though the vision for *Battlestar Galactica: Blood & Chrome* has evolved over the course of the past year, our enthusiasm for this ambitious project has not waned. We are actively pursuing it as was originally intended: a groundbreaking digital series that will launch to audiences beyond the scope of a television screen." Stern told the *Pittsburgh Post-Gazette* that the channel was still "trying to figure out the economics right now."

Eventually, *Blood & Chrome* received both a web and a Syfy airing, but it was never picked up as a series on either platform. Some fans were asking other questions, such as, If not *Blood & Chrome*, what can Syfy air that is, well, sci-fi-ish? As Meredith Woerner wrote on i09, "Where is the serious space opera on Syfy? There are vampires, ghosts, werewolves, gadgets, detectives, and even monster movies. But what happened to our big juicy spaceship drama steak?"

Blood & Chrome would have been a bit more futuristic than its predecessors in terms of production. TV special effects have long ago left behind spaceship models and miniaturized planetary mockups in favor of digital creations. *Blood & Chrome* would have out-Lucased them all by relying on digital sets, including reconstructions of the bridge (or CIC) of the battlestar.

Rock performer Kyle Toucher, who has moved into the world of creating visual special effects, told Noisecreep.com in June 2012 that he disagreed with claims that *Blood & Chrome* simply cost too much. "The show was monstrously affordable, considering what you were getting," he told the music website. "It was like $7.5 million, which is the craft service budget on a *Transformers* movie."

Calling it "a sci-fi-space-opera-hardware-action show," Toucher added, "This is the show we've always wanted to do. . . . Everything you see there is CG; the sets, the *Galactica* bridge, the ice planet. We had tons of ideas. If the series had gone on, we would have seen sea battles, a giant air battle over Caprica City, Cylon basestar taking out planets. Crazy shit."

If there is a *Chrome* silver lining to all of this, it is that we at least got to see the pilot movie (and it can still be rented or purchased on various platforms). I loved what I saw, and I would have happily watched a series of *Blood & Chrome*. The show promised to give audiences all of the action and backstory they have sought about the Twelve Colonies for decades. It is tempting to chastise Syfy for not going forward with it as a series, but a fairer evaluation is probably that Syfy had in fact taken lots of chances with *Galactica*, including the miniseries itself, the hit series it spawned, innovative interstitial webisodes, special TV movies, and two attempted spinoffs.

Yes, we can want more, but I think we have to acknowledge that we've already gotten quite a lot.

CHAPTER FOUR

Star Trek: The Next Generation 1987–1994

It all has something to do with William Shatner, sooner or later. Classic *Star Trek* star Shatner wasn't thrilled with the J.J. Abrams *Trek* films. But director Abrams probably wasn't too unthrilled; Shatner wasn't excited about *Star Trek: The Next Generation*, either, when it premiered in September 1987, and that sequel series went on to become a monster ratings hit and a critic-pleaser.

Unlike his costar Leonard Nimoy, Shatner has yet to appear in an Abrams-era *Trek*, and he never appeared in *Next Generation* or its fellow sequel series (albeit he did co-star in the mixed-series movie *Star Trek Generations*). We'll leave that to you to conclude if it is coincidence or Hollywood vengeance.

Nonetheless, the show about which he had some initial qualms would become the most successful TV *Trek* series ever, becoming a favorite feature for genre magazine covers and the most successful syndicated TV series of its day. Its success helped establish syndication as a viable platform for first-run—and first-rate and pricey—genre television series, and many such shows would follow in its path, including others from the Gene Roddenberry non-*Trek* collection, such as *Andromeda* and *Earth: Final Conflict*. *Babylon 5*, which in many ways was the un-*Trek* science fiction space series, arguably would not have happened or at least not in the same format if TNG hadn't confirmed original syndication as a sound platform for big-idea SF TV that could last more than a season or two.

How did this come to be? How did a low-rated three-season '60s series become a mega-hit two decades later? A few thoughts:

Quality: The Next Generation was top quality in terms of acting and production, a far cry from the tight finances of the 1960s *Trek*. In terms of writing, the series had its weak episodes, but it had a large number of strong outings, ranging from extravaganzas such as "Best of Both Worlds" to quiet character studies such as "Home."

Continuity: The Next Generation did not reboot the *Trek* universe (something Abrams would do to spectacular effect two decades later); it was set in the 24th instead of the 23rd century, and it paid homage to what went before in the adventures of Kirk, Spock, Bones, Uhura, and others.

Discontinuity: It takes courage to mess with an established formula, but that is what it takes to create something worthwhile and not just to create "product." *Next Generation* didn't just bring us the same characters or the same era, it resolved some issues from the previous incarnation of the series (such as Federation–Klingon warfare), changed the chemistry of the core unit (yes, they actually put a psychiatrist on the bridge), and let the characters develop over time, deepening our knowledge of them and our appreciation of their individual stories.

Salvage: A number of the early stories featured in *Next Generation* were originally conceived as episodes for a never-produced *Trek* series in the late 1970s. That series, initially dubbed *Star Trek: Phase II*, never came to fruition, as studio Paramount wavered between supporting a TV series or a film; after much work and money had been sunk into television pre-production efforts, Paramount eventually went with the film option, and the result was 1979's *Star Trek: The Motion Picture*. When *Trek* was resurrected (following the successful launch of the film franchise featuring the original actors), a number of *Phase II* stories and conceits came along with it (including calling the first officer of *Enterprise* "Number One," an idea that harkens back to creator Gene Roddenberry's original pilot for *Trek*, when the first officer was a—*gasp!*—female).

Real Danger: What began as a fairly safe science fiction series became a wonderfully complex storyline, as we will see when we get to season three. Many programs decide to "shake things up" by having cataclysmic happenings (major characters dying, locations shifting, cast changes); *Trek* didn't need to do that, but it did need to prove that it was a show that was willing to take its characters and the series' thematic challenges seriously, and that was something the show did extremely well. When the writers showed the Klingon Lt. Worf allow someone to die rather than have him assist his enemy, it was true to the character and his outlook on life, even if in 20th century human terms it was morally wrong. This helped make the series more adult than juvenile, letting it stand head and shoulders above typical SF series.

Science fiction: Plenty of science-fiction shows make little or no use of their genre tools. Science fiction stories, pretty broadly and classically speaking, are extrapolations and explorations of the effects and possibilities of human progress, often technological. Most SF space-based shows are futuristic westerns; *Star Trek: The Next Generation* had its share of shows that weren't strictly genre, but the show had many, many that explored the effects of advanced weaponry, different ways of organizing society, medical advances, improvements in space travel, and more.

UNNECESSARY INTERRUPTION

If you were a bystander in 1986, you would not have said a new *Star Trek* series was the missing piece to the cultural puzzle at the time. Things were going rather smoothly back then. The economy was humming along nicely; visual science fiction had reoriented itself to the new possibility of storytelling on a broader canvas and the use of prosthetic special effects; and space exploration had been shunted aside in favor of a global endgame with communism. Even just in the *Trek* world, the focus was on the successful films.

In short, *Star Trek: The Next Generation* never *needed* to happen.

Gene Roddenberry made it happen. A much-loved but still controversial creator and producer of *Trek* since the mid-1960s, the former police officer turned TV producer had not had any big hits—to be honest, he hadn't had any hits at all—since the early years of *Star Trek*. But the TV series had proved to be an enduring success in syndication; it had spawned a well-regarded animated Saturday morning series from 1973-74; there was the continuing movie series (with only limited Roddenberry participation following the first one); lucrative merchandising activity; and successful *Star Trek* conventions were educating the rest of the public on what exactly a science fiction convention was.

So by the mid-1980s, two decades after his better-than-it-needed-to-be science fiction series premiered on NBC, Roddenberry unleashed *Star Trek: The Next Generation*. It should have failed.

But it didn't. It became one of the biggest success stories in television history. Instead of actors trying to ape the styles or characterizations of Walter Koenig and William Shatner and George Takei, the show featured a brand new cast of actors confidently creating new characters. It might not have been at the cutting edge of racial or gender equality, even for the 1980s, but it was quite advanced in terms of its predecessors in both *Trek* and non-*Trek* science fiction TV. When it debuted, there were three female characters in important roles, and though Tasha Yar would make a quick exit, additional women were added to the staff in ensuing years. African American actors would play a larger role in this series, including not just the chief engineer and later addition Guinan, but the wonderful Worf and many of his Klingon compatriots, many of whom were portrayed by African American actors.

In the 1970s, science fiction on TV had some brief hits and a never-ending supply of disappointments. Cheap production values, unimaginative writing, rushed acting, and usually poorly executed special effects did much to inure audiences to low expectations. Networks might offer higher budgets (such as for the original *Battlestar Galactica*), but they also came with all sorts of time-slot restrictions and network interference from executives who wouldn't know the difference between a nebula cluster and a peanut cluster. Syndication offered a bit less interference, but budgets were lower and it came with a constant sales job needed to get the show on enough stations to pay the bills. In the mid-1980s, *Star Trek: The Next Generation* changed much of that.

The reborn *Star Trek* became a syndicated behemoth, at one point garnering the top ratings of any syndicated show in its era, and it managed to please both critics and fans. Despite the change-up of a major cast member in the second season (and then the switch back to the original cast member in the third season), the show continued to get stronger and stronger, developing characters in ways the original *Star Trek* series never did, producing stories that were many steps above the westerns-in-space fodder so often served up in the 1970s, and cultivating an entire new generation of science fiction screenwriters and producers who would go on to transform the small screen SF of the 1990s and 2000s.

It wasn't all goodness and crumpets; the show initially suffered from some mid-1980s political correctness (putting a psychological counselor on the bridge is like sticking a Soviet political commissar in a military unit) and the show's leaders weren't always exactly inspiring (Captain Jean-Luc Picard abandoned his ship with disturbing frequency in the early days of the show).

But, oh, what Patrick Stewart's Picard *became*. Stewart—not Roddenberry's first choice; the producer wanted a Frenchman and only reluctantly settled on an Englishman portraying a Frenchman—performed Picard as a principled leader, not afraid to be unpopular if it meant making the correct tough decision, but not unwilling to show his human side to his friends and crew. After that first season, Picard quickly became an icon of good leadership, and Stewart got to show himself as the icon of great acting that he is. In so doing, Stewart established Picard as arguably the most popular *Star Trek* captain of all time, which undoubtedly didn't sit well with William Shatner.

Because it all has something to do with Shatner, sooner or later.

Creator and Executive Producer: Gene Roddenberry
Studio: Paramount
Producers (various titles and timeframes): Rick Berman, Peter Lauritson, David Livingston, Robert Justman, Robert Lewin, Burton Armus, Mike Gray, John Mason
Theme Music by: Alexander Courage
Composer: Jerry Goldsmith
Consultant: David Gerrold (season 1)
Associate Producer: D.C. Fontana (season 1)
Production Associate: Susan Sackett
Script Supervisor: Cosmo Genovese
Casting Executive: Helen Mossler
Special Effects: Dick Brownfield
Scenic Art Supervisor: Michael Okuda
Senior Illustrator: Rick Sternbach
Set Designer: Herman F. Zimmerman
Consulting Senior Illustrator: Andrew Probert
Captain Jean-Luc Picard: Patrick Stewart
Commander William Riker: Jonathan Frakes

Lt. Commander Data: Brent Spiner
Lt. Commander Geordi la Forge: LeVar Burton
Dr. Beverley Crusher: Gates McFadden (seasons 1, 3–7)
Counselor Deanna Troi: Marina Sirtis
Lt. Tasha Yar: Denise Crosby (season 1)
Lt. Worf: Michael Dorn
Wesley Crusher: Wil Wheaton
Dr. Katherine Pulaski: Diana Muldaur (season 2)
Transporter Chief Miles O'Brien: Colm Meaney
Guinan: Whoopi Goldberg (seasons 2-6)

SEASON ONE

Encounter at Farpoint

Writers: D.C. Fontana, Gene Roddenberry. **Director:** Corey Allen. **Airdate:** September 28, 1987.

The maiden voyage of the newly rebuilt starship *Enterprise* takes it to Deneb IV to pick up the rest of its crew and to open diplomatic relations with the Bandi. The Bandi have built Farpoint Station, where items appear seemingly created by the thoughts of people and which is powered by a large, unknown source of energy. But on its way to the station, the *Enterprise* confronts the super-powerful alien being Q, who says their actions in this mission will determine whether humanity deserves to survive or be extinguished.

At Farpoint Station, counselor Deanna Troi detects the presence of an unknown being in despair. Another ship arrives and attacks a Bandi settlement; Captain Picard orders an away team to visit the alien ship, where they discover a structure similar to what's found underneath Farpoint Station. The ship transforms into a large space-going creature, and Picard and his *Enterprise* crew help it rescue its mate—the unknown being whose powers were being milked by the Bandi to produce their wondrous station.

Q deems the humans' actions to be worthy of survival. For now.

McCoy: I don't see no points on your ears, boy, but you sound like a Vulcan.
Data: No, sir. I am an android.
McCoy: Hmph. Almost as bad.

Notes: This episode includes a special cameo appearance by DeForest Kelley, portraying a well-advanced-in-age Dr. Leonard McCoy (now an admiral) making a quick visit to the new *Enterprise*. He arrives via shuttle, of course, so he can avoid that gosh-darn confabulated newfangled transporter technology. The character's age is 137 years old.

As a premiere episode, "Encounter at Farpoint" gets the job done. All of the annoying starchness of the first season is present in the debut story, but it still manages to bring together the ongoing crew and wrap it in a typical *Star Trek* morality play. For a more flavorful telling of the same story, I recommend you pick up David Gerrold's novelization of "Encounter at Farpoint."

This is the first time we see the new *Enterprise* separate its saucer section from the rest of the ship. Apparently the crew liked this (or, more accurately, the writers thought it added tasty drama to the story), because we will see it again in "The Best of Both Worlds," "The Arsenal of Freedom" and almost in "Hollow Pursuits"—oh, yes, and one last time in the *Star Trek Generations* film.

Elements of "Encounter at Farpoint" will be played out again in "All Good Things . . . ," the series-ending episode that once again brings Picard and the *Enterprise* to Q's French Revolution-inspired kangaroo court for their much-delayed judgment.

The Naked Now

Writers: J. Michael Bingham (pseudonym for D.C. Fontana), John D. F. Black. **Director:** Paul Lynch. **Airdate:** October 5, 1987.

In this installment, we learn that Dr. Noonien Soong, creator of the android Data, apparently obsessed over details so much that he designed, built, and perfected Data's nether regions to be "fully functional" to engage in sexual relations.

But that exciting/titillating/disturbing revelation will have to wait. First, the *Enterprise* comes to the aid of the SS *Tsiolkovsky*, a science craft observing an unstable giant star. They find that the crew is frozen to death. Upon returning to the *Enterprise*, Geordi LaForge begins suffering from an ailment and he unwisely (and unbelievably unprofessionally) abandons sick bay, spreading whatever illness he carries. The *Enterprise*'s medical and scientific crewmembers study the effects of the illness that affected the *Tsiolkovsky*, and Data learns that it is similar to something that struck the *Enterprise* under Captain Kirk (see notes below); meanwhile, various crewmembers begin exhibiting symptoms of odd behavior.

It is at this point that we learn that Data's USB port functions fully and that Tasha Yar likes cyber sex with real cybernetics. Wesley Crusher meanwhile takes control of the ship from Engineering, leaving the starship in danger from the collapse of the nearby star. Dr. Crusher, herself dealing with the effects of the disease, has to create a new cure for it, because the one used on the original *Enterprise* no longer works.

Dr. Crusher: It is definitely like alcohol intoxication. The same lack of good judgment. For example, right now, I find you extremely, extremely—of course, we haven't time for that sort of thing.
Picard: What sort of thing?

Notes: As an homage or follow-up of some sort to the original series episode "The

Naked Time," this go-around follows much the same formula: Have the characters act up and put the ship at risk as they shed their Starfleet duties and occasionally their clothes (Data and Yar in the new one, a shirtless sword-wielding Sulu in the original). "The Naked Time" was the fourth episode of the first season of original *Trek*, and "The Naked Now" was the second episode of the first season of *Next Generation*. In both cases, the episodes might have been improved simply by appearing later in the series, when we would know the characters better and could appreciate just how un-naturally they were acting.

Code of Honor

Writers: Kathryn Powers, Michael Baron. **Directors:** Russ Mayberry, Les Landau. **Airdate:** October 12, 1987.

Oh, dear; thank goodness there is no cancel culture in the 24th century.

Anchilles fever is ravaging the planet of Styris IV, and the only place to get the vaccine is on Ligon II, so naturally Picard and crew head there to get some. The Ligonian leader, Lutan, is intrigued that the *Enterprise*'s security chief, Tasha Yar, is female. On Ligon, though women own the property, they are secondary to men in terms of wielding power. Lutan kidnaps Yar and pits her against his "first one," Yareena, in a fight to the death.

Hagon (*to Tasha Yar*): Out of my way, woman!

Notes: It is hard to avoid noticing the cringe-inducing depiction of the Ligonians as a proud but violent race, and then having all of them portrayed by African American actors. The kudos owed to the producers for hiring an often-overlooked group of actors are tarnished by their presentation in a stereotypical space-tribal society. A number of *Next Generation* actors have agreed, referring to this episode as a racist story and/or the worst episode of the series. It probably is an *and*.

The physical fight between Yar and Yareena—oh, hey, I just realized their names are similar—that is the deciding factor in a relationship makes this episode quite similar to the fight between Spock and Kirk in the original *Trek* episode "Amok Time," which had the benefit of being one of that series' best entries.

And not being racist.

The Last Outpost

Writer: Herbert Wright, Richard Krzemien. **Director:** Richard Colla. **Airdate:** October 19, 1987.

In one of *Cinefantastique*'s giant annual *Star Trek* issues, someone involved in the early years of *Next Generation* claimed that Gene Roddenberry had expounded enthusiastically to his coworkers about the significant sexual endowments of the male alien Ferengi. If true, it's just one more weird aspect of Hollywood, not to mention

TMI and what would earn him a #MeToo moment today.

In this episode, the viewers aren't the only ones being introduced to the Ferengi; this is also the first contact the Federation has with this species. Chasing a Ferengi spaceship to the planet Gamma Tauri IV, the *Enterprise* and its quarry are both disabled by some unknown power. On the planet, they discover a system running on automatic pilot, apparently left there by the long-extinct Tkon Empire.

The away teams from the Ferengi vessel and the *Enterprise* begin to struggle, and when a firefight breaks out, they encounter a humanoid projection called Portal 63. The projection accuses humanity of being barbaric, but Commander Riker is able to convince it that the Federation is worth preserving. Convinced, Portal 63 grants Riker the ability to destroy the Ferengi vessel. Riker refuses, and both away teams go back to their vessels. The Ferengi return the energy converter they had stolen, which had kicked off the chase in the first place.

Data: Something to write home about.

Notes: It's worth noting that this is a recurrence of the theme of humanity being put on some sort of trial on charges of being barbaric and undeserving of existence, just like in the "Encounter at Farpoint" opener. (And, it should be noted, like the entire reimagined *Battlestar Galactica.*) Hollywood SF writers are very judgy.

The Ferengi Letek in this episode is played by Armin Shimerman, who would go on to essay the role of another Ferengi, Quark, in the spinoff *Star Trek: Deep Space Nine*. And though the Ferengi in this episode are loathsome creatures, Shimerman's Quark is a sympathetic and ultimately likable character, who even turns some of the Ferengi's pilloried characteristics, such as their greed, into virtues, in that they might be greedy and acquisitive, but at least they don't commit mass murder and genocide. Point for the Ferengi.

Also of note is that Richard Colla, who helmed this episode, also directed the original *Battlestar Galactica* movie and one additional episode of that series.

Where No One Has Gone Before

Writers: Diane Duane, Michael Reaves. **Director:** Rob Bowman. **Airdate:** October 26, 1987.

This episode sees the first appearance of occasional character the Traveler, who would eventually lure Wesley Crusher into a new life. But first things first: We're spared any details about the Traveler's sex life. As C3PO would say: Thank the Maker!

Starfleet engine whiz Kosinski and his assistant, the Traveler, board the *Enterprise* to run some tests on its warp engines. However, the tests go badly, with the ship surging faster than it's supposed to be able to go; when the ship stops, they find themselves in a different galaxy.

Wesley Crusher earns the admiration of the Traveler for his talents. Crusher notices that the Traveler phases in and out of existence during the warp tests, which turns out to be due not to Kosinski's efforts but to something going wrong with the Traveler, who heads to sick bay.

The crew of the *Enterprise*, stuck in the Outer Rim after a partial return from the other galaxy, find themselves having visions of the past. The Traveler tells Picard that he is able to change thought into reality, and he can also tell that Wesley is a scientific whiz kid who deserves to have his talents nurtured. After the young Crusher and the Traveler are able to return the *Enterprise* to Federation space, Picard makes Wesley an acting ensign.

Kosinski: Do you realize how many great advancements of mankind have been tied to speed? This is a moment in history, right here, right now—and your names will be forever linked with mine.

Notes: Writer Diane Duane is the author of about a dozen *Star Trek* novels, including 1983's *The Wounded Sky*. That novel concerned an adventure involving James Kirk and his generation of *Enterprise* crew. Duane adapted that storyline into "Where No One Has Gone Before."

Duane is an exception in the seven-year run of TNG in that she's an established science fiction writer. This show would feature a lot of unknown writers as well as producer-writers and the frequent gang-up of multiple writers for episodes, and the result was often stellar. But the original *Star Trek* boasted many already established science fiction writers, such as Harlan Ellison, Fredric Brown, Richard Matheson, Robert Bloch, Theodore Sturgeon, Norman Spinrad, and others. One can argue the benefits of either approach; the first series used those established names to validate the series when SF was still suspect on network TV; on the other hand, the sequel series introduced a lot of new writers into the fold. One of whom we'll eventually see is a young lad named Ronald Moore.

Lonely Among Us

Writers: D.C. Fontana, Mark Halperin. **Director:** Cliff Bole. **Airdate:** November 2, 1987.

The aptly (or lamely) named planet Parliament is the site for a meeting of delegates from two different species. Passing an energy cloud of some sort, as one does in space, the *Enterprise* experiences some strange phenomena when Worf and Dr. Crusher both exhibit rather odd behavior due to the cloud.

The *Enterprise* itself suffers from the cloud; dropping out of warp and with Captain Picard being taken over by the energy field. After a struggle between the *Enterprise* crew and Picard, the crewmembers are able to separate their captain from the energy being and continue on to their Parliamentary appointment.

Data: It's elementary, my dear Riker. Sir.

Notes: The recurring trope of Sherlock Holmes makes its appearance in this episode, as Data takes on the great detective's guise to solve the mystery of the crew's behavior. Shakespeare was the literary touchstone of the original *Star Trek*. Just sayin'.

Justice

Writers: Worley Thorne, Ralph Wills. **Director:** James L. Conway. **Airdate:** November 9, 1987.

The *Enterprise* visits the planet Rubicun III for the first time. Young Wesley Crusher joins a landing party and goes off to play with some of the children of the local inhabitants, the Edo. While playing, he accidentally breaks the glass of a greenhouse.

Tasha Yar had said that the Edos' laws weren't anything unusual, but she should have cleared her browser's cache and googled the latest info on the Edo, for they turn out to punish even minor infractions of the law with the death penalty. Minor infractions such as breaking some greenhouse glass. The locals try to immediately kill Crusher for committing a crime, but Worf and Yar stop them.

Meanwhile, in orbit, Data has discovered another craft of some sort orbiting the planet. The *Enterprise* crew learns that the Edo worship the ship as a god, and the god in turn is committed to protecting them. It's up to Picard to extricate Crusher from the planet below while not angering the orbiting god.

La Forge: [The Edo are] wild in some ways, actually puritanical in others. Neat as pins, ultra-lawful, and they make love at the drop of a hat.
Tasha Yar: Any. Hat.

Notes: As a commentary on the death penalty as a deterrent to crime, this show is an "*eh*." The Edo somehow fear that allowing Wesley Crusher to escape the death penalty would lead to the collapse of their civilization. As if they faced a plague of greenhouse glass-breaking teens. Even weirder are the attempts to make the Edo society seem Utopian. Just as you would expect from *L.A. Law*-era Hollywood writers, utopia seems to connote people dressed in skin–bearing clothes, a willingness to engage in wanton sexual encounters, and the people run everywhere. If you were expecting Arnie Becker to pop up in his terrycloth robe, maybe it's in the deleted extras on the DVD.

Considering how wildly popular "Wesley Crusher" actor Wil Wheaton has become with movie and tech fans over the past couple decades, it can be hard to remember that his character was a wildly controversial one, especially in *Next Gen-*

eration's early years. One feels sorry for the young actor, because there was a fair amount of "kill Wesley Crusher" sentiment espoused by the usual rabble. All of that is worth noting only because the producers here present an entire story around the idea of killing Wesley Crusher, but of course they don't carry through with it. Again, in light of Wheaton's geek godhood today, the rabble is probably glad they didn't.

The Battle

Writers: Herbert Wright, Larry Forrester. **Director:** Rob Bowman. **Airdate:** November 16, 1987.

Ferengi Captain DaiMon Bok meets up with the *Enterprise* and presents Captain Picard with a gift: the Constellation-class starship *Stargazer*, aboard which Picard used to serve and on which he won a victory at Maxia, as DaiMon Bok reminds him, by destroying an unidentified attacker that turned out to be Ferengi.

Retrieving some of his old personal items from the *Stargazer*, Picard finds a round, glowing object that seems to be linked to serious headaches he has been experiencing. Bok lures Picard back to the *Stargazer*, where he has another round object that creates the illusion in Picard's mind that he's once again fighting the battle of Maxia. That battle, it turns out, had included Bok's son at the command of the Ferengi ship, and Bok wants payback.

It's up to Riker and Data aboard the *Enterprise* to think two steps ahead of Picard, who thinks he's in a pitched battle with them. Luckily, they know about the Picard Maneuver, a deception their captain had used to win at Maxia.

Riker: I hope you're right, Data.
Data: No question of it, sir.

Notes: In this episode, Captain Picard explains that he was able to win the battle when he was aboard the *Stargazer* due to a short warp-jump trick. That trick became known as the Picard Maneuver.

The Picard Maneuver also became the popular name for actor Patrick Stewart's habit of tugging the bottom of his uniform tunic when he stood up (from the third season onward). This was a result of the tunic's bunching up on the actors when they sat down. All of the actors adopted this in some form, though leave it to Jonathan Frakes to take it one step further. As Wil Wheaton explained on his blog on February 12, 2007: "I also recall Jonathan Frakes always making a huge deal about doing the Picard Maneuver with the jacket on his space suit, pulling it down, tugging it from side to side, standing back up, yanking it down, sitting back down and tugging on his sleeves . . . I don't think I'm conveying how incredibly hilarious it was, but maybe you had to have been working on the Bridge for 12 hours to be in the same comedy space we were whenever he'd do it."

In the early 1990s, Stewart was touring with a one-man stage show in which he played short vignettes of famous leading men, many of them Shakespeare creations. He was, of course, marvelous, and this writer remembers being in an Indianapolis auditorium filled to the brim with Stewart fans who were naturally hoping, assuming, expecting that Stewart would break into a Captain Picard soliloquy. Stewart did us one better: About midway through the performance, he made a comment about how he's sure most of the people there were familiar with a certain spaceship captain he essayed; he then did the Picard Maneuver—and moved on to other, more classic characters. It brought down the house.

Hide and Q

Writers: C.J. Holland, Gene Roddenberry. **Director:** Cliff Bole. **Airdate:** November 23, 1987.

In the first appearance of the omnipotent alien Q since the premiere episode, he steals some of the *Enterprise* bridge crew to take part in a competition. He tells Captain Picard (who was left aboard the starship when the others were taken) that he is there to test Riker to see if he's capable of being granted the powers of a member of the Q Continuum.

Q returns to the planet where he has secreted the others and tries to give Riker the powers, but the commander refuses. When in the course of the struggles there Worf and Wesley Crusher are killed, Riker finally assumes the powers and brings them back to life. But he tells Picard he will not use the powers again. When Q continues to test his resistance, Riker vacillates until he finally grants his friends' wishes—which they reject, and he realizes he prefers the mortal company of his friends and crewmates.

Picard: A marshal of France? Ridiculous!
Q: Well, one takes the jobs he can get.

Notes: Wesley Crusher dies in this episode. Was this an early form of fan service? Luckily, this was not Wheaton's exit from the series. Nonetheless, from now on, technically we should refer to Zombie Wesley and Zombie Worf.

This is also our first real glimpse of the comedic side of Q, as opposed to the all-powerful and malevolent Q of the first episode.

Haven

Writers: Tracy Tormé, Lan O'Kun. **Director:** Richard Compton. **Airdate:** November 30, 1987.

There are many people who wish a plague upon their in-laws, but leave it to the Troi family to take that to its logical conclusion. Mother Lwaxana Troi draws her daughter Deanna and the *Enterprise* to the planet Haven to honor a pre-arranged marriage to Wyatt Miller, a doctor. There is only one small problem: Deanna doesn't want to marry Wyatt, and Wyatt is really in love with a woman he dreamt about. Sounds like a match made in heaven—er, Haven—but that would not turn out to be.

A Tarellian ship nears Haven and is intercepted by the *Enterprise*, which holds it in a tractor beam because its inhabitants are afflicted with a very dangerous plague. Wyatt learns that a woman on board the plague ship is the woman about whom he has been dreaming, and he engages in a little subterfuge to get himself transported to the ship, despite its quarantine. Picard can't retrieve Wyatt, because the doctor has become infected with the plague, and Wyatt and Deanna therefore are able to break their arranged engagement.

What some people will do to get out of a commitment . . .

Troi: Stop this petty bickering—all of you! Especially you, Mother!
Data: Could you please continue the petty bickering? I find it most intriguing.

Notes: Majel Barrett, the wife of *Trek* creator Gene Roddenberry, debuts as Troi's mother, Lwaxana, in this episode. She already played the voice of the *Enterprise* mainframe computer and of course had played Nurse Christine Chapel in the original *Star Trek* TV series and in *Star Trek: The Motion Picture* and *Star Trek IV: The Voyage Home*. In ST:TMP, we learned that Chapel had become a doctor in her own right. Said Dr. McCoy: "Well, Jim, I hear Chapel's an M.D. now. Well, I'm going to need a top nurse, not a doctor who will argue every little diagnosis with me."

Co-writer Lan O'Kun, who passed away in 2020, had a long career writing for many shows. But he might be most remembered for his extensive 44-year collaboration with his sister-in-law Shari Lewis and her Lamb Chop puppet character.

The Big Goodbye

Writer: Tracy Tormé. **Director:** Joseph L. Scanlan. **Airdate:** January 11, 1988.

In one of the first season's stronger episodes, we get to see a side of the characters beyond their Starfleet roles. Jean-Luc Picard is a big fan of the detective stories of Dixon Hill, and he has a holodeck program written to allow him to play in that fictional world. (Let's face it: If we had holodecks today, more than a few fans would create programs that allowed them to live in a *Trek* fictional world.) The captain, Data, Dr. Crusher, and a guest named Dr. Whalen are dressed up in their 1940s gangster garb and playing in the Dixon Hill holo-program when a computer glitch traps them inside.

Meanwhile, an alien race known as the Jaradan are about to start negotiations with the Federation, but their protocols are very strict. They are upset when they try to open contact with the *Enterprise* but can't speak with the captain. That's because the *Enterprise* crew inside the holodeck have realized something's gone wrong when the safety mechanisms fail to prevent a wound to Dr. Whalen when he is shot.

Picard tries to describe what the holodeck is to the gangsters who are threatening them, but they don't believe him until the holodeck program is successfully reset by Wesley Crusher and the two gangsters try to walk out of the holodeck.

Still awaiting Picard's attention are the Jaradan.

Madeline (*to Picard*): There's a lady named Bradley waiting in your office; nice legs. Not you—her!

Notes: "The Big Goodbye" won *Next Generation* a Peabody Award, as well as an Emmy for costuming.

Audiences get their first extended look at the holodeck in this episode, and like it frequently does, the contraption malfunctions. As one friend noted after watching the umpteenth episode in which the holodeck malfunctions (the better to move along the plot): Don't they have some sort of 24th-century OSHA that would make them fix it?

Datalore

Writers: Robert Lewin, Gene Roddenberry, Maurice Hurley. **Director:** Rob Bowman. **Airdate:** January 18, 1988.

Data, the artificial lifeform created by Dr. Noonien Soong, turns out not to have been an only child. The *Enterprise* visits Omicron Theta, the planet where Data had been found by an earlier starship. The away team discovers that what had once been a farming colony is now a lifeless, barren landscape of rock. They find the lab where Dr. Soong created Data, and there they also discover another, nonworking (but presumably anatomically correct) android, and take it back with them to the *Enterprise.*

When they bring the other android to "life," he calls himself Lore and describes himself as a more advanced model than Data, though he later admits it was the other way around. More disturbing is what he says about how the planet became barren: a strange "Crystalline Entity" destroyed the colony and all life on the planet.

Lore turns off Data and pretends to be him to the other crew members, to whom he also offers his help when the Crystalline Entity shows up. His impersonation of his brother lacks polish, and mother and son Crusher figure it out, revive Data, and arrive at the cargo hold in time to see Lore make plans with the entity to destroy the *Enterprise* crew.

Wesley Crusher: Since I am finished here, may I point out that everything I said would have been listened to, if it came from an adult officer!

Notes: "Shut up, Wesley," Captain Picard tells Acting Ensign Crusher, who is the first one to notice something's wrong with Data (as impersonated by Lore). His mother repeats the order a couple minutes later, though she is more open to Wesley's point of view. Wesley's complaint (see featured quote above) is exactly correct, and it shows that Picard and other senior officers aren't taking this seriously. This is particularly bad judgment by the captain, because earlier in the episode, security chief Tasha Yar asks him if Data can be trusted, and Picard makes a point of loudly saying that was a proper security question to raise.

If Lore had somehow incapacitated Data and taken his position, that would be a very big deal, especially with the Crystalline Entity right outside the ship. But even after Lore calls Riker "Riker" instead of "commander" and fails to understand Picard's "Make it so" direction, the most Picard does is order a small security detail to find "Data." So that must mean Picard doesn't actually think Lore is Data, or else he would have issued a shipwide alert and had the imposter android hunted down. But Worf and two security men locate "Data" (accidentally) when "Data" traps Worf in a turbolift with himself, something the other two security people notice, yet still none of them trips a shipwide alert. Worf in the turbolift does fight with "Data," but he could also have tapped his badge and broadcast his interaction to the bridge. Nope. Once Wesley and Beverly Crusher revive the real Data, neither of them sends a message to Captain Picard (and neither does Data, for that matter), and again, no shipwide alert is given. Considering the fake Data had just gotten permission from Picard to use the cargo transporter in some sketchy communication with the Crystalline Entity, one would think Picard and his senior staff would be a bit more savvy about ratcheting up the alert level in what is clearly an emergency.

That is, unless the writers simply wanted to end up with a Lore confrontation with Data and the Crushers in the cargo bay, and wrote the rest of the episode backwards.

In addition to building up Lt. Data's back story, "Datalore" lets us see Brent Spiner's acting chops. Here, he portrays both innocent good-guy android Data as well as his not-so-nice "brother," Lore.

Angel One

Writer: Patrick Barry. **Director:** Michael Ray Rhodes. **Airdate:** January 25, 1988.

Seven years earlier, the Odin spaceship crashed on the planet Angel One. The *Enterprise* sends an away team to meet with the planet's matriarchal leaders and convince them to let the Starfleet crew search for Odin's survivors. The leader, Beata, agrees, and the search turns up four male survivors who have taken local wives and do not want to leave. Beata, worried about the disintegration of her social system, has the four men taken into custody and threatens to have them killed.

Meanwhile, a virus from the holodeck sweeps through the *Enterprise*, leaving Dr. Crusher in charge. She has only 48 hours to find a cure before the starship has to leave.

Riker: It's not my function to seduce or be seduced by the leader of another world.

Beata: It's not the reason.
Riker: No, it's not. But will you still respect me in the morning?

Notes: Yes, a virus on the holodeck. No Starfleet FDA, either?

So the writers relied on some hokey holo-crutch for their b-plot. But there is less defense for the show's ham-handed attempt to tell a story about sexism without itself being sexist. Like the casual racism in "Code of Honor," "Angel One" was a low point for a show that tried to be about a post-prejudice society.

11001001

Writers: Maurice Hurley, Robert Lewin. **Director:** Paul Lynch. **Airdate:** February 1, 1988

Arriving at Starbase 74 for maintenance, the *Enterprise* is assigned some Bynars to help out while most of the crew takes shore leave. Despite all of the recent problems caused by the contraption, Riker and Picard nonetheless head to the holodeck for a jazz program, where they meet a surprisingly sophisticated character who charms them, Minuet.

Meanwhile, the Bynars create a warp core problem that forces the evacuation of most of the rest of the crew, and Data and La Forge take the ship at warp speed to a location where its explosion won't harm anyone else. But before they know it, the ship sets off on a new course: the Bynar system. The Bynars hope to upload to the *Enterprise* all of the data in their planet's computer, which contains all of their knowledge and on which the Bynars effectively rely for everything.

Riker: What's a knockout like you doing in a computer-generated gin joint like this?

Notes: "11001001" earned *Next Generation* another Emmy Award, this time for its sound editing.

Too Short a Season

Writers: Michael Michaelian, D.C. Fontana. **Director:** Rob Bowman. **Airdate:** February 8, 1988.

As the *Enterprise* nears Mordan IV to help broker a peace settlement, the elderly Admiral Mark Jameson is growing younger and stronger. He had negotiated the previous peace agreement on Mordan, and he has been requested by that planet's governor, Karnas, to negotiate the new pact.

Jameson, intent upon righting a wrong he committed in that previous negotiation, has been taking a lot of drugs that reduce the effects of age. With an *Enterprise* away team, he beams down to Mordan in an attempt to meet with a group of terrorists, but instead they beam into a trap and Jameson is shot. Picard then decides on a new gambit: Show up at Karnas' headquarters and straighten out everything face to face.

Jameson: I'm strong. I'm alert. I'm fit. I'm fitter than you are, Picard, and I'm getting younger.

Notes: In a quick game of six degrees of separation, Admiral Jameson actor Clayton Rohner has a long series of credits on his resume, including a guest appearance on the William Shatner police show *T.J. Hooker*.

When the Bough Breaks

Writer: Hannah Louise Shearer. **Director:** Kim Manners. **Airdate:** February 15, 1988.

The *Enterprise* is searching for the planet of Aldea, which has managed to conceal itself from outsiders but reveals itself to Picard's vessel long enough to request some of the ship's children to help replenish its population, because the Aldeans have become sterile. The answer from the *Enterprise*, not surprisingly, is no, so the Aldeans kidnap five of the ship's children, including Wesley Crusher, and uses its advanced technology to push the *Enterprise* a three days journey away.

Crusher and his mother discover that the planet's cloaking shield is what has made its inhabitants unable to bear children. After Crusher instigates a passive resistance movement among the other kidnapped Starfleet children, Picard is able to reopen negotiations to return the kids and help the Aldeans have their own.

Data and the Ferengi can help out, if they're asked.

Picard: The legend will die, but the people will live.

Notes: This is the only *Next Generation* outing for director Kim Manners, who would go on to become a genre hero with his work on *The X-Files*. Not to take this six-degrees thing too far, but starring in this episode is Jerry Hardin, who would become a household genre name for his work as the Deep Throat character in *The X-Files*.

Home Soil

Writers: Robert Sabaroff, Karl Geurs, Ralph Sanchez. **Director:** Corey Allen. **Airdate:** February 22, 1988.

The Velara III colony is falling behind in its efforts to terraform its planet. The *Enterprise* shows up with Darth Vader to get them back on schedule—no, wait, that's a different SF story. But the ship does show up to find out what is going wrong, and they discover equipment that's been programmed to attack humans and a crystal that acts oddly. Dr. Crusher thinks the crystal might be a lifeform, and she is proven correct when it begins to act up and then fends off attempts to get it off the ship and out of the ship's computers, which it has accessed.

The crew learn that the crystals become very intelligent when linked together by saline solution, but their environment was disrupted by the terraforming process. Data and LaForge try to find a way to save the ship and to save the crystal lifeforms on the planet.

Luisa Kim: Terraforming makes you feel almost god-like.

Notes: If you have seen the episode or have just read the summary and you think, "Original series' 'Devil in the Dark,'" then you're not alone.

Coming of Age

Writer: Sandy Fries. **Director:** Mike Vejar. **Airdate:** March 14, 1988.

Wesley Crusher takes the Starfleet Academy entrance exam. He helps his fellow cadets, but he finds himself challenged and without help when it comes to dealing with the psychological part of the exam.

Meanwhile, the *Enterprise*'s senior staff is subjected to an investigation of their loyalty and competence by their higher-ups in Starfleet. After they are cleared of wrongdoing, Picard turns down an offer of promotion to admiral.

Wesley: I failed, sir. I didn't get into the academy. I failed you, and I failed the *Enterprise.*

Notes: Look for further elements of the Starfleet mystery from this episode to show up in "Conspiracy" near the end of the first season. Also, just as we'll note later on Riker's reputation for turning down promotions, here Captain Picard does the same.

Heart of Glory

Writers: Maurice Hurley, Herbert Wright, D.C. Fontana. **Director:** Rob Bowman. **Airdate:** March 21, 1988.

Following a freighter's distress signal, the *Enterprise* finds the ship damaged but with life still aboard it: three Klingons. They are brought to the *Enterprise*, where they discover Lt. Worf.

The three survivors from the freighter say that they had been on the ship when it was attacked by Ferengi, but later they admit they had taken it over in an attempt to go somewhere they could live "authentically" Klingon lives. After a failed attempt to take over the *Enterprise*, none of the fugitives remain to live authentic lives.

Worf: Cowards take hostages. Klingons do not.

Notes: This is the first episode in which the producers start to flesh out the lifestyles and society of 24th-century Klingons. Michael Dorn's Lt. Worf would deservedly become one of the viewer-favorite characters, not just because he's a good actor but because he nicely brought to life the role of a Klingon unafraid to go against the niceties of human society.

The Arsenal of Freedom

Writers: Richard Manning, Hans Beimler, Maurice Hurley, Robert Lewin. **Director:** Les Landau. **Airdate:** April 11, 1988.

The *Enterprise* arrives at the planet Minos, the last known location of the USS *Drake*. There they discover a holographic salesman hawking weapons. While an away team does battle with drones, the *Enterprise* is being attacked by different weapons. Captain Picard and Dr. Crusher, down on the planet with the away team, fall into a hole and Picard finds a computer, which reveals that the battles they are fighting are just a demonstration of a weapons system—one the *Enterprise* crew surmises destroyed both the *Drake* and the inhabitants of Minos.

Picard: Mr. La Forge, when I left this ship, it was in one piece. I would appreciate your returning it to me in the same condition.

Notes: The arsenal's "Peddler" is played by none other than veteran character actor Vincent Schiavelli, whose resume includes roles in everything from *Batman Returns* to *The Happy Hooker.*

Symbiosis

Writers: Robert Lewin, Richard Manning, Hans Beimler. **Director:** Win Phelps. **Airdate:** April 18, 1988.

Our heroes fly to the rescue of a freighter for the second time in three episodes. Those freighters must be produced by the same guys who make holodecks. Anyway, the *Enterprise* rescues four crewmen from the endangered ship, who then begin to fight among themselves over the contents of a barrel. The men come from two different planets that are quarreling over medicine needed to combat a plague (from which two of the survivors of the freighter are believed to be suffering). But Dr. Crusher sees that the "medicine" is really just a narcotic, being used for a nonexistent plague.

The four are returned to their planets, and Picard throws a wrench into the symbiotic customer-dealer relationship by refusing to provide replacement parts to the ships that plied the drug trade.

Picard: What is the matter with these people?

Notes: Judson Scott, who portrays freighter crewman Sobi, had previously appeared in *Star Trek II: The Wrath of Khan* as Khan Noonien Singh's number-one aide, Joachim. He would also play a Romulan in an episode of *Star Trek: Voyager*.

Merritt Butrick, Sobi's pal T'Jon, had previously portrayed James Kirk's son, David Marcus, in *The Wrath of Khan* and *Star Trek III: The Search for Spock*. His promising career and life were ended a year after his appearance on *Next Generation*, when he died reportedly of AIDS-related causes.

Skin of Evil

Writers: Joseph Stefano, Hannah Louise Shearer. **Director:** Joseph L. Scanlan. **Airdate:** April 25, 1988.

While returning from a conference, Deanna Troi's shuttle crashes on Vagra II. An away team from the *Enterprise* arrives and discovers Armus, a puddle of black goo. Think a thousand gallons of melted Hershey's chocolate. But Armus isn't just a puddle of goo; Armus is a sentient being that is preventing the away team from reaching Troi's shuttle. When Tasha Yar tries to get to the shuttlecraft, Armus kills her.

The *Enterprise* crew learns that Armus is a remnant of evil from a long-dead ancient race. Picard beams down to the planet to negotiate directly with Armus to get Troi back—or at least distract it long enough so that the *Enterprise* can get a transporter lock on her position and rescue her.

Tasha Yar: Hello, my friends. You are here now watching this image of me, because I have died. It probably happened while I was on duty—and quickly, which is what I expected. Never forget I died doing exactly what I chose to do. What I want you to know is how much I loved my life, and those of you who shared it with me. You are my family. You all know where I came from and what my life was like before. But Starfleet took that frightened, angry young girl and tempered her.

Notes: Chevy Chase was vocally unhappy with the NBC sitcom *Community*, in which he co-starred, but he still stuck with it into the fourth season before calling it quits (and after calling the show a number of names in the press). But Denise Crosby didn't even wait a full year of *Star Trek: The Next Generation* before asking out of her contract.

The manner of her death has been debated and criticized from the beginning, and the program itself addressed it in the spectacular third-season episode "Yesterday's Enterprise," in which her death is described as having been meaningless. The best fan activity associated with this first-season episode that I can cite is a report many years ago in *Starlog* magazine about a convention costume contest in which the contestant walked to the stage and poured a container of dark syrup over themselves as their representation of "Skin of Evil."

We'll Always Have Paris

Writers: Deborah Dean Davis, Hannah Louise Shearer. **Director:** Robert Becker. **Airdate:** May 2, 1988.

Following a disruption in space-time, the *Enterprise* responds to a distress signal from Dr. Paul Manheim, who is taken aboard the ship along with his wife, Jenice. Captain Picard recognizes Jenice as his former lover from many years earlier. She spills the beans on her husband, who is incapacitated but had been working on unknown projects.

Meanwhile, localized time distortions are occurring on the ship and causing difficulties. Manheim awakens and reveals that his projects involve time and connections to other universes, and he thinks his experiments have gotten out of control, causing the time distortions. Data must go to Manheim's laboratory and try to stabilize the experiment and end the time-space problems.

Picard: Enough of this self-indulgence.

Notes: The title, a *Casablanca* reference, regards the place where Picard and Jenice ended their affair. They recreate some of that in a holodeck scene in this episode. Jenice is portrayed by Michelle Phillips, formerly a member of The Mamas and the Papas singing group and stepmother to *One Day at a Time*'s Mackenzie Phillips.

Conspiracy

Writers: Tracy Tormé, Robert Sabaroff. **Director:** Cliff Bole. **Airdate:** May 9, 1988

After being alerted to a possible conspiracy at the top of Starfleet, the *Enterprise* heads to Earth to find out what's happening. Several admirals greet the *Enterprise,* and Picard comes to believe that one of them, Quinn, is not the same Admiral Quinn he dealt with a few months earlier (in the episode "Coming of Age"). Quinn tries to infect Riker with a parasitic creature, but the *Enterprise* crew is able to subdue the admiral.

At Starfleet, Picard arrives for an *Indiana Jones and the Temple of Doom*-style gross-out dinner with his superiors. Riker, pretending to have been taken over by the parasite, prevents Picard from leaving, and in some helpful exposition the Starfleet leaders explain that the parasites are aliens who are planning to invade Federation space. Picard and Riker are able to kill the hosts and their parasites, but they learn that one of them was able to send a signal far away into the galaxy—perhaps summoning more like itself?

Tryla: The one thing both races share is a love of theater, and you've put on a fine show.

Notes: "Conspiracy" won an Emmy award for best makeup. Some of that makeup was blown to smithereens in an exploding head scene, which gave some people worries that the episode was too violent. *Scanners* it isn't, however, and no one is likely to have nightmares from it.

The Neutral Zone

Writers: Maurice Hurley, Deborah McIntyre, Mona Clee. **Director:** James L. Conway. **Airdate:** May 16, 1988.

After several decades of silence, the Romulans make themselves known again, and the *Enterprise* is sent to the Neutral Zone. On board are three humans who had been picked up on Earth after being revived from cryogenic stasis. The three are from the 20th century, their bodies preserved until a time when their incurable illnesses could be cured. Bingo—welcome to the 24th century.

Several destroyed outposts along the Neutral Zone are found, as is a Romulan warbird and its commander, Tebok. He and Picard face off, but they need to figure out who destroyed the outposts. Picard realizes that the Romulans aren't going to go back into radio silence for another 30 years. But *Star Trek: The Next Generation* will go into several months of silence until the second season debuts in the fall of 1988.

Tebok: Your presence is not wanted. Do you understand my meaning, Captain? We. Are. Back.

Notes: Milwaukee-born actor Michael Alaimo booked numerous trips to outer space. In "The Neutral Zone," he portrayed Romulan Commander Tebok. He also appeared in more than three dozen episodes of spinoff series *Star Trek: Deep Space Nine* as Gul Dukat. And he portrayed a Romulan and a Cardassian in episodes of *Next Generation.*

SEASON TWO

The Child

Writers: Jaron Summers, Jon Povill, Maurice Hurley. **Director:** Rob Bowman. **Airdate:** November 21, 1988.

Troi gives birth after being, er, impregnated by an alien entity. She names the child Ian, and he grows extraordinarily quickly. Meanwhile, the *Enterprise* is transporting a special cargo of a plague that is causing trouble in the Rachelis system. When the plague sample begins to grow as a result of Eichner radiation (don't bother googling it; it's fictional), the crew learns that Ian is the cause of the radiation. He informs his mother that it is time for him to leave—his mission to learn about life among the humans complete.

Riker: I don't mean to be indelicate, but who's the father?
Troi: Last night, while I slept, something, that I can only describe as a presence, entered my body.
Picard: A life form of unknown origin and intent, is breeding, right now, inside of Counselor Troi. Our purpose here today is to determine what course of action we need to take.
Worf: The decision is clear—the pregnancy must be terminated to protect the ship

Notes: A Hollywood writers' strike left the *Star Trek* producers with a shortage of available scripts, so they turned to "The Child," a script originally written for the unrealized *Star Trek: Phase II* series from the 1970s.

The idea of a mysterious child growing at an absurdly accelerated rate is a recurring one in science fiction, but here it is married with the queasy idea of Troi being impregnated without her knowledge. Rape? Or are unwanted pregnancies so common in the 24th century that this doesn't raise any eyebrows?

In other news, after the first season of *Star Trek: The Next Generation*, the producers decided they wanted something different than Dr. Beverly Crusher on board the *Enterprise*. Actor Gates McFadden was let go, and Diana Muldaur was cast as Dr. Katherine Pulaski. Muldaur had appeared in two guest-starring roles in the original series, "Is There in Truth No Beauty?" and "Return to Tomorrow."

Pulaski brought a bit of an outsider's perspective to the happy mall-ship that was the *Enterprise*. She sees Data as a machine and treats him that way. She doesn't treat Worf as the moral disappointment that many of the other crewmembers do; she seems to like and respect him, and she is knowledgeable about his culture and his needs. She comes across at times a bit colder than McFadden's Dr. Crusher, but that was because she was often offering alternative ideas and opinions than what was offered by the other characters, and when producers decided not to have her back for season three, the show lost what was becoming a breath of fresh air. It would have been a suffocating situation if the first season's heavy-handed political correctness hadn't been steadily dissipating.

Next Generation producers reportedly let Muldaur go after one season because they didn't see the necessary chemistry evolve between her and the other characters. It was perhaps a case of art imitating life, because Muldaur herself has noted that she did not enjoy herself on the show because the other cast members didn't seem to want her there and it was not the imaginative, creative experience she had hoped for.

The loss of Pulaski did not hold back the series, but it does give rise to thoughts of how she might have played a role in the remaining five seasons. Muldaur is a great actor—she went on to earn two Emmy nominations for her role as Rosalind Shays on *L.A. Law*—and she added some weight to what was an often ill-defined position on the *Enterprise*.

Outsiders can only guess about any conflicted feelings McFadden might have had about returning to a series that had rejected her and then invited her back; Hollywood can be a brutal place for an actor's feelings. One source reports that she resisted the initial invitation to return but was convinced by Patrick Stewart to resume her former role. If her character was sometimes hesitant and weakly played in the first season (and at times in the third), she nonetheless grew into a stronger and convincing central player in the remainder of the series, becoming more and more a good counterpoint to Stewart's Captain Picard.

Where Silence Has Lease

Writer: Jack B. Sowards. **Director:** Winrich Kolbe. **Airdate:** November 28, 1988.

The *Enterprise* encounters an area of pitch black. In space, yes. But this is blacker than normal; if the ship sends probes into the blackness, they just . . . disappear. The area of blackness soon expands and takes in the *Enterprise*. A Romulan warship appears and the *Enterprise* destroys it, easily. Then a Federation ship appears, and Riker and Worf beam over to investigate, but they find nothing.

There are occasional openings to "real" space in the blackness, but when the *Enterprise* tries to approach any of the openings, they quickly close up. With Riker and Worf back aboard, some sort of space being—Nagilum, by name—makes itself present and promptly kills a crewman to learn about the human body. Picard pulls the Corbomite maneuver and threatens to destroy the ship if anyone else is injured. Nagilum tries subterfuge to get Picard to change his mind, but eventually he relents and says humans and Nagilum's race have nothing in common.

Dr. Pulaski: Why do I get the feeling this was not the time to join this ship?

Notes: Even more than awkwardly executed sexual concepts, *Star Trek* loves to explore the interaction of the *Enterprise* crew with a godlike higher power that toys with it. The first and fifth *Trek* films were given over to that idea, as was the premiere and finale (and a handful of Q-laden episodes in between) of *The Next Generation*.

If this episode's writer seems familiar, that's because Jack B. Sowards is the screenwriter of the much-loved original-cast film *Star Trek II: The Wrath of Khan*, which arguable saved the franchise.

Elementary, Dear Data

Writer: Brian Alan Lane. **Director:** Rob Bowman. **Airdate:** December 5, 1988.

Data and La Forge use the holodeck to create a Sherlock Holmes mystery for them to play in. But when Data quickly solves the mystery, Geordi is upset. Dr. Pulaski tells them that the problem is that Data, as an android, simply can't do the independent reasoning necessary to figure out a mystery to which he doesn't already know the answer. So the three of them head back into the holodeck for a new mystery, but this time Geordi has told the holodeck to create a new story with a villain who is able to defeat Data.

The story unfolds, and Dr. Pulaski is kidnapped by Professor Moriarty; Data must solve the abduction. They find that Moriarty knows that he's in a holodeck simulation, and he even creates a drawing of the *Enterprise*. Data and Geordi flee the holodeck and get Captain Picard. Geordi figures out how the problem came to be: He told the holodeck to create someone who could defeat Data, not Sherlock Holmes, and therefore the computer made Moriarty knowledgeable about everything that could trip up Data.

It gets worse. Moriarty uses his knowledge of the ship to gain control of some of its computers, and Picard has to negotiate the return of Pulaski and convince Moriarty to be content to stay in the holodeck.

Moriarty: The more you proclaim your ignorance, the more you try to mislead me, the more I'm on to you. Your every silence speaks volumes.
Doctor Pulaski: Good. Then if you know what I'm saying when I'm not saying anything, what do you need me for? Thank you for the tea and crumpets. I guess I'll be going.

Notes: This is one of the stronger second-season episodes. Diana Muldaur's Dr. Katherine Pulaski gets her first real opportunity to show her acting talent in this episode. It also highlights her skepticism of the idea that Data is more than an emotionless computer, instead seeing him as nothing more than the sum of his programming.

The Outrageous Okona

Writer: Burton Armus, Les Menchen, Lance Dickson, David Landsberg. **Director:** Robert Becker. **Airdate:** December 12, 1988.

The *Enterprise* offers help to a cargo ship and its one-man crew, comprised of a handsome and apparently very randy man named Okona. Once aboard the Federation starship, he sets about trying to charm the women.

But the *Enterprise* soon also encounters two other ships, both of them too weak to harm the starship but very interested in its newly acquired passenger. The leader of one of the ships says that Okona got his daughter pregnant; the other claims Okona stole the Jewel of Thesia. Each of the aliens wants to take Okona, who proclaims himself innocent of both accusations. Picard helps uncover the truth.

While all of that is going on, Data is inspired by Okona to explore the concept of humor. Naturally he employs the one instrument on the ship that breaks down the most, the holodeck. It doesn't break down, but it lets him down with its unnatural environment. Guinan proves a better resource.

Guinan: Data, you spoiled the joke. It could have been your timing.

Data: My timing is digital.

Notes: The actor who brings Okona to life is William O. Campbell, who is of course best known to many SF fans as Billy Campbell, the star of the underappreciated 1991 comic book adaptation film *The Rocketeer*. He almost did not get that movie role because studio executives reportedly wanted a bigger name.

The holodeck comedian who teaches Data about comedy is real-life standup comic Joe Piscopo. The *Saturday Night Live* alum reportedly wrote his own comedy bits in this episode.

And, finally, the transporter operator was portrayed by an uncredited Teri Hatcher, who would go on to star in *Lois & Clark*.

Loud As a Whisper

Writer: Jacqueline Zambrano. **Director:** Larry Shaw. **Airdate:** January 9, 1989.

The *Enterprise* takes on a new passenger, Riva, a deaf-mute federation mediator who communicates via a three-person backup group that speaks his ideas. But when he beams down to the planet Solais V, his "chorus" trio is killed by someone hoping to stop the peace negotiations between two tribes.

Back on the *Enterprise*, Data and Troi learn to communicate with Riva and how he uses his inability to hear or talk to get opposing sides in a negotiation to deal with each other. Despite the loss of his backup, Riva decides to return to the planet, where he will try once more to turn a problem into a tool.

Riker: You will be careful, sir?
Picard: Oh, cluck, cluck, cluck, Number One.
Riker: Sir?
Picard: You're being a mother hen.

Notes: We met Spock's parents, including his ambassador father, on the original *Star Trek* series episode "Journey to Babel." In the first season of *Next Generation*, the *Enterprise* ferries ambassadors to the unimaginatively named planet of Parliament. And there would be other episodes, this one included, in which the *Enterprise* is a very expensive transit service for ambassadors.

The Schizoid Man

Writer: Tracy Tormé, Richard Manning, Hans Beimler. **Director:** Les Landau. **Airdate:** January 23, 1989.

Dr. Ira Graves is one of only two people on a planet that is appropriately called Gravesworld; the other inhabitant is Kareen Brianon. In response to a request for medical help, the *Enterprise* sends a team headed by Dr. Pulaski to help Graves. When they arrive, they learn that Kareen requested the help unbeknownst to

Graves. Graves realizes that Data is the creation of Noonien Soong, who was Graves' protégé. But he wants more than credit; the dying scientist wants to transfer his consciousness into Data by using a computer he developed.

The crew returns to the *Enterprise*, where they slowly realize what has happened. After a confrontation with Captain Picard, Graves leaves Data and transfers everything he knows into the ship's computer, but not his consciousness.

Data: Perhaps it is best that I do not remember. I trust I did nothing . . . unbecoming to a Starfleet officer?
Riker: Does wrestling with a Klingon targ ring a bell?
Picard: Mr. Crusher, take us out of orbit.
Wesley: Aye, sir.
Data: Did I win?

Notes: Generally, I can happily fast-forward through predictable consciousness-possession episodes of science fiction programs. The plots are almost always the same; but this one provides some twists, we learn more about Data, and of course it's got a nice tinge of humor.

One of the *Enterprise* medical team members is the Vulcan Dr. Selar, who is portrayed by Suzie Plakson. Her other *Trek* roles include Worf's mate in two *Next Generation* episodes, as well as several other characters in *Next Generation*, *Voyager*, and *Enterprise*. Writer Tracy Tormé is known for his work on *The Next Generation* and *Sliders* (which he co-created). His father was known as The Velvet Fog—he was singer Mel Tormé.

Unnatural Selection

Writers: John Mason, Mike Gray. **Director:** Paul Lynch. **Airdate:** January 30, 1989.

The *Enterprise* finds that the entire crew of the USS *Lantree* has died of old age—despite their actual ages being no more advanced than the *Enterprise* crew's. The starship then heads to the last known place visited by the *Lantree*, the Darwin Genetic Research Station. There they discover that the station's staff is also beginning to age rapidly.

Dr. Pulaski investigates genetically engineered children who were supposedly kept isolated from the researchers; she finds that the rapid aging is caused by the teenager she is examining. She begins to undergo the deterioration herself, and the *Enterprise* must rush to find a solution to the process before it takes her life. They find that the transporter can be used to filter out the aging-causing virus, but Pulaski doesn't use transporters.

Captain Taggert [*Pulaski's former captain*]: The moment she heard of the opening on the *Enterprise*, she put in a request for transfer. Knew your service record

backward and forward. Apparently, she has been an admirer of yours for some time.
Picard: Extraordinary.

Notes: If some of this sounds familiar, that might be because you remember "The Deadly Years," the original *Trek* series episode that also involves super-fast aging of the *Enterprise* crew. Don't forget that *Star Trek* is a creation of Californians, for whom growing old is the greatest terror.

A Matter of Honor

Writers: Burton Armus, Wanda M. Haight, Gregory W. Amos. **Director:** Rob Bowman. **Airdate:** February 6, 1989.

It's time for an officer exchange, so the *Enterprise* gets a Benzite named Ensign Mendon and Riker is sent to a Klingon ship, the IKS *Pagh*. Worf gives Riker a transponder that he can use in case he needs to signal for help.

The *Enterprise* discovers that it and the *Pagh* have somehow taken on an unwanted life form. Mendon figures out how to remove it from the ships, but before they can let the Klingons know, the *Pagh*'s captain discovers the lifeform eating away at his ship and, thinking it's a Federation weapon, prepares to attack the *Enterprise*. Riker, playing the good Klingon officer, helps with the attack plans, but he makes use of the transponder to trick the Klingon captain into being beamed aboard the *Enterprise*. Riker then takes control of the *Pagh*—and gets Picard to surrender. The Federation crew then helps the *Pagh* get rid of the alien organism.

Kargan: To be ordered to die is an expectation for any officer at any time.
Klag: For a Klingon perhaps, but Riker's people do not volunteer for death so easily.

Notes: If you want to see a Klingon punch Riker, then this is your episode.

The Measure of a Man

Writer: Melinda M. Snodgrass. **Director:** Robert Scheerer. **Airdate:** February 13, 1989.

When is an android a piece of property and when is it an independent being with its own "human" rights? Commander Bruce Maddox brings the theoretical question to reality when he wants to use Data's positronic brain in the computer at a starbase, which would mean the end of everyone's favorite android.

If Data wants to avoid this fate, he has to resign from Starfleet, but Maddox argues that he is the property of Starfleet and therefore not an individual with sentience and rights. A legal hearing is held to determine Data's rights, with Riker serving as Maddox's legal representative and Picard as Data's lawyer. The captain turns the case into a question of slavery.

Picard [*regarding a portrait of Tasha Yar*]: You have no other portraits of your fellow crew members. Why this person?
Data: I would prefer not to answer that question, sir. I gave my word.
Picard: Under the circumstances, I don't think Tasha would mind.
Data: She was special to me, sir. We were . . . intimate.

Notes: Poker, which will become a recurrent feature of stories right through to the final scene of the final episode of the series, appears here for the first time. In terms of character development, it's an effective way of showing the crew off-duty and giving them some background. A very *M*A*S*H* touch.

Writer Melinda Snodgrass served as a story editor for TNG's second and third seasons.

The Dauphin

Writers: Scott Rubenstein, Leonard Mlodinow. **Director:** Rob Bowman. **Airdate:** February 20, 1989.

Salia could be the key to peace on Daled IV, where her parents' deaths left the planet vulnerable to renewed conflict. Salia's protector, Anya, watches over her, going so far as to try to kill a sick crew member she thought could infect Salia. Meanwhile, young Wesley Crusher is getting sweet on Salia, showing her around and getting dating advice from others on the *Enterprise*. But when Anya reveals her true form in an attempt to scare away Wesley, Salia reverts to the same alien form, and Wesley begins to think he's too young to be dating.

Wesley Crusher: Are you telling me to go yell at Salia?
Worf: No. Men do not roar. Women roar. Then they hurl heavy objects. And claw at you.
Wesley Crusher: What does the man do?
Worf: He reads love poetry. [Worf clears his head.] He ducks a lot.

Notes: Co-writer Leonard Mlodinow is a theoretical physicist who is author most recently of *The Upright Thinkers: The Human Journey from Living in Trees to Understanding the Cosmos*. He has also worked in computer gaming and, in addition to *Trek*, wrote scripts for *MacGuyver*, *Hunter*, and *Night Court*.

Contagion

Writers: Steve Gerber, Beth Woods. **Director:** Joseph L. Scanlan. **Airdate:** March 20, 1989.

After trying unsuccessfully to help the disabled U.S.S. *Yamato*, a Federation ship stuck in the Neutral Zone, the *Enterprise* goes to the planet that the *Yamato* had just visited. A probe launches from the planet; before it can be destroyed it manages to infect the *Enterprise's* computer; Data is similarly infected while on an away team to investigate the probe's launch site. A Romulan warbird shows up, similarly infected with the virus.

Data is able to clear himself of the computer virus by basically doing a hard reboot, so La Forge suggests the same treatment for the *Enterprise* computer. It works, and with the solution shared with the Romulan ship, they flee the planet as the probe's base is destroyed.

Wesley Crusher: Sir, the shields are back up.
Riker: Impeccable timing!
Wesley Crusher: Sir, the shields are back down.
Williams: Phaser banks are down.
Wesley Crusher: Shields are back up.
Troi: In another time and place, this could be funny.

Notes: Now you know why Commander Adama wouldn't network his ship's computers in the SyFy *Battlestar Galactica*. Of course, he had other problems.

The Federation starship named *Yamato* was named after a real World War II battleship, an Imperial Japanese Navy flagship that represented the heights of Japan's naval power. The name was used most famously for the groundbreaking anime series *Space Battleship Yamato* (redubbed *Star Blazers* for syndication in the United States, where the ship itself was also disappointingly renamed the *Argo*). In that show, the original battleship was dug up and converted into a spaceship—I know, just go with it—representing the indomitable spirit of an Earth fighting off certain destruction by its enemies.

Co-writer Steve Gerber is the award-winning creator of *Thundarr the Barbarian* and *Howard the Duck*.

The Royale

Writer: Tracy Tormé, aka Keith Mills. **Director:** Cliff Bole. **Airdate:** March 27, 1989.

A casino Royale, indeed. Looking for information to explain the wreckage of an Earth spaceship around an alien planet, Riker, Worf, and Data beam down to discover a hotel and casino called The Royale; but it's like a roach motel—when they enter, they can't get back out.

The trio discovers what's left of NASA astronaut Steven Richey, along with *Hotel Royale*, a book that some aliens used as a template to create what they thought was Richey's ideal life. Instead, they unwittingly built him a gilded cage that he couldn't escape, and now Riker, Worf, and Data find they, too, are stuck there.

Data realizes that he and his fellow Starfleet officers need to assume the roles of some characters in the book who leave the hotel; when they play through their roles as high-roller gamblers, they finally find their release.

Data: Baby needs a new pair of shoes!

Notes: Writer Tracy Tormé used his pen name Keith Mills after being unsatisfied with rewrites to his script. Audiences might be a bit unsatisfied by remembering "A Piece of the Action," a 1968 episode of the original *Star Trek* in which the *Enterprise* discovers a planet that had been visited years earlier by an Earth ship, which had left behind a book called *Chicago Mobs of the Twenties*, and the people of the planet modeled their whole society on the book. Kirk, Spock, and McCoy have to play mobsters themselves in order to get out of the situation.

Time Squared

Writer: Kurt Michael Bensmiller. **Director:** Joseph L. Scanlan. **Airdate:** April 3, 1989.

The *Enterprise* encounters a shuttlecraft that is adrift and brings it aboard. The shuttle's pilot is an unconscious Captain Picard—a double from six hours in the future. The "current" Picard orders that the future Picard be awakened, but the crew is unable to learn anything from him. The future Picard is slightly out of phase sync with the "current" time. But a sensor log on the future Picard's shuttlecraft shows the destruction of the *Enterprise*. Time's a-tickin'.

Then the *Enterprise* comes across a vortex, and the future Picard tries to flee into the shuttle, perhaps in a bid to draw away possibly damaging rays from the vortex. The "current" Picard ends the cycle by destroying his future self, and then orders his ship to go right into the vortex, which it does, resulting in the dissolution of his double and of the extra shuttle.

Picard: They say if you travel far enough you will eventually meet yourself. Having experienced that, Number One, it's not something I would care to repeat.

Notes: This is a strong outing that really has some dramatic fun with the science fictional elements of the story.

Director Joseph Scanlan counts many film and television credits in his resume, including working on 1973's *The Starlost*, a 16-episode SF series created by Harlan Ellison. The short-lived Canadian-made syndicated series involved a doomed space ark. It's a show filled with painful 1970s haircuts and computerized music, but it also loaded up on the science fiction luminaries. Besides Ellison, the show also had Ben Bova as a science advisor and starred *2001: A Space Odyssey*'s Keir Dullea, with guest stars including future *Battlestar Galactica* villain (and later *Star Trek: Deep Space Nine* Klingon) John Colicos, future *Space: 1999* star Barry Morse, and *Star Trek* star and writer Walter Koenig; one of the producers was special effects wizard

Douglas Trumbull.

Dissatisfied with budget cuts and other problems, Ellison essentially disowned *The Starlost*, using his pseudonym Cordwainer Bird rather than have his real name appear in the credits.

The Icarus Factor

Writers: David Assael, Robert L. McCullough. **Director:** Robert Iscove. **Airdate:** April 24, 1989.

One can be forgiven for thinking that almost as soon as Captain Picard ended up with Commander Riker as his "Number One"—his executive officer—he was trying to rid himself of the man. Out of respect, of course. The idea that Riker is ready and able to command his own ship but simply refuses to accept it is one that will recur throughout the *Next Generation* saga; it would not find resolution until the final *Next Generation* film, *Star Trek Nemesis*, which ends with Riker and Troi going off to Riker's new command, the USS *Titan*.

But first we have this episode, in which Riker has the opportunity to command his own starship; his father's involvement in the matter complicates things. Riker and his father do not get along, but the older man is trying to make amends with his son. Things are not helped by the discovery that the elder Riker is Dr. Pulaski's old flame.

Meanwhile, Worf is weirding out over not being able to perform an Age of Ascension anniversary ceremony, so his friends on the *Enterprise* use the holodeck to help him recreate the typically brutal Klingon ritual.

In the end, Riker and his father come to terms with each other, finally dealing with their conflicted emotions over the death of Riker's mother. And Riker decides he's not ready to leave the *Enterprise* just yet.

Riker [*sees Dr. Pulaski hugging his father*]: They know each other.
Miles O'Brien: No kidding. I know her, too; but we don't do that.

Notes: Playing a holographic Klingon warrior in this episode is none other than John Tesh, who at that time was working for entertainment television as a host and was on set reporting about the show, which led to a quick acting gig.

Pen Pals

Writers: Melinda Snodgrass, Hannah Louise Shearer. **Director:** Winrich Kolbe. **Airdate:** May 1, 1989.

Data receives a message from a young girl on a primitive planet that is being racked by earthquakes. The girl, Sarjenka, uses some old-fashioned radio technology to carry on a conversation with Data. When Data informs Picard about the girl and the peril to her planet, Picard orders him to end the pen pal-ship, due to the Prime

Directive, the Federation rule that would allow genocide to take place rather than risk "infecting" a primitive planet with advanced Starfleet ideas, such as non-genocide. Eventually, the *Enterprise* team finds a way to stop the earthquakes, but in the course of the effort Data brings Sarjenka up to the *Enterprise*. Picard orders Dr. Pulaski to ensure that the girl's memories are erased, so she doesn't remember her visit to a better place.

Meanwhile, Ensign Wesley Crusher is chosen to head up a science away team, but he finds that not all of his team members respect his authority.

Worf: There are no options. The Prime Directive is not a matter of degrees; it is an absolute.
Pulaski: I have a problem with that kind of rigidity. It seems callous, and even a little cowardly.
Picard: Doctor, I'm sure that is not what the lieutenant meant. But in a situation like this, we have to be cautious. What we do today may profoundly affect the future. If we could see every possible outcome—"
Riker: —we'd be gods, which we are not. If there is a cosmic plan, is it not the height of hubris to think that we can or should interfere?
La Forge: So what are you saying, that—that the Dremans are—are fated to die?
Riker: I think that's an option that we should be considering.
La Forge: Consider it considered and rejected!

Notes: Don't get me started on the Prime Directive, a rule dreamed up by *Trek*'s creators but one that should trouble anyone in a civilization that should be advancing faster than it is but is instead stuck under the thumbs of fundamentalists and anti-rationalists. Sound familiar?

Actress Nikki Cox, who portrays Data's pen pal Sarjenka, has acted in a number of roles over the years and is a dancer in addition to being an actor. But what interests us here is that from 1997 to 2005, she was the partner of comic Bob "Bobcat" Goldthwait. She's currently married to comedian Jay Mohr, so she obviously likes the funny guys.

Q Who

Writer: Maurice Hurley. **Director:** Rob Bowman. **Airdate:** May 8, 1989.

Out of small things come great villains. Q, the man who set the entire *Next Generation* tale in motion in the premiere episode, returns and stirs up a storyline that will return in some of the series' greatest moments, including arguably the best *Trek* film.

Q decides to teach the *Enterprise* a lesson by throwing the ship into another part of the galaxy, where its crew comes across the Borg. Guinan knows who/what the Borg are, and she warns Picard that they are incredibly powerful—they destroyed her people, and the *Enterprise* should get away from there right away to save its skin.

The Borg manage to infiltrate the *Enterprise* and access its systems; they then demand that the *Enterprise* surrender. Resistance being futile and all. Captain Picard won't do it, so the Borg attack and kill 18 *Enterprise* crew members.

After a visit to the Borg ship, the *Enterprise* tries to flee, but the Borg ship easily catches up to it. Totally outgunned and out-powered, Picard is forced to call upon Q for help. Q helps, but warns that the Borg are something that the Federation is going to have to deal with sooner or later.

Guinan gives Picard the bad news that the Borg, now aware of the Federation's existence and knowledgeable about its capabilities, will make an appearance in Federation space.

Picard: Why?
Q: Why? Why, to give you a taste of your future—a preview of things to come. Con permiso, capitán? The hall is rented, the orchestra engaged—it's now time to see if you can dance.

Notes: Aaaand the Borg finally arrive. They're the ultimate villains of the entire *Trek* franchise, never before nor later surpassed in terms of major menace. They were also at the heart of two of the franchise's best outings, "The Best of Both Worlds" and *Star Trek: First Contact.* Just like the first season's "Conspiracy," "Q Who" ends with a warning that some scary aliens have been alerted to Earth's location and vulnerability and they will be back. Unlike "Conspiracy"'s rather comic critter aliens, the Borg do of course return to spectacular and creatively successful effect.

This episode earned three Emmy nominations, for outstanding special visual effects, outstanding sound editing for a series, and outstanding sound mixing for a drama series. It won the second and third of those awards.

Samaritan Snare

Writer: Robert L. McCullough. **Director:** Les Landau. **Airdate:** May 15, 1989.

Captain Picard is heartless. At least, he doesn't have a "real" heart but instead an artificial heart. It's due for replacement, so he heads to a starbase because he doesn't want to look weak in front of his crew by having Dr. Pulaski do the operation.

Picard uses a trip by Wesley Crusher for Starfleet Academy tests as an excuse to visit the same starbase, where he will get his operation. But there are complications in the procedure, and the only person who can save Picard's life is Dr. Pulaski.

Meanwhile, La Forge is sent over to a Pakled ship that has asked for help. The aliens are big, dopey-looking and dopey-acting, and they appear unable to fix their ship or properly understand how it operates. But once the Federation officer is aboard, the Pakled kidnap La Forge in the hopes of having him help them with defense. The *Enterprise* gets its engineer back after running a ruse to convince the Pakleds that the *Enterprise* can easily defeat them.

Picard [*awakening from surgery*]: What in the hell are you doing here?
Pulaski: Saving your life. This may be a commonplace procedure, but it appears that you are not a commonplace man. . . . Don't worry, you're still the captain. Invincible.

Notes: *Star Trek: The Next Generation* became famous or infamous in Hollywood for becoming a producer-driven series, often employing multiple producers and a series of writers to craft a story. One might expect those franken-stories to be disjointed and a hodgepodge, but frankly *Next Generation* produced some truly great science fiction television drama both for its time and for all time. But this episode, with only one writer credited, seems a hodgepodge of two mismatched stories.

The storyline about Picard is a great example of how *Next Generation*, so much more than the original *Trek* series, was able to focus on back story and character development, even in a quieter tale. It teaches us more about Picard, and it feeds our growing appreciation of Patrick Stewart's fine acting. It also lays some good groundwork for how a mutually respectful relationship between Picard and Pulaski could develop, which unfortunately apparently wasn't in anyone's plans.

But the story about the Pakleds is awkward, and viewers can be left wondering about a (hopefully unintended) impression that the aliens were somehow representing mentally retarded or impaired individuals. This storyline seems like it's from a different script and a different outlook than the Picard storyline. Most likely, as we saw with some reimagined *Battlestar Galactica* episodes, it was an attempt to add some sort of dramatic tension to a story that was feared to be too quiet. Producers really need to have more confidence in their characters and actors. As we'll see, *The Next Generation* does develop this confidence and delivers some fine stories as a result.

Up the Long Ladder

Writer: Melinda Snodgrass. **Director:** Winrich Kolbe. **Airdate:** May 22, 1989.

Dr. Pulaski helps Worf cover up his embarrassment over having a childhood disease, and Worf starts to realize he has an ally on board. He rewards her with a Klingon tea ceremony.

Meanwhile, the *Enterprise* comes across travelers who are a throwback to old-timey Europe—Ireland, to be exact. These travelers are primitive farmers, but their ship also includes cargo for an advanced colony on a different planet from the one to which the farmers are headed.

The modern colonists turn out to be seeking new genetic injections into their gene pool. They have been forced to use cloning because their numbers were too small; but after many generations of cloning, they are facing the cumulative negative effects of the process being too often repeated.

Picard, perhaps eager to rid his ship of the barnyard animals and their colorful overseers, brokers an agreement by which the Irish farmers join with the modern colonists to help create a more survivable gene pool. The cost? They can't be monogamous and the woman should have children from several different men.

Brenna Odell: Will, is something wrong?"
Riker: What do you mean?
Odell: Do you not like girls?
Riker: Of course I do. Oh—is there a certain technique to this foot washing?"

Notes: What to make of this episode? A wildly stereotypical view of the Irish? A teenage boy's fantasy of multiple sex partners? Another simplistic solution to a genetic problem? It's all that and more.

If the Irish immigrants aren't enough to make you cringe, perhaps the one Irishman's search for alcohol shocked you so much that you blanked out for the rest of the episode. Then there's the ultimate solution, in which the agrarian immigrants are offered as mates and genetic banks for the advanced colonists, a happy solution as long as they want to mate like rabbits. In January 2020, writer Rob Bricken wrote on Gizmodo that he would nominate this as the worst episode of the series: "Everyone has their pick, but 'Up the Long Ladder' is my dark horse contender for the title, because it manages to be racist, sexist, and terrible sci-fi, all at once." Bricken correctly notes the middle school-level stereotypes of the Irish as well as the callous repurposing of them as nothing more than breeding stock.

All around, the weakest show of an otherwise fine second season.

Manhunt

Writer: Terry Devereaux. **Director:** Rob Bowman. **Airdate:** June 19, 1989.

Once again, the *Enterprise* is pressed into service as a very well-appointed ferry for ambassadors, this time a group of dignitaries heading to the planet Pacifica for a conference. Everyone who's anyone is aboard, including the Antedeans (traveling in an unconscious state) and Lwaxana Troi, Deanna Troi's oversexed mother.

The elder Troi is seeking a new husband, and she targets various men on the ship, starting with an uninterested Captain Picard and moving on through Riker and a character in a holonovel.

When the Antedeans are awoken before the conference, Lwaxana Troi reveals them to be assassins. Their hidden explosives are discovered, and the Antedeans are arrested.

Deanna Troi: Why did you stop me [from putting Lwaxana in her place]? Somebody needs to set her straight.
Riker: I think I'll leave that to the captain.

Deanna Troi: Coward.

Notes: The Antedean ambassador is portrayed by Mick Fleetwood, one of the founding members of the Baby Boomer supergroup Fleetwood Mac.

No insult intended to Majel Barrett, but I'll admit to being unmoved by Lwaxana Troi as a character. She's a rather preposterous person who presumably is included because she has the ability to say things other characters would not. Sort of a science fiction Sophia Petrillo. But with rare exception, she is also an unsympathetic character who serves mainly to test the patience of Deanna Troi, Picard, Riker, and me.

The Emissary

Writers: Richard Manning, Hans Beimler, Thomas H. Calder. **Director:** Cliff Bole. **Airdate:** June 26, 1989.

Starfleet orders the *Enterprise* on a secret mission, which turns out to be a rendezvous with a Federation agent. Pressed for time, the agent arrives in a small space probe and turns out to be a woman who is half human and half Klingon. Worf in particular is not pleased with her appearance aboard the *Enterprise*. But after a holodeck combat exercise outing, Worf and K'Ehleyr are intimate, and he's apparently honor bound to marry her now. In his mind, and in Southern Baptist backwoods tradition. But not in her mind, and she rejects him.

She informs the crew that a Klingon ship, the *T'Ong*, carries a crew of warriors (well, every Klingon is a warrior, no?) in suspended animation; they are due to awaken soon. The problem? When they went into hibernation, the Federation and the Klingon Empire were at war. It's up to the Klingon/human K'Ehleyr and the *Enterprise* to meet the *T'Ong* and educate them about the peace that exists between the two dominions. If they fail, the *Enterprise* must destroy the *T'Ong*. When the Klingon sleeper ship shows up, it fires upon the *Enterprise*, and Worf and K'Ehleyr pull a ruse to convince the Klingon warriors that the war is over. K'Ehleyr then goes to the *T'Ong* to continue educating them about the new realities since they went into hibernation 75 years previously.

K'Ehleyr: Worf! So this is where you've been hiding. I told you we would meet again.
Worf: I have nothing to say to you.
K'Ehleyr: Haven't changed a bit, eh? Well, I missed you, too.

Notes: The discovery and recovery of sleeper ships and/or generation ships must be added to the list of recurring *Trek* themes. From "Space Seed" onward, the Buck Rogers-ian need to introduce out-of-time characters into a far-future storyline is a *Star Trek* favorite.

In the world of *Trek* tie-in novels, a highlight is my favorite *Star Trek* novel, David

Gerrold's 1980 *The Galactic Whirlpool*, in which the Kirk-era *Enterprise* encounters a generation ship with warring populations that don't even realize they are on a spaceship.

Peak Performance

Writer: David Kemper. **Director:** Robert Scheerer. **Airdate:** July 10, 1989.

The events of the earlier episode "Q Who" reverberate in this episode when Starfleet tries to ready its forces to face a possible Borg attack. The *Enterprise* is ordered to join a combat test, with Picard commanding the *Enterprise* and Riker helming the challenger, the *Hathaway*. A Zakdorn strategist named Kolrami shows up to observe the test, but that's only after he annoys everyone with his overblown ego.

During a simulated attack by the *Hathaway*, a real attacker shows up. Not the Borg, but a Ferengi ship; nonetheless, the *Enterprise* is unable to respond with its systems in simulation mode.

The Ferengi think there must be something of value on the *Hathaway*, so they threaten the *Enterprise*. But the Federation crews take advantage of some quick thinking by Wesley Crusher (to allow the *Hathaway* to appear to be destroyed when it really just makes a short warp jump away) and Worf (to fool the sensors of the Ferengi into thinking there is another Starfleet ship nearby).

Data: For over nine millennia, potential foes have regarded the Zakdorns as having the greatest innately strategic minds in the galaxy.
Worf: So no one is willing to test that perception in combat?
Data: Exactly.
Worf: Then the reputation means nothing.

Notes: Armin Shimerman, who would go on to portray the beloved Ferengi Quark in *Star Trek: Deep Space Nine*, makes another visit to *The Next Generation* here, playing the role of the Ferengi commander DaiMon Bractor. Another Ferengi is played by David Lander, who has a zillion TV and film credits, but he probably has the most fans from his work as the weird Squiggy on the 1970s sitcom *Laverne & Shirley*.

Shades of Gray

Writers: Maurice Hurley, Richard Manning, Hans Beimler. **Director:** Rob Bowman. **Airdate:** July 17, 1989.

While on an away mission, Riker is injured by a thorn that gives him a deadly infection. With only hours to save him before the virus reaches Riker's brain and kills him, Pulaski uses technology to stimulate his brain and resist the infection. Thus under the control of the machine, Riker has memories of his various past adventures on the *Enterprise*. In an attempt to drive away the infection, Pulaski has the machine draw up negative memories, which help chase down and destroy the virus.

Riker: Deanna, facing death is the ultimate test of character. I don't want to die, but if I have to, I'd like to do it with a little pride.

Notes: *Star Trek: The Next Generation*'s second season was so expensive, they managed to go over budget. That led to the need to do a cheap episode, one accomplished by stringing together some clips from previous episodes. It resulted in an episode that does not make many people's Top Ten lists. In fact, it makes some "worst" lists, but people need to skip the hyperbole and keep things in perspective. If an infinite number of monkeys at an infinite number of typewriters sat writing an infinite number of *Galactica 1980* episodes, they'd still never write anything as good as this weak episode.

This episode is a budget-forced low point for the series, and it's a sad way to end a relatively good season. But much better things would be around the corner when *Next Generation* returned for its third season. Speaking of which . . .

SEASON THREE

Every television series is going to have its share of weak episodes, and *Star Trek: The Next Generation* is no exception. The first season saw entries such as the embarrassing "Code of Honor" and "Angel One," and the second season ended with "Shades of Gray," a dreary compilation of clips from past shows united by a thin new story. But *Next Generation*'s third season simply wowed as it pushed stories and characters into new directions and complexity.

Michael Simpson, writing for *Sci Fi Now*, noted "Sure, there would be classic episodes in years to come, but no other season produced quality as consistently as the third. Looking down the list of episodes . . ., there is barely a weak link in the chain that runs from the premiere, 'Evolution', to the seminal 'The Best of Both Worlds, Part One'."

My choices for the season's strongest episodes are "The Enemy," "Yesterday's Enterprise" (more on which in a moment) and the first part of "The Best of Both Worlds." From looking at other people's "best episodes" lists, I can see that my choices are not unique. All three of these episodes rank among the best of the third season but also among the best of the entire seven-year run of the show. That is saying a lot, because as we'll see in later seasons, there is a lot of really good *Next Generation* to come, including great character studies, Picard's torture by Cardassians, Dr. Crusher's excellent "Remember Me" adventure in season four, and many others.

A sound case can be made that season three was the very best season of *Star Trek: The Next Generation*, and perhaps it was the best season of *Star Trek* in any televised form. The show would not miss a beat when it started season four. But with the third season, the stories and characters clicked, and the audience and critics took note. Including, in some small way, me.

HOW I TOOK NOTICE

This entire book is a personal review of these science fiction series. But let's get even more personal for this short essay: "How I Fell in Love with *Star Trek: The Next Generation*." It all has to do with my friend Jamie and the third season.

When *Next Generation* premiered back on September 28, 1987, I was an editor at an independent student daily newspaper on the campus of the University of Wisconsin–Madison. The paper was distributed in the morning, so in the afternoons and deep into the evenings, we were in the offices writing and editing and laying out the next day's paper. For that premiere episode, many of us crammed into the paper's grimy little lounge and watched the show on our television set mounted high up on the wall. We enjoyed it, but we were not blown away. I watched a few other episodes that first season, but none of them grabbed me, and my attitude changed from excitement about this new series to detached appreciation that the show was surviving.

Frankly, I found the show to be a bit boring, way too politically correct, with a captain of Starfleet's flagship who simply didn't seem that strong or admirable. My feelings were somewhat echoed by *Newsday*'s Marvin Kitman, who wrote in 1988 that *Next Generation* "is somewhat boring and derivative. . . . The new *Star Trek* tries to make the characters 'realistic,' and they turn out to be unbreakably plastic."

So I drifted away; college is a busy time, and I had much more interesting things to do. I soon forgot what day and time the syndicated show was even on, only catching it by chance when I was home and flipping channels.

It continued through the second season, when I was even more detached; I don't remember if I saw a single second-season episode in its original run.

But during that second season, the newspaper gained a new employee, a news reporter named Jamie who was smart, funny, a good person, and she liked science fiction. We became friends, and our circle of friends grew together over the next year or so. It was not unusual for Friday or Saturday evenings to see six or ten of us having dinner at someone's apartment, maybe going out to a movie or watching a video, and talking for hours. A good group.

Then one Friday night, we all came back to Jamie's apartment after an evening at a movie, and before we could do anything else—such as play cards or open a bottle of wine—Jamie said we had to watch *Star Trek*, which aired at that time. It was her home, so her rules. Reluctantly, we gathered around her little television set, prepared to pepper the show with wisecracks and ironic remarks.

The episode was "Yesterday's Enterprise," and I don't believe we had any wisecracks or ironic remarks. Instead, we were enthralled. This was great drama, great television, and great science fiction. They actually sent the old *Enterprise* back into the temporal rift! Tasha Yar sacrificed her life! A number of us complimented the show, and Jamie told us we didn't know what we'd been missing. She was right.

That episode so impressed me that I began paying attention once more to *The Next Generation*. I now knew what time it aired in our market (late Friday evenings), and I began to watch the first-run and the repeat episodes. I saw "The Enemy" and marveled that this show that I thought I had pigeonholed as too precious in its politically correct attitudes would let an enemy die, but they did, and it was one of the heroes—Worf—who made it happen.

The first part of "The Best of Both Worlds" completed my conversion; I was a *Next Generation* fan. This show was a quality program like no other science fiction program on the air then or ever before, and it could go toe-to-toe with any drama on television, genre or not.

I wasn't the only one who was converted by *Next Generation*. Years later, another friend of mine would come home from work in Washington, D.C., and he started viewing ST:TNG repeats while he recuperated from his stressful day. He was hooked, and he was in no way a science fiction fan. My mother—never an SF fan before—also got hooked through ST:TNG. And, of course, the series set new records for syndicated television, so it was bringing in new viewers across the country. I later enjoyed myself during a business trip to Berlin by catching episodes in German. Different language, same great series.

Thanks to Jamie's example and the many people who put together this show, especially but not exclusively season three, *Star Trek: The Next Generation* earned my lasting appreciation and enjoyment.

Evolution

Writers: Michael Piller, Michael Wagner. **Director:** Winrich Kolbe. **Airdate:** September 25, 1989.

Wesley Crusher is a god. No, really. The young acting ensign has a project in which he uses nanites (super-teensy-weensy robots, if you will), but a couple of them escape and get into the *Enterprise*'s computer core. There, they evolve—hence the episode's name—and are fruitful and multiply. Meanwhile, his mother, Dr. Beverly Crusher, has returned from a year at Starfleet Medical, and she's concerned about whether her son is "normal." She thinks he is overly involved in experiments and other work on the starship, and not involved enough in causing trouble and dating.

Complicating matters is that the *Enterprise* is trying to launch a probe to study an explosion of stellar material in a nearby binary star system. Dr. Paul Stubbs tries to expose the nanites to gamma radiation in an attempt to wipe them out, but the nanites fight back, attacking the bridge of the *Enterprise*. Before Captain Picard can take drastic action, Commander Data makes contact with the nanites, who use him to speak to Picard and establish peace, forcing an apology out of Stubbs.

The new sentient life that was created by Wesley Crusher is then sent to Kavis

Alpha IV. Wesley's children have been set free into the universe on their own.

Dr. Crusher: What were you doing when you were 17?
Picard: Probably getting into more trouble than Wesley, I can assure you.
Dr. Crusher: So was I. Isn't that what 17's supposed to be?

Notes: This episode includes the return of Gates McFadden's Dr. Beverly Crusher following her one-season replacement by Diana Muldaur's Dr. Kate Pulaski.

A great deal is made of Wesley's supposed unnatural development because his mother is always around him, as if this is automatically understood to be a stultifying thing. But children growing up in multi-generational homes is more the rule on Earth today than the exception. It is of course the exception in the modern United States and some other places, but plenty of people live their entire lives with their parents in the house (until they pass away) and then with their own children and grandchildren in the house. And people who live in smaller communities are also conscious of always having the eyes of family, neighbors and authorities on them. None of that is to say that this episode's writers are making an incorrect point—personally, I love my family but do appreciate the anonymity and freedom to establish myself on my own terms that I find possible in a modern big city—but just to note that it is reflective of a minority and relatively moneyed viewpoint.

The Ensigns of Command

Writer: Melinda M. Snodgrass. **Director:** Cliff Bole. **Airdate:** October 2, 1989.

Data is a god. Not really, but the android commander is sent down to the surface of the planet Tau Cygni V to try to convince the 15,000 people there to evacuate immediately. Unable to convince the colonists that they need to leave, he takes it upon himself to prove that they are too puny and weak to defend themselves against him, much less against the Sheliak.

The Sheliak are an alien race that has served notice that the colonists have four days to get off the planet so they can colonize it themselves, according to a long-standing if apparently poorly written treaty with the Federation.

Data is the only one of the *Enterprise* crew that can go to the planet, because lethal hyperonic radiation (don't bother googling, apparently not a real thing) would make it too dangerous for the non-androids on board. Nonetheless, the human colonists on the planet were able to survive after initial troubles adjusting to the radiation. But the *Enterprise*'s transporter won't work through the radiation, and it would take three weeks to evacuate the colonists with shuttles. Captain Picard finds a rule in the treaty that calls for using a third-party arbitrator, and he selects a species that won't be done hibernating for another six months. Faced with waiting six months or allowing three weeks for evacuation, the Sheliak finally relent and allow the three-week delay.

Meanwhile, Data has no luck talking the colonists into abandoning the planet they've known as their only home. So he destroys their water supply and convinces them that if they can be so easily defeated by him, they couldn't possibly win against the Sheliak. Mission accomplished.

Riker [*to Data*]: The lives of 15,000 people are riding on you. You'd better get innovative.

Notes: This was not the first *Next Generation* appearance for Sheliak actor Mart McChesney, who had also appeared under heavy prosthetics in the much-maligned first-season episode "Skin of Evil," which was the swan song for the Tasha Yar character. Until she returned. And returned.

The Survivors

Writer: Michael Wagner. **Director:** Les Landau. **Airdate:** October 9, 1989.

The *Enterprise* receives a distress call from Delta Rana IV, a Federation colony. But upon arrival, the crew finds the colony to have been wiped off the face of the planet, save for one tiny spot of greenery with a house and its two occupants, Kevin and Rishon Uxbridge. They want the *Enterprise* to leave them alone, but Picard refuses to leave until he finds out what happened and knows that they are safe—and why they alone seem to have survived the attack on the colony.

Counselor Troi finds herself being driven insane by the effects of a music box discovered on the planet, and she is put into a medically induced coma. A strange ship appears in orbit and twice draws away the *Enterprise*; a third time it appears and destroys the Uxbridge home. The *Enterprise* moves away from the planet far enough to appear to have gone away, and the Uxbridge home and its occupants soon reappear on the planet's surface.

Picard has the Uxbridges brought aboard the *Enterprise*, where he learns that the strange ship was created by Kevin, a Douwd who has immense powers, to keep others away from the planet. He had been living with his human lover Rishon when aliens known as the Husnock arrived and attacked. Because he doesn't believe in violence, he refused to join the fight, though Rishon did fight and she got killed along with the rest of the colonists. Kevin reacts by wiping out the entire species of Husnock, and consigns himself to living on this little patch of land with an artificially recreated Rishon.

Worf: Sir, may I say your attempt to hold the away team at bay with a non-functioning weapon was an act of unmitigated gall.
Kevin Uxbridge: Didn't fool you, huh?
Worf: I admire gall.

Notes: This episode is an interesting exploration of violence, revenge, and pacifism. Surprisingly—and refreshingly—it isn't a black-and-white portrayal of the issues involved, simplified though it might be to fit into a one-hour teleplay. Kevin survives the attack by the Husnock because he is a pacifist and doesn't fight them. That would seem to suggest pacifism is a viable alternative to even defensive violence. But he loses everything he loves, showing the possible cost of such an approach. Further, he had the power that could have saved the people around him, yet he did not use it. And finally, when he does strike out in vengeance, he commits a genocide that takes the lives of 50 billion Husnock.

In the end, Kevin is left alone on his planet, there to contemplate the costs and moral issues raised by his experience, with the audience to do the same.

Who Watches the Watchers

Writers: Richard Manning, Hans Beimler. **Director:** Robert Wiemer. **Airdate:** October 16, 1989.

Picard is a god, at least to the Mintakans, a primitive pre-Warp species on the planet Mintaka III who are being observed by a camouflaged Federation monitoring station. The Mintakans develop this odd belief after one of their own talks about "The Picard" as a godlike figure, all the result of a mind-wipe that didn't work after he was treated aboard the *Enterprise* for injuries sustained in an accident at the monitoring station.

In an attempt to learn what is going on in the colony, the *Enterprise* crew makes some visits to the planet. When there, a crewmember is taken captive and, in an attempt to get him back, the real Picard shows up, unfortunately during a thunderstorm, which increases his godlike visuals a bit. But there's nothing like proving a man is not a god like shooting him with an arrow, as Picard and the Mintakans find out.

Liko: I believe I have seen the Overseer. He is called The Picard.

Notes: This episode is another example of the ridiculous Prime Directive creating and complicating conflicts. The humans were watching this pre-warp society, but they weren't supposed to be seen. But they are. Doctor Crusher breaks the Prime Directive by healing the injured Mintakan. After trying to adhere to the Prime Directive, Picard has to intervene anyway. Much ado about an unnecessary to-do.

The stupid prime directive: The Gene Roddenberry-written rule, present from the original *Star Trek* series onward, decrees that Starfleet personnel can't interfere with the internal development of a pre-warp alien civilization. The intent was that highly developed civilizations shouldn't affect the development of lesser-developed ones, lest they create unnatural effects in societies unadvanced enough to have become nice and shiny awesome like the Federation is.

That's obviously a prejudicial interpretation, but the point remains. All civilizations are always developing (and sometimes regressing), so if the ideology behind the Prime Directive was literally followed, no two civilizations could ever interact. Except for a few undeveloped societies on islands or deep in the Amazon, all peoples and societies have undergone interaction/warfare/trade/cultural "contamination" or exchange with other peoples. Interaction with other societies is one of the ways cultures grow, expand, change; humans see that better ways exist, that they don't have to keep doing things the same old way. So why does *Star Trek* assume that we can all be contaminated just fine, but it's wrong if it happens to some humanoid alien group in space?

In specific application, it focuses on not getting involved in an alien civilization that has not yet achieved warp power. Roddenberry and Starfleet assumed that if a civilization can develop warp power, by that time it has supposedly also shed its primitive prejudices and warlike spirit. But technological advance doesn't necessarily mean psychological and moral growth; Nazi Germany was one of the most technologically advanced nations on earth, but it was a moral atrocity. And as much as I love technology and advanced science, I'll point out that a society might have rejected warp powers and space travel but focused on moral and ethical development. It wasn't warp drive that made the Vulcans intellectual and rational giants; it was attending to the mind and morals.

If the imposition of this rule was initially spawned by a sincere desire to prevent more powerful civilizations from taking over and destroying smaller, weaker ones, it surely should not have survived the encounters with the warlike Klingons, or the warlike Romulans, or the warlike Borg, or the warlike Dominion, or any of the many other warlike and often quite prejudicial Warp-capable civilizations *Enterprise* crews have encountered and fought with since 1966. It is especially worrying, with regards to the futuristic and moral standing (not to mention writing skills) of the franchise's creators and producers over the years, because it is a problem that could have been pretty easily solved by tweaking the directive to target the specific harmful behavior it allegedly hopes to prevent.

In *Star Trek into Darkness*, if the *Enterprise* had not interfered in the alien civilization at the beginning of the film, the race would have died. How is that better than knowing there were other more-developed beings in the universe?

The power differential between the civilizations is the point, but it's not the real problem. If Earth were about to be destroyed, I would love it if a more highly developed species appeared and interfered with our natural development into dead people.

The Bonding

Writer: Ronald D. Moore. **Director:** Winrich Kolbe. **Airdate:** October 23, 1989.

During a visit to a planet, Lt. Marla Aster is killed when a mine is tripped. The woman's son, Jeremy, blames Lt. Worf for his mother's death.

The *Enterprise* crew finds more mines on the planet's surface. Troi detects a consciousness on the planet, and Jeremy is visited by a vision of his dead mother, trying to convince him that she is still alive and trying to bring him back with her to the planet. The crew stops that from taking place. The fake mother reappears and again tries to take Jeremy, but she's again stopped. Under questioning, she reveals that she wants to help Jeremy deal with his mother's death, because her species has seen so many others die on that planet.

In the end, Worf—like Jeremy, an orphan—helps the kid deal with the loss of his mother and honor her through the Klingon ritual of R'uustai.

La Forge: Let's just hope it doesn't blow us to kingdom come while it's figuring out how to blow us to kingdom come.

Notes: This is a strong example of how *The Next Generation* could handle a smaller, quieter story, something that scares away most science fiction producers; that's their loss, because "The Bonding" demonstrates how this type of an episode deepens the reality of the fictional series, increases the depth of the characters, and lets the audience live in this fictional environment more.

In the third season of the 1960s *Star Trek*, creator Gene Roddenberry was effectively sidelined and a new producer—Fred Freiberger—took over. The third season had a few high points, but it was easily the weakest season of that iteration of *Trek*. "Spock's Brain." Nuff said.

But with *Star Trek: The Next Generation*, it was almost as if the calculus were reversed. Gene Roddenberry's health declined throughout the seasons of *Next Generation*, and yet the show got better. Roddenberry would pass away in 1991 while the show was still in production, but he had bequeathed this sequel series with a deep bench of talent to take the show to new heights. We can already see many of those talented new faces starting in the third season.

Perhaps the biggest name is Ronald D. Moore, who joined as a writer of this very episode and became a script editor and producer for *Next Generation*, co-wrote the first two *Next Generation* feature films, was an executive producer for a couple seasons of *Deep Space Nine*, produced *Roswell*, developed and executive produced the critically lauded *Battlestar Galactica* reboot, created *Caprica*, developed the *Outlander* series, and worked on many other series and potential series. Not a bad legacy for a college dropout who wormed his way onto the staff of *Next Generation*.

Michael Piller also joined the ST:TNG staff as a writer, became a producer, co-created the spinoffs *Deep Space Nine* and *Voyager*, and developed *The Dead Zone* as a TV series.

Melinda Snodgrass began contributing stories to *Next Generation*, and over the next couple decades would write many short stories and novels.

Producer Rick Berman assumed increasing control and authority on the series as Roddenberry's health got worse, and he eventually became an executive producer. He would go on to lead Paramount's *Star Trek* franchise for nearly two decades, until *Star Trek: Enterprise* was taken off the air in 2005.

Ira Steven Behr joined as a producer in the third season, and he would later work for *Deep Space Nine* as well as non-*Trek* productions *Dark Angel*, *The Twilight Zone*, *The 4400*, and *Alphas*.

These voices and others came to prominence with the second and third seasons of *Star Trek: The Next Generation*, but they would go on to influence SF TV and film for decades.

Booby Trap

Writers: Ron Roman, Michael Piller, Richard Danus, Michael Wagner. **Director:** Gabrielle Beaumont. **Airdate:** October 30, 1989.

The *Enterprise* explores an area of space that had been the scene of a big battle between two species, the Menthars and the Promellians. A Promellian battleship sends out a distress call, and the *Enterprise* finds it adrift in space and its crew long dead. Before expiring, the Promellian captain had left a message explaining that they were the victims of a trap by their enemy, the Menthars.

Back on the *Enterprise*, the crew discovers that their own ship has fallen prey to the Menthar trap. The ship begins to lose power, and Geordi La Forge calls up a holodeck program to help him find a way to make the engines work despite the effects of the Menthar weapons. A holographic version of Dr. Leah Brahms, the developer of the *Enterprise*'s warp engines, aids LaForge in his search, but they are unable to find a solution before Picard is forced to cut off all extraneous energy use.

La Forge convinces the captain that the holodeck simulation is crucial to finding a solution, and indeed two solutions soon present themselves. First, the holo-Brahms suggests letting the computer take control, able to make decisions and moves faster than a living crewmember could. But La Forge comes up with the solution that Picard implements: manually steer the ship away from the Promellian ship and the Menthar trap using just a couple basic thrusters.

Guinan: I'm attracted to bald men.

Notes: In the fourth season, watch for the real Dr. Brahms to make a visit to the *Enterprise*, and La Forge must fess up about his holodeck version of her.

Also, I just want to note apropos the quote included above, I once had a friend (who was also a big *Next Generation* fan) who accompanied me to a Patrick Stewart one-man performance. She, too, readily admitted that she was attracted to bald men.

The Enemy

Writers: David Kemper, Michael Piller. **Director:** David Carson. **Airdate:** November 6, 1989.

The *Enterprise* discovers a Romulan craft that crash landed on the planet Galorndon Core. Upon investigation, they come across a badly injured survivor, who is brought back to the *Enterprise* for treatment. La Forge is separated from the rest of the away team and is captured by another Romulan survivor. They are both now stuck on the planet and must work together to devise a way to adapt La Forge's VISOR to give them direction to a place where they can be beamed back to their ships.

Above the planet, the *Enterprise* is in a standoff with a Romulan ship, and it turns out that Worf is the only crewmember on the *Enterprise* with the matching ribosomes that can save the injured Romulan's life. But Worf refuses to make the donation, and the Romulan dies. When Picard informs the Romulan captain of the death, the two ships gear up for a battle until they learn that La Forge and his Romulan pal have made it to the beam-out site. The two are beamed directly to the *Enterprise* bridge, where the Romulan convinces his captain that the *Enterprise* isn't at fault. Battle is averted, and the *Enterprise* escorts the Romulan ship back to the nearby Neutral Zone.

Dr. Crusher: Worf, you are the only one who can save his life.
Worf: Then he will die.

Notes: This is a stellar episode, because it lets Worf play out his character as his character would actually behave and not succumb to the wishes of a Hollywood wishy washy last-minute reprieve. The good-and-nice thing for Worf to do would be to help save the Romulan; the usual television writer thing to do would be to have Worf at the last minute be convinced that he should change his mind. But Worf is not a liberal Episcopalian youth pastor. He is a Klingon, and if you introduce a warrior race onto the *Enterprise*, you have to be willing to follow that to its natural conclusions, beyond just having him appear gruff. Klingons have consequences, and it is a sign of the maturation of *Next Generation* and it's a sign of the producers' and writers' trust in the maturity of their audience that they could have one of the show's heroes behave in a way that pretty much everybody would say is wrong.

The Price

Writer: Hannah Louise Shearer. **Director:** Robert Sheerer. **Airdate:** November 13, 1989.

In a thematic precursor to the spinoff series *Deep Space Nine*, the Federation is one of several parties vying to win rights to control the entrance to a wormhole. Troi immediately falls for Ral, the negotiator for one of the other groups. What she only learns later is that Ral is, like her, an empath and he has been using his abilities to manipulate the proceedings and undercut the Federation.

Meanwhile, La Forge and Data are sent through the wormhole to test it out; a Ferengi ship makes the journey as well. Arriving at the other end of the wormhole, they find themselves in the Delta quadrant. Unfortunately, the Delta end of the wormhole is unstable, and before it collapses the Federation shuttle is able to make the return trip, but the Ferengi ship stubbornly refuses to follow and its two crewmembers are stuck there.

La Forge and Data arrive back at the site of the negotiations with the news that the wormhole isn't worth it, but Ral has already won the rights for his employers, and his trickery has been unmasked by Troi. All in all, a bad day to be Ral.

DaiMon Goss: See to it that we get some chairs.
Picard: Let me explain—
DaiMon Goss: Fine, fine. Just have your Klingon servant get us some chairs.
Worf: I'm in charge of security!
DaiMon Goss: Then who gets the chairs?

Notes: In the *Star Trek: Voyager* episode "False Profits," we once again meet up with the two Ferengi who are stranded in the Delta Quadrant. The *Voyager* discovers that they have set themselves up as gods on a primitive planet. They struggle to undo the Ferengi ploy, finally extricating them from the clutches of the now-indignant natives, only to have the Ferengi escape with their shuttlecraft into the wormhole, which has once again appeared but doesn't stick around long enough to let *Voyager* take it home.

The Vengeance Factor

Writer: Sam Rolfe. **Director:** Timothy Bond. **Airdate:** November 20, 1989.

Internecine conflict is a messy thing. The *Enterprise* is on the hunt for the perpetrators of an attack on a Federation outpost. Their search leads them to Acamar III, where they are told that the guilty party was probably the Gatherers, an Acamarian offshoot that survives by piracy. Picard tries to establish a peaceful resolution to the Gatherer-Acamarian divide, but Yuta, the assistant to the Acamarian leader, complicates matters when she kills one of the Gatherer leaders.

After studying Acamarian data, the Federation crew learns that Yuta is on a long-term mission to seek vengeance for the destruction of her clan. Riker is forced to destroy her in order to prevent her from ruining the negotiations, which are finally concluded successfully.

Worf: Your ambushes would be more successful if you bathed more often.

Notes: *Star Trek: The Next Generation* brought in a lot of new or young writers during its seven-year run, but as with "The Vengeance Factor," it also drew upon some serious veterans. Writer Sam Rolfe created *Have Gun – Will Travel*, a well-regarded western television series, and he played an important part in the development of *The Man from U.N.C.L.E.* His very first screenplay, for the 1953 western *The Naked Spur*, earned him an Academy Award nomination. Not bad for a beginner.

The Defector

Writer: Ronald D. Moore. **Director:** Robert Scheerer. **Airdate:** January 1, 1990.

Data acts in a Shakespeare play to try to learn more about humanity and iambic pentameter. But his work is interrupted by the arrival of a Romulan scout vessel that is being chased by a Romulan warbird. The warbird returns to Romulan space, but the scout's pilot boards the *Enterprise* and announces his intention to defect. Declaring that he is Sub-Lieutenant Setal, the defector says he has information about a secret Romulan base on a planet in the Neutral Zone.

Picard suspects that Setal is not what he claims. The *Enterprise* crew is concerned that Setal might be a trap set by the Romulans to lure them into the Neutral Zone. Data takes Setal into a holodeck recreation of Romulus after hearing the man's sorrow at never again being able to see his home or family. Setal isn't comforted, but it does help make up his mind to come clean. Picard was correct; Setal isn't what he claimed. He now reveals that he is actually Admiral Jarok. Picard persuades him to give up the information needed to confirm his claim about a secret base.

The *Enterprise* goes into the Neutral Zone and finds there is no base there, but two Romulan warbirds promptly show up and attack the *Enterprise*. Luckily, Picard and Worf had prepared for such an eventuality—Picard had worried about a trap from the beginning, remember—and three Klingon birds of prey appear, countering the warbirds. The *Enterprise* is allowed to leave, and it becomes clear that Jarok had been set up by the Romulans, who were able to lure the *Enterprise* into the forbidden area and disgrace Jarok. The defector, utterly defeated, commits suicide.

Picard [*to Jarok*]: You already betrayed your people, Admiral! You made your choices, sir! You're a traitor! Now if the bitter taste of that is unpalatable to you, I am truly sorry; but I will not risk my crew because you think you can dance on the edge of the Neutral Zone. You crossed over, Admiral. You make yourself comfortable with that.

Notes: This is another excellent episode, one more example of the strong, well-told stories that make *Next Generation*'s third season stand out. It is a well-acted, well-executed story that manages to merge both hope and tragedy into one taut story. As with "The Enemy" and as we'll see in "Yesterday's Enterprise," "The Defector" does not take the easy way out of making everything nice, simple, and happily resolved at the end.

Also, Shakespeare is almost required reading for any long-term *Star Trek* viewer. The Bard's work was a favorite of *Trek* creator Gene Roddenberry, and it pops up in many episode titles, storylines, and quotes in the original series, *Next Generation*, and even in the movies. (Remember the Klingon Chang quoting *The Merchant of Venice* in *Star Trek VI: The Undiscovered Country*—a movie whose very title comes from Shakespeare's *Hamlet*?)

The Hunted

Writer: Robin Bernheim. **Director:** Cliff Bole. **Airdate:** January 8, 1990.

The inhabitants of the planet Angosia III want to join the Federation, so the *Enterprise* is sent to check them out. Picard agrees to a request from Prime Minister Nayrok to help find a convict, Danar, who is soon located but turns out to have been a genetically enhanced soldier. Deanna Troi sticks up for Danar, and looks into his police record (which turns out not to exist.) The Angosians consider him a criminal unfit to live in their society any longer, but Danar says soldiers like him were just imprisoned after serving because the government didn't undo the effects of their military training and modifications.

Danar manages to escape aboard an Angosian transport ship, which he uses to attack a colony and free some of his colleagues. They then attack the Angosian leaders, who call upon Picard for help, but Picard refuses. He leaves them to fix their own problems, holding out the possibility of help with deconditioning the soldiers and eventual re-application to the Federation.

Picard: Prime Minister, even the most comfortable prison is still a prison.

Notes: Picard and Riker are told that Danar is extremely dangerous and a serious threat. Yet when the *Enterprise* beams him aboard, there are only two security officers in Transporter Room 4. This also comes after the bridge crew witnessed Danar outwit them multiple times. Those two security officers are swatted away with ease by Danar, and he is only brought under control after Riker and Worf arrive and have a fight with him. Does "extremely dangerous" mean *nothing* to Picard and Riker?

Prime Minister Nayrok is portrayed by veteran actor James Cromwell, who had roles in several other *Trek* episodes and of course played the colorful inventor of the warp drive in the film *Star Trek First Contact*.

The High Ground

Writer: Melinda Snodgrass. **Director:** Gabrielle Beaumont. **Airdate:** January 29, 1990.

While the *Enterprise* crew is on Rutia IV dropping off medical supplies, a terrorist bombing takes place. Dr. Crusher is ordered to return to the ship, but she stays to tend the wounded. In the process, she is taken captive by Ansata separatist rebels. The Rutian government wants to use the *Enterprise*'s superior technology and firepower to search for and destroy the rebel base, but Picard refuses. Meanwhile, the *Enterprise* crew investigates the inverter transportation/shifting technology used by the rebels. Crusher finds out from her captors that the inverter is making the rebels sick from its overuse.

The rebel leader, Kyril Finn, uses the inverter to attack the *Enterprise*, plant a bomb (swiftly removed by the Starfleet crew), and kidnap Captain Picard. Aboard the *Enterprise*, Data and Wesley Crusher are able to locate the rebels, and the Federation and the Rutian government invade the base and put them down.

Dr. Crusher: I'm sorry; if I'd only gone back to the ship.
Picard: I should've beamed you up.
Dr. Crusher: You wouldn't dare.
Picard: Oh, yes, I would, and should.
Dr. Crusher: Without my permission?
Picard: If you don't follow orders.
Dr. Crusher: If you'd give reasonable orders, I'd obey.
Picard: Doctor, I will be the judge of what is reasonable!

Notes: Just a handful of episodes ago, Dr. Crusher broke the Prime Directive to heal an injured Mintakan in "Who Watches the Watchers." Her captivity in this episode is the result of her disobeying an order and healing a wounded person. Apparently her year-long assignment at Starfleet Medical did not include a primer on following rules.

And anyway, it all happens in a rather ham-handed story about terrorism that reportedly didn't leave anyone happy—producers, the writer, or the British authorities, who were unhappy about the show's rather lame framing of the Northern Ireland situation.

Déjà Q

Writer: Richard Danus. **Director:** Les Landau. **Airdate:** February 5, 1990.

Q is no longer a god. The *Enterprise* crewmembers are distracted from their mission to prevent a moon from falling into a planet when Q appears on the starship's bridge, stripped of his clothes and his powers. Picard is not pleased with Q's story that he has lost his powers and been kicked out of the Q Continuum, exiled as a mortal human. Q is thrown into the brig.

Eventually, Q is called upon to help the crew figure out how to save the planet's population from being destroyed by the moon. But when the Calamarain, one of the species that had previously been the target of Q's interference, show up trying to get at him, they succeed in getting past the *Enterprise*'s shields and inflicting harm on Data, who is trying to protect the *Enterprise*'s unwanted passenger.

Q decides to flee the ship in a shuttle so the Calamarain won't harm the *Enterprise*'s crew any more. That causes the appearance of another member of the Q Continuum (also called Q, naturally), who says that the first Q's actions show that he has demonstrated behavior that qualifies him for a restoration of his powers. Duly re-powered, Q gets ready to take vengeance on the Calamarain, but Q is stopped by Q (you get the idea) and instead lets the aliens go.

As a reward for trying to save him, Q grants Data a gift: an outburst of laughter.

Picard: Return that moon to its orbit.
Q: I have no powers! Q the ordinary.
Picard: Q the liar! Q the misanthrope!
Q: Q the miserable; Q the desperate! What must I do to convince you people?
Worf: Die.
Q: Oh, very clever, Worf. Eat any good books lately?

Notes: Is Q an evil omnipotent being or not? He's an interesting recurring character, mixing sympathetic humor with malevolence, curiosity with indifference, ultimate power with an interest in puny powerless humans. And it is nice to see him powerless for once.

The second Q is played by Corbin Bernsen, who portrayed divorce lawyer Arnie Becker on *L.A. Law* and Henry Spencer on *Psych*, among other roles.

A Matter of Perspective

Writer: Ed Zuckerman. **Director:** Cliff Bole. **Airdate:** February 12, 1990.

Commander Riker is accused of killing a Tanugan doctor, and the Tanugans want Riker to be extradited. Picard draws on the doctor's relatives and coworkers, records and testimony, and even the holodeck to try to recreate what happened.

The late Dr. Apgar had been working on an energy source for the Federation, but there's much behind-the-scenes politicking going on, including Riker and Apgar's wife getting too close for comfort or propriety. But a discovery of energy beams continuing to strike the *Enterprise* leads to the conclusion that Apgar had tried to kill Riker and ended up an unintended casualty of his devious deed.

Riker: We can't both be telling the truth.
Troi: It is the truth—as you each remember it.
Riker: But her version puts a noose around my neck.

Notes: Filmmakers love the idea of retelling a story from different viewpoints. In "A Matter of Perspective," the incidents leading to Apgar's death are told from the vantage points of various actors. Similarly, the 1950 Akira Kurosawa classic *Rashomon* is the touchstone for all such stories, with different characters giving their versions of an event.

Yesterday's Enterprise

Writers: Ira Steven Behr, Richard Manning, Hans Beimler, Ronald D. Moore, Trent Christopher Ganino, Eric A. Stillwell. **Director:** David Carson. **Airdate:** February 19, 1990.

In Ten Forward, while Guinan is having a TMI conversation with Worf about drinking, companionship, and the well-being of females who get, um, close to Worf, a temporal rift is spotted out in space. On the bridge, the crew is trying to figure out what they have found. Suddenly, a starship emerges from the temporal phenomenon: The *Enterprise* C. Captain Picard learns that bit of information from Tasha Yar. Gone are Worf and Troi, but Tasha Yar is back, and things are definitely different aboard the *Enterprise* D.

The *Enterprise* C has clearly been in a battle and is suffering visible damage. It is under the command of Captain Rachel Garrett, and it had been responding to a call for help from a Klingon outpost when it entered the rift. Thanks to the space phenomenon, the *Enterprise* C has unwittingly time traveled to the future, and that action has changed the timeline. The reality Garrett's ship arrives in is grim: The Federation is locked in a war it is losing against the Klingons, and the *Enterprise* D is not the family-friendly 1980s shopping-mall of a starship we have known and loved; it is a warship.

Only Guinan realizes something has happened, that things are not as they should be. She tells Picard to send the *Enterprise* C back into the rift, which could restore the correct timeline, but he resists.

In an attack by the Klingons, Captain Garrett is killed, and her first mate, Richard Castillo must take command. Tasha Yar has gotten close to Castillo. When she learns that her death in the real timeline is meaningless, she opts to join the *Enterprise* C on its suicide mission back into the rift. If the older ship rejoins the fight in the old timeline and is destroyed in the process, it would be seen as an honorable sacrifice by the Klingons. While several Klingon warships attack the *Enterprise*s, Castillo's ship limps back into the abyss.

Tasha Yar: There's something more when you look at me, isn't there? I can see it in your eyes, Guinan. We've known each other too long.
Guinan: We weren't meant to know each other at all. At least, that's what I sense when I look at you. Tasha, you're not supposed to be here.

Notes: Usually when you see a plethora of writers attached to a script, you can confidently predict a muddle of embarrassing proportions. This time, instead, we get one of the greatest hours of *Star Trek: The Next Generation*—or any science fiction television drama, for that matter.

Season three of *Next Generation* is often called the year that the show came into its own, when it reached its potential. It's also the year that the show did a lot of serious adult programming—and not "adult" in the sexual sense; adult in that it dealt with serious, often life-and-death matters without taking the easy outs in which no one is killed or no one makes a morally questionable choice (remember "The Enemy").

If you enjoyed this episode but think it's just a normal good episode, consider all of the other ways it could have been done. Lesser writers could have turned it all into a dream, so it wouldn't matter. It could have taken place in an alternate universe, so it wouldn't really affect the world of our heroes. It could have been resolved in a way where everyone is safe in the end, including Tasha Yar in her escape into a different timeline. That's not what these writers did, and by dealing with difficult choices and letting their characters make excruciatingly painful, life-or-death decisions with consequences, they made the story count.

It does matter, because—in the *Star Trek* universe—it is real and it took place. And the head of a Starfleet starship had to send to a certain death other Starfleet officers, all for a greater good. Those officers don't want to die, but they do it because they understand the greater good. There is no easy way out. There is no last-minute quickie-save for the characters or the storyline. There is only the need to end a horrible war that has taken untold lives. Picard doesn't know that his real timeline is (relatively) peaceful and in that timeline he is an explorer and scientist, not a warship captain. Therein lies the drama, and it is aided by great acting by everyone from Picard to the returning Denise Crosby as Tasha Yar.

And, last but not least, credit must be given to the writers, director, and producers for giving a stellar take on one of the hoariest cliches in *Star Trek*dom: the time travel story. Instead of presenting characters who go back in time knowing that they are traveling back in time (such as in the original series' "Assignment Earth," the movies' *Star Trek IV: The Voyage Home*, or *Next Generation*'s own "Time's Arrow" or even the film *Star Trek: First Contact*, for examples), the characters here do not know that things have changed. They do not know that the hellish lives they are living, including fighting a disastrous war they are losing, is not the natural, actual way things should be going. It is only Guinan who realizes something is wrong and things shouldn't be this way. She tells Tasha Yar that the younger woman shouldn't be there. The audience already knows it, and because many of us miss her character, we share her sad but true realization that she does not in fact belong there and the only way to make things right is to sacrifice her life.

The Offspring

Writer: René Echevarria. **Director:** Jonathan Frakes. **Airdate:** March 12, 1990.

Data is not a god, but he does become a life-creating parent. The android creates a "child," and like a Marin County parent, he lets the child choose its own gender and appearance. Data names his offspring Lal, who has chosen to be a humanoid young woman. At first, she appears to outdo even her creator in language and the display of emotion, and she learns human concepts quickly, albeit awkwardly. But her emotions turn out to be the result of problems with her positronic brain.

Hearing about the creation of the new android, Starfleet Admiral Haftel comes aboard to try to get Data to give up Lal so she can be taken to a science lab elsewhere. Picard resists the move, telling Haftel that Data is sentient and can make his own choices. Their tug-of-war is interrupted by Lal's positronic problems, which have reached a critical point. Even with Haftel's help, Data is unable to save his offspring.

Data downloads her memories into his own positronic brain.

Data: He is questioning my ability as a parent.
Picard: In a manner of speaking—
Data: Does the admiral have children, Sir?
Picard: I believe he does. Why?
Data: I am forced to wonder how much experience he had as a parent when his first child was born.

Notes: This is the first episode directed by actor Jonathan Frakes, who has gone on to turn in numerous assignments in television and film, including of course the top-rated film *Star Trek: First Contact*. If that doesn't impress you, then know that Frakes worked as a costumed Captain America at conventions in the 1970s while in the employ of Marvel Comics.

"The Offspring" is a great story to run after "Yesterday's Enterprise." The producers follow the high drama and cataclysmic time-travel tale with this deceptively quiet "character" story that nonetheless explores issues of sentience, parenting, and—as ever, when dealing with androids—humanity.

Sins of the Father

Writers: Ronald D. Moore, W. Reed Moran, Drew Deighan. **Director:** Les Landau. **Airdate:** March 19, 1990.

Viewers have to start remembering those weird Klingon names that get thrown around in Klingon-heavy episodes, because they are starting to carry a lot of backstory, as this episode demonstrates.

Duras is a powerful Klingon who is the son of the rival of Mogh, Worf's late father. Duras is charging the dead Klingon with having been a traitor and causing a massacre at the Khitomer colony by betraying security codes to the Romulans. Worf goes to the Klingon homeworld to defend his father's honor, and he learns that he has a brother, Kurn, who agrees to help him in the defense. The other Klingons, however, do not know of Kurn's family ties to Worf and Mogh.

K'mpec, the Klingon chancellor, tires to get Worf to drop the challenge to Duras' prosecution, but Worf refuses. When Kurn is seriously injured in an attack, Picard steps in to serve as Worf's backup, and the Starfleet captain also orders his crew to examine the evidence against Mogh. They discover that the evidence was faked, but when Picard attempts to demonstrate in court that Mogh was innocent, K'mpec interrupts the proceedings. He privately tells Worf and Picard that the Klingon High Council knows that Mogh is innocent and, worse, that Duras' father was the actual traitor, but because Duras holds a powerful position in the empire, revealing that information would lead to civil war. The chancellor and Picard come to loggerheads over the Klingon plan to condemn Worf and his brother Kurn despite the truth, and Worf opts to let the chancellor cover up the truth in the interests of peace in the empire. In the end, the council condemns Worf.

Duras: You are a fool, and your challenge can only result in a fool's death.
Worf: It is a good day to die, Duras. And the day is not yet over.

Notes: To have two stories centering on parents and their children air in consecutive weeks probably was not planned, because "Sins of the Father" and "The Offspring" have very different stories. But both are still about the relationships, responsibilities, and even the mistakes of parents and their offspring.

Allegiance

Writers: Hans Beimler, Richard Manning. **Director:** Winrich Kolbe. **Airdate:** March 26, 1990.

Unknown aliens kidnap Picard from the *Enterprise* and replace him with a double. The fake Picard proceeds to give unusual orders and act in unexpected ways, eventually leading the bridge crew to refuse to carry out an order they deem dangerous to the ship and its crew.

Meanwhile, the real Picard is stuck in a prison cell with three other captives. The Starfleet captain organizes the others into an effective team to attempt a breakout from their jail. But after managing to get their cell door open, they find themselves facing a blank wall.

Picard realizes this is a test of some sort, and one of the prisoners, Haro, admits the jig is up and shows herself to be a different alien who explains that his race had set up this experiment to test out the idea of leadership.

The aliens return Picard to the *Enterprise*, where he teaches them a brief lesson about captivity.

First alien: Captain, our species cannot bear captivity!
Second alien: We were merely curious; we meant no harm.
First alien: We did not, after all, injure you in any way.

Picard: Imprisonment is an injury, regardless of how you justify it.

Notes: One of the things that makes the *Enterprise* crew suspicious of the fake Picard is his flirtatious behavior around Dr. Crusher. This would be followed up in future episodes, of course, including the series finale, which has one timeline in which Crusher and Picard had been married and divorced.

As for the plot line that the whole experience was a test—eh. That seems like a weak explanation and an unlikely setup. They kidnap members of other species for the purpose of learning about the concept of leadership? What line of thought led them from "Hmm, I'm curious about this leadership thing" to "I know, we'll take some aliens captive and put them in an unnatural situation that might or might not allow us to see them display leadership"? At least a couple problems with that. First, if observing members of other species is going to inform these curious aliens about something as vague as leadership, couldn't they just get the interstellar equivalent of cable TV and watch countless fiction and nonfiction displays of leadership? They'd get a much broader pool of examples from which to draw conclusions. Second, why do it secretly? Starfleet would have welcomed the chance to meet them, discuss and display leadership (it's not like it's a military secret), probably give them access to decades or centuries of research on the topic (which could ultimately save the aliens the cost of that interstellar Comcast)—and the aliens would not run the risk of creating a political or even military dustup with the subjects of their test.

Captain's Holiday

Writer: Ira Steven Behr. **Director:** Chip Chalmers. **Airdate:** April 2, 1990.

Captain Picard bows to pressure from his crew to take a vacation, so he heads to a resort on the planet Risa, where he is soon kissed by a strange woman named Vash. Later, relaxing by the pool, the woman returns with Sovak, a Ferengi. Sovak is trying to recover an optical disc that he believes Vash has stolen. In fact, she does have the disc, and she secretly slips it into Picard's pocket before leaving.

In his hotel room, Picard meets two Vorgons, who say they're from the 27th century and are in search of the Tox Uthat, a weapon they say was hidden in their "past" to keep it out of dangerous hands. After the aliens depart, Picard finds the disc. He learns from Vash that she was given the disc by an archaeologist who knew where the Tox Uthat is, and she's trying to prevent Sovak from getting it. The two of them head off to the location where they think the Tox Uthat is buried, and—despite hearing that Vash was working with Sovak and has double-crossed him—Picard begins to fall for her.

The next day, the Vorgons and Sovak arrive, but the Tox Uthat is not found. Picard realizes Vash already has the weapon, and he stops her from leaving. She tells him the Vorgons tried to steal the weapon from its creator in the future, and Picard destroys the Tox Uthat.

Vash leaves. For now.

Picard: Tell me, Number One, is the entire crew aware of this little scheme to send me off on holiday?
Riker: I believe there are two ensigns stationed on deck 39 who know nothing about it.

Notes: Vash, an ethically impaired archaeological explorer portrayed by Jennifer Hetrick, would go on to appear in the episode "Qpid" and in *Deep Space Nine's* "Q-Less." Among her many television credits, she also portrayed the wife of FBI Assistant Director Skinner in an episode of *The X-Files*.

Tin Man

Writer: Ira Steven Behr. **Director:** Chip Chalmers. **Airdate:** April 2, 1990.

Federation ambassador Tam Elbrun is ferried by the *Enterprise* to a faraway star to make contact with a giant sentient starship, which they call *Tin Man* but who reveals its own name to be *Gomtuu*. Elbrun is a mentally unstable telepath of enormous powers, so strong that he has trouble focusing with all of the *Enterprise* crew's mental noise around him.

Also trying to deal with *Tin Man/Gomtuu* is a Romulan warbird, which tries to attack the alien ship but is destroyed by it after Elbrun telepathically warns it. Elbrun learns from *Gomtuu* that the ship is thousands of years old and from a very distant place. It is in orbit around a star that is about to go supernova; it wants to die with the star, because it is lonely and sad about the loss of its crew in an accident.

Elbrun becomes *Gomtuu's* new crew, giving it a purpose in life again. Just before the star supernovas, *Gomtuu* sends the *Enterprise* to safety and gets itself out of danger, too.

Data: You said . . . that you could not read my mind.
Tam Elbrun: True enough, but I think I understand you pretty well. It worries you that I can't read your mind?
Data: Perhaps there is nothing to read, nothing more than mechanisms and algorithmic responses.
Tam Elbrun: Perhaps you're just different. It's not a sin, you know. Though you may have heard otherwise.

Notes: Yep, the *Enterprise* is carting around an ambassador once again. That aside, a simple but good story (and a nice reminder that *vive la différence*).

Writer David Bischoff penned the short story "Tin Woodman" in 1978. It was nominated for a Nebula award that year and later was turned into a novel. Bischoff's story was adapted into this episode of *Next Generation*. Bischoff's list of books includes many genre licensed novels, including for *Space Precinct*, *SeaQuest DSV*, *Jonny Quest*, *Farscape*, and others, as well as the best-selling *Next Generation* novel *Grounded*.

Hollow Pursuits

Writer: Sally Caves. **Director:** Cliff Bole. **Airdate:** April 30, 1990.

Engineer Reginald Barclay is having trouble relating to his fellow crewmembers aboard the *Enterprise*, and Chief Engineer Geordi La Forge wants him off the ship. But Captain Picard tells La Forge to bear with it, making it a project to help Barclay. La Forge tries to do so, but when he finds Barclay using a holodeck program to interact with fictional versions of the *Enterprise* crew, the chief engineer sends Barclay to Counselor Troi.

Barclay's distracted work and absences are particularly noticeable when the *Enterprise* is carrying some tissue samples that are to be used to fight an epidemic on Nahmi IV. One of the containers of samples leaks; that batch is destroyed to prevent it from contaminating the other samples. When the starship unexpectedly goes to warp, it is Barclay who comes up with the key piece of data that helps the crew find the element that has contaminated the system and caused the ship to accelerate. The ship's matter/antimatter injectors are cleared, and it heads to a nearby starbase to make sure the contaminant is all gone.

Barclay stands on the bridge, thanks the bridge crew for their time with him, but explains that he should leave them. He then deletes the holodeck program of the bridge crew.

Barclay: Being afraid all of the time, of forgetting somebody's name, not . . . not knowing—what to do with your hands. I mean, I am the guy who writes down things to remember to say when there's a party. And then, when he finally gets there, he winds up alone, in the corner, trying to look comfortable examining a potted plant.
La Forge: You're just shy, Barclay.
Barclay: Just shy. Sounds like nothing serious, doesn't it? You can't know.

Notes: In a season that accomplishes so much by adding subtlety and complexity to the stories' science fictional concepts, "Hollow Pursuits" is an anomaly. Actor Dwight Schultz's Barclay is over-the-top in its awkwardness, and La Forge is surprisingly unsympathetic to a member of his crew who is different and a loner; aren't Starfleet officers supposed to be more open-minded and sensitive than that? La Forge loosens up a bit, under orders, but if a well-oiled machine like Starfleet saw fit to put Barclay on board its flagship, surely its crews are typically more accepting of eccentricities and individuals than is the *Enterprise* crew here, which avoids Barclay and calls him names behind his back. After all, this is literally one episode after Data (and viewers) are reminded that being different isn't a bad thing.

All of that is done, of course, to make the script's points about Barclay's outsiderness, but it's an unsubtle and inelegant way to make a point. What saves the episode is Schultz's incredibly sympathetic portrayal of the character, turning him from what could have been a comedic schlub into a lovable and honest character with whom many in the audience could identify.

The Most Toys

Writer: Shari Goodhartz. **Director:** Tim Bond. **Airdate:** May 5, 1990.

The *Enterprise* arranges to transport hitridium, something that can neutralize the trycyanate contamination on a colony. Trader Kivas Fajo can get it for them, but the hitridium is too unstable to be beamed aboard, so Data goes to Fajo's ship to help with the transport. During the final transport, Data's shuttle explodes. With most of the hitridium it needs and its crew believing Data to be dead, the *Enterprise* leaves to deliver the decontaminant. But when it completes its mission, the contamination clears up too quickly, leading our heroes to conclude that they had been tricked, the contamination faked, the whole thing a setup. They head back to find Fajo.

However, Data isn't dead; he has been kidnapped and his death faked so he could be added to Fajo's private collection. Data refuses to play the role of obedient museum piece, until Fajo threatens to kill one of the trader's own crewmembers, Varria. When Data and Varria finally get their opportunity to escape, Fajo kills Varria, and Data is beamed aboard the *Enterprise* just as he threatens to kill Fajo, who ends up in the starship's brig.

Kivas: Data, you will be catered to, fawned over, cared for, as you never have been before. Your every wish will be fulfilled.
Data: I wish to leave.
Kivas: Almost every wish.

Notes: Actor Saul Rubinek took over the role of Kivas Fajo following the attempted suicide of the character's original actor, David Rappaport. Rappaport survived that attempt but, sadly, the *Time Bandits* actor who suffered from depression did later kill himself.

Sarek

Writers: Peter S. Beagle, Marc Cushman, Jake Jacobs. **Director:** Les Landau. **Airdate:** May 14, 1990.

Ambassador Sarek, father of Spock, comes aboard with his wife Perrin on a mission to establish trade relations with the Legarans. Sarek is old and ready to retire after this final duty. But when the stoic Vulcan ambassador begins crying during a classical music concert, Picard knows things are not well. Then emotional and hostile outbursts spread throughout the ship. Dr. Crusher concludes Sarek might have a degenerative neurological condition that makes him lose control of his emotions, sending those emotions to those around him. Sarek's staff confirms that this is the case, but Sarek denies it to Picard until the ambassador breaks down in front of the captain.

Picard makes arrangements to cancel the meetings with the Legaran delegation, but Perrin suggests that Sarek mind meld with someone else, transferring his emotions to that other person so Sarek can finish this last mission. Picard agrees to become the host and take on the pain of the elder ambassador.

Picard: I saw you crying.
Sarek: I do not cry.
Picard: I was there, I saw the tears.
Sarek: You exaggerate, Captain, I recall only one tear.

Notes: Mark Lenard originated the character of Spock's father in the original series episode "Journey to Babel," but that was not the first alien he portrayed in *Trek*. In the first season of that series, he played a Romulan in "Balance of Terror," and he was later the leader of a Klingon warship in *Star Trek: The Motion Picture*. He reprised the Sarek character on the big screen in the second-through-fourth *Star Trek* films.

Ménage à Troi

Writers: Fred Bronson, Susan Sackett. **Director:** Robert Legato. **Airdate:** June 10, 1990.

Love or at least lust is in the air when Ferengi DaiMon Tog tries to seduce Lwaxana Troi following a trade conference on Betazed; the Betazed ambassador has her own concerns about love, when she urges her daughter Deanna Troi to find a mate and, well, to mate. Lwaxana rebuffs Tog but tags along when Deanna and Commander Riker take a quick vacation in the hope that she can rekindle her daughter's relationship with Riker. But Tog isn't so easily put off; he kidnaps Riker and the mother-daughter Troi team aboard his ship the *Krayton*, where the Ferengi doctor Farek plans to probe Lwaxana's mind-reading abilities to see if the Ferengi can make use of it for their own purposes.

Riker manages to trick a guard and escape his cell. Unable to use the Ferengi ship's protected communications system to send an SOS to the *Enterprise*, he instead modifies the ship's engine system to create a distortion in the warp field that he hopes will be recognized by his Starfleet colleagues.

Back on the *Enterprise*, Wesley Crusher misses his ride back to Earth for another crack at the Starfleet Academy entrance exam when he notices Riker's SOS and alerts the bridge crew. The *Enterprise* catches up to the *Krayton*; Lwaxana bargains with the Ferengi to let Riker and Deanna return to the *Enterprise* if Lwaxana stays behind as Tog's partner. But Picard plays the jealous lover, claiming his intention to attack the *Krayton* unless his beloved Lwaxana is returned. A frightened Tog complies.

Lwaxana Troi: I must admit, when you, uh, first approached me aboard the *Enterprise*, I was . . . intrigued.
DaiMon Tog: You mean revolted.
Lwaxana Troi: Perhaps a little.

Notes: There's something about the Ferengi that resembles a teenage boy's sexual fantasies. As noted in the first season, the Ferengi males were conceived (pardon the word) as having extraordinarily large sexual organs. Here, Deanna and Lwaxana are shorn of their clothing aboard the Krayton; Tog makes sexual advances with abandon; and the Trois are both important figures as well as sexual objects throughout the story. There's nothing wrong with a story about sexual desire, but *Trek* could do better than a juvenile look at it.

Star Trek carries a weighty legacy, and it's not one that was foisted upon it by fans or critics. It was proclaimed by the show's creators and producers: This show imagines a better future, when problems and prejudices of the past are overcome, when humans are no longer held back by old ideas of racial and sexual superiority.

That's a tremendous claim to make, but it dedicates one to high ideals and goals; it tells people that this is not just escapist fun, it is a vision of a better world, not significantly different from utopian novels of the past such as *Zwei Planeten*. There are many excellent science fiction productions that make no claim about prophesying or guidance for a preferred future; *Alien* and *The Empire Strikes Back* come to mind. *Star Trek* chose to announce its ambitions, and what it promised was to show us a future that had solved the many problems that have held us back today.

Then there's the reality.

One of the best ways of building a better future is to model it, to show the unusual as usual, not even worthy of comment. *Star Wars* might not be a proposed guide to the future, but creator George Lucas did a great job at making the unusual seem normal, whether it was peppering conversations with unknown concepts—kessel runs or clone wars, anyone?—or getting us to believe there was a grand galactic republic that was represented in the early films in no way other than by a tired old man who supposedly represented a knight of said republic. (For the sake of speed, we'll overlook Princess Leia's "Will someone get this big walking carpet out of my way?" racist outburst, and chalk it up to frustration at her torture; it's hard being a galactic princess, after all.)

Star Trek aimed higher. Gene Roddenberry's creation has arguably done better in matters of race than sex. The first season *Next Generation* episode "Code of Honor" was an uncomfortable and rare example of the writers and producers erring in their attempt to handle racial issues. That episode was truly cringe-worthy in its portrayal of a race using entirely African-American actors who lived in a macho, tribal society.

The selection of comedian and actor Whoopi Goldberg to play the new character of Guinan, beginning in second season's "The Child," was not the result of a cattle call of performers to find the right fit. It was instead the result of Goldberg's determination to be a part of the show; she lobbied Gene Roddenberry directly (and repeatedly; he reportedly did not think she was serious and suspected her request to join the cast was a joke). Part of her motivation for joining the series came from her identification with Lt. Uhura in the original series, which presented a rare African-American face on the command bridge in a science fiction series.

Truth be told, Uhura and the other regular cast members of the original series were given very little to do to expand their characters or show their acting chops—unless they were Kirk, Spock, or McCoy. That is very different in ST:TNG, where all of the regular characters had numerous opportunities to shine. The role of Geordi La Forge was quickly expanded from that of a blind navigator to the chief engineer, and actor LeVar Burton got many stories in which he was a central character or even *the* central character.

Also, if the "Code of Honor" portrayal of the all-black society as warlike and tribal produced revulsion, even three decades ago, the producers pulled off something entirely different with their fleshing out of Klingon society and characters. The Klingon actors, though under heavy makeup, were very often African American, beginning with series co-star and fan favorite Michael Dorn. The Klingon society is also warlike, but its presentation in *Next Generation* and subsequent sequel series is rich and respectful, including the treatment it receives from second-season doctor Kate Pulaski, who built a bond with Worf through her appreciation of and respect for his rituals.

Star Trek: The Next Generation never dealt well with issues of sexuality, particularly homosexuality or bisexuality. We never got to see writer David Gerrold's "Blood and Fire" script, until it was produced by the fan-made *Star Trek: New Voyages*; Gerrold also served as the director of that episode. And when it came to good ol' fashioned man-and-woman sexuality, *Star Trek* frequently treated it with all of the subtlety and depth that would be expected of a teenage boy. I once was a teenage boy, and I'm not denigrating them. But if you are going to tell a story with a teenage boy's outlook on sexuality, love, and lust, then focus the story on Wesley Crusher and/or introduce other teenage boys to be the focus of that story. When you've got older characters doing the story, tell an adult story.

When it comes to sex and *Star Trek*, it's easy to remember the juvenile aspects of it. Captain James Kirk having sex with numerous color-coded alien females. Lt. Ilia needing to have an oath of celibacy on record. *The Next Generation* crew visiting a planet where people were nearly naked and health-obsessed. The Ferengi males designed to be extremely well-endowed you-know-how. The Betazed practice of nude weddings.

Deep Space Nine would finally give us a female first officer, something Roddenberry tried to do in the original series but had to jettison in the face of network opposition. *Voyager* would finally give us a female captain, and a good one at that. But it took until the third J.J. Abrams rebooted series of films for *Star Trek* to finally come to terms with the apparently controversial idea that some men are attracted to men and some women are attracted to women and that it's simply not a big deal.

Even the fifth-season *Next Generation* episode "The Outcast," a well-intentioned story about androgynous aliens and gender identity, was undercut by having Riker fall for an alien who was obviously played by a female. More explicit suggestions of the show's leanings were evident in the fourth-season episode "The Host," in which a gender-switching Trill is rejected by Dr. Crusher after it moves from a male to female host.

In 2002, Kate Mulgrew, who portrayed *Star Trek: Voyager*'s Captain Janeway, told *Metrosource* in a widely quoted statement that she supported the inclusion of gay characters "because of its both political and potentially incendiary substance. I'm in a minority as well, as a woman [captain]. It took a lot of courage on their part to hire a woman. I think that right up until the end they were very dubious about it. It's one thing to cast a subordinate black, Asian or woman, but to put them in leading roles means the solid endorsement of one of the largest studios in the world. And that goes for a gay character as well. It requires a terrific social conscience on their part and the pledge of some solidarity and unanimity, which I think is probably at the source of most of this problem to get every one of those executives on board regarding this decision."

It took 'em a long time.

Transfigurations

Writer: René Echevarria. **Director:** Tom Benko. **Airdate:** June 17, 1990.

John Doe just might be becoming godlike, but first he has to regain his memory.

The *Enterprise* rescues a humanoid passenger from a crashed ship; the passenger has no memory of his identity, so the crew call him John Doe. Dr. Crusher says the man's cells are mutating, and John Doe experiences occasional pain and power emissions; he also has the power to heal people's injuries, as Worf learns following an accident.

Another spaceship arrives, and its captain, Sunad, declares that John Doe is a condemned criminal and should be returned to their home planet Zalkon. Doe refuses to go, and Picard refuses to force him to leave until he learns more about why he was condemned. Sunad attacks, but John Doe counteracts the effects and brings Sunad to the *Enterprise*. John Doe's memory has recovered, and he tells everyone that he is the next stage in his people's evolution; Sunad represents the government's efforts to stop the development of their species, capturing and killing anyone who exhibits these new powers. He sends Sunad and his ship on their way, and he completes his transformation into a being of pure energy.

Worf: I have much to teach you about women.

Notes: Writer René Echevarria is a very significant contributor to the genre world. He went on to write dozens of *Star Trek: The Next Generation* episodes, and he also wrote for its sequel series *Star Trek: Deep Space Nine*. He created the science fiction series *The 4400*, which ran for four seasons on the USA Network; he was a producer on the short-lived Steven Spielberg series *Terra Nova*, and he contributed to series ranging from *Dark Angel* to *Intelligence*.

The Best of Both Worlds, Part I

Writer: Michael Piller. **Director:** Cliff Bole. **Airdate:** June 18, 1990.

A Federation colony has been destroyed, and the Federation thinks the Borg did it. Admiral Hanson arrives on the *Enterprise*, and he brings along a Borg expert, Lt. Commander Shelby. Just like we saw in Season Two's "The Icarus Factor," Commander Riker is being pressed to accept the job of commanding his own starship, only this time Shelby is present and expecting to succeed Riker as Captain Picard's Number One. Hanson suggests that Picard give Riker a "kick . . . in the rear end for his own good" and get him to take the offered command.

The *Enterprise* heads off to intercept what is believed to be a Borg cube, after reports from another Starfleet ship are abruptly cut off. It is indeed the Borg, and with typical Borg bureaucratic bravado, it demands the surrender of Captain Picard. He, of course, refuses, and the Borg chase the *Enterprise* into a nearby nebula; Shelby, La Forge, and Wesley Crusher try to modify the ship to produce a weapon capable of destroying the cube, but the *Enterprise* is forced out of the nebula and is boarded by the Borg, who kidnap Picard and go back to their ship. The cube then zooms toward Earth, closely followed by the *Enterprise*.

Shelby leads an away team to the cube to try to rescue Picard, but they find that their captain has already been assimilated. Picard declares himself to be Locutus of Borg, and he orders the *Enterprise* to prepare to be assimilated.

Riker, in command of a starship under unexpected circumstances, prefers to fight, and he orders the *Enterprise* to fire its new weapon at the cube.

Riker: When it comes to this ship and this crew, you're damned right I play it safe.
Shelby: If you can't make the big decisions, commander, I suggest you make room for someone who can.

Notes: "The Best of Both Worlds, Part I" is justifiably considered one of the best episodes of the series, an even more amazing feat considering how many strong episodes appeared in the show's third season.

Writer Michael Piller's script reflected a Mario Cuomo-esque should-I-or-shoudn't-I angst, played out in Commander Riker's indecisiveness about leaving the *Enterprise*. "[W]hile Riker is going through a personal dilemma of whether or not to leave the *Enterprise*, I was going through the dilemma of whether or not I was leaving *Star Trek*, and a lot of that bled into the script," Piller told *Starlog* in October 1990. Talking about himself in the third person, he added that "Riker's musing to himself is sort of like Michael Piller musing to himself. . . . I found it very difficult to walk away from the show that I had fallen in love with, a TV series that mattered."

"The Best of Both Worlds" is a cliffhanger episode, designed to keep fans thirsty for the resumption of the series in the fall. It accomplished that, and if, as we'll see next issue, Part II was not as strong as Part I (albeit still a good episode), the show then followed up with an episode that demonstrated beyond a doubt how *Star Trek: The Next Generation* had come into its own as a high-quality, confident dramatic series.

SEASON FOUR

The Best of Both Worlds, Part II

Writers: Michael Piller. **Director:** Cliff Bole. **Airdate:** September 24, 1990.

The Borg cube uses the knowledge from its new Locutus/Picard component to thwart an attack by the *Enterprise*, which is left crippled. The cube zooms off toward Earth. The *Enterprise*, meanwhile, has a new captain, William Riker, who takes the ship to Wolf 359, where Starfleet is staging a last stand against the Borg. The *Enterprise* arrives to find that the Borg won and that the fleet was obliterated.

The *Enterprise* sets off after the cube, which refuses to negotiate with them. Riker sends Data and Worf into the cube on a mission to kidnap Locutus.

With Locutus/Picard back on board the *Enterprise*, Data and Dr. Crusher try unsuccessfully to use him as a conduit to the Borg's collective mind. But when the cyborg utters a one-word message, he is at first thought to be referring to his own need for rest until Data recognizes it as advice. They use Locutus to send a message to the cube to go into sleep mode and, thus caught off guard, the Borg cube is destroyed.

Riker is offered his own permanent command, but he turns it down in favor of continued service as Picard's Number One.

Locutus/Picard: Sleep.

Notes: Finally, a space TV show survived to its fourth season. The first two *Trek*s (original and animated) didn't make it this far; the original *Galactica* didn't survive to its second season; *Buck Rogers in the 25th Century* basically had one and a half seasons; *Space: 1999* and *Lost in Space* both failed to get to fourth seasons. But *Star*

Trek: The Next Generation sailed into its fourth season with strong ratings, critical support, and top-flight production.

What would it do with that newfound security and confidence? Some shows go off the rail just after they finally become big hits, as their writers get bored with established characters and situations and try to reinvent the shows with increasingly outlandish plots.

What *The Next Generation* did was grow up. This is the season in which the show really started sharing the spotlight with a wider range of crew members, and we got to see them in some relatively "quiet" episodes that didn't need to be tarted up with slam-bang action, because the producers knew the fans were happy with the characters.

Episodes such as "Data's Day," "The Loss," and others let us get a feeling for life on the *Enterprise* that was almost "behind the scenes"—impossible in a totally fictional story, but earning my appreciation for building out back stories of characters and letting actors other than Patrick Stewart stand out.

The result was a fine season that showed perhaps for the first time how a space-centered SF series could shine on the small screen, making fans and Paramount shareholders alike happy.

And a quick casting note: Commander Shelby, who jostles with Riker for leadership of the *Enterprise*, is played by Elizabeth Dennehy, the daughter of famed actor Brian Dennehy.

Family

Writers: Ronald D. Moore, Susanne L. Lambdin, Bryan Stewart. **Director:** Les Landau. **Airdate:** October 1, 1990.

While the *Enterprise* undergoes some needed repairs following its bruising battles with the Borg in the previous two episodes, the ship's crew members spend some quality time with their families. For Worf, that means an initially embarrassing but ultimately comforting reunion with his human adoptive parents. For Beverly and Wesley Crusher, that means fully digesting the death of husband/father Jack Crusher. For Captain Picard, that means a trip to France to spend time with his brother Robert on the family's vineyard. He and his brother have long been estranged, with Robert not wanting his son René to follow Picard into Starfleet. But the two brothers soon make up (after fighting in the muck), and Robert lets René do what he wants.

Worf: I do not believe any human can truly understand my dishonor.

Notes: There is no more obvious sign of the maturity and confidence of the series than this, following up a high-stakes action-packed two-part episode with a quiet story centered on family. It also is a good counterpoint to all of the action movies and TV programs over the decades that have heroes and heroines get beaten up, punched, kicked, knocked unconscious, and then they're back on their feet minutes later, with nary a sign of the violence's impact on them physically or psychologically. (The absurdity of that was nicely parodied in the 1985 action film *Commando,* which included a scene in which Arnold Schwarzenegger and Rae Dawn Chong are in a car that crashes into a telephone pole—an accident that in real life would have caused serious injury or even death; instead, in the film, Schwarzenegger's character just asks "Are you all right?" and they move on as if they had experienced nothing more violent than parallel parking.) Picard is seriously affected by his experience as Locutus, and he heads to the quiet family vineyards of France to recover.

There's also a sad payoff from this story four years later in the 1994 film *Star Trek Generations*, when Picard learns that Robert and René have both been killed.

Brothers

Writer: Rick Berman. **Director:** Rob Bowman. **Airdate:** October 8, 1990.

Data has a family get-together of an entirely different sort. He takes control of the *Enterprise* and forces it to go to the planet Terlina III. There, he beams down to the home of his creator, Dr. Noonien Soong, who tells him he summoned Data to him because he is dying and wants to give the android an emotion chip. Lore, his other android creation introduced in first season episode "Datalore," also shows up, apparently called by the same signal from Soong. Lore tries to take the emotion chip meant for Data; he eventually tricks Soong into installing the chip in him.

The *Enterprise* crew arrives and finds Data deactivated and Soong dying. Before expiring, Soong helps Data undo the damage he had done to the *Enterprise* when he was summoned.

Lore [*to Dr. Soong*]: You didn't fill Data with substandard parts—did you, old man? No. That honor was bestowed upon me. You owe me, old man. Not him. *Me.*

Notes: Brent Spiner played Dr. Soong, Lore, and of course Data. Wonder if he got three paychecks.

It's also worth noting how far film and television technology had come that by the 1990s, we no longer watched episodes with twin characters and looked for the lines or blue screens that would give away the illusion. We (most of us anyway) probably knew we were being tricked, but we couldn't see how and we could just enjoy the story.

Suddenly Human

Writers: John Whelpley, Jeri Taylor, Ralph Phillips. **Director:** Gabrielle Beaumont. **Airdate:** October 15, 1990.

Responding to a distress signal, the *Enterprise* rescues five teenagers from a Talarian spaceship. Four are Talarian, but one is a human named Jono, the grandson of a Starfleet admiral who had been orphaned when his parents were killed by Talarians a decade earlier.

Jono, as politically woke folks in the 21st century would say, "identifies as Talarian." He doesn't want to return to his human family, but instead wants to go with Endar, a Talarian captain who tries to retrieve his adopted son. Despite thinking he has made some progress in reconnecting Jono to his human past, Picard is stabbed by Jono; luckily, the injury isn't serious. Picard finally relents and lets Jono go with Endar, preferring not to impose his values on Jono and the Talarians.

Jono: I am Talarian.
Worf: You are confused.

Notes: Another family-based episode. And despite the danger posed by Endar threatening the *Enterprise* in an attempt to get his adopted son back, the drama here is appropriately focused on the emotional push and pull going on inside Jono.

This episode led to claims that the story excused child abuse. The *Enterprise* crew notice that Jono has some indications that he had been physically harmed, and that becomes part of the reason Captain Picard is so resistant to letting Jono stay with the Talarian who raised him after the deaths of his parents.

Remember Me

Writer: Lee Sheldon. **Director:** Cliff Bole. **Airdate:** October 22, 1990.

They say that as people get older, their worlds get smaller, their circles of friends contract, they are alone more. Dr. Crusher's not old, but she's finding those effects to be happening in a very real way to her life.

People on the *Enterprise* keep disappearing, and when Dr. Crusher inquires, she is told that those people never existed. It keeps going that way until only she and Picard remain on the *Enterprise*; the captain of course thinks that's how it has always been and should be. And then there was one—only Crusher remains, and she realizes that her entire universe is a bubble surrounding the *Enterprise*, and the universe is contracting.

The incredible shrinking universe is the result of yet another failed experiment by Wesley Crusher, who was trying to create a static warp bubble. The Traveler appears and helps stabilize the experiment and retrieve Wesley's mother.

Dr. Crusher: It's all perfectly logical to you, isn't it? The two of us roaming about the galaxy in the flagship of the Federation. No crew at all.
Picard: We've never needed a crew before.

Notes: All in all, a nicely played script and a well-done science fiction tale. The actual reason behind (and the solution to) the disappearances is less interesting than the way Crusher, Picard, and the others so beautifully play out the perfectly natural absence of all that we expect on the ship.

The Traveler, portrayed by Eric Menyuk, first appeared in the first-season episode "Where No One Has Gone Before." He would have appeared more often if he had gotten the *Next Generation* role he had really wanted: Data, the role that of course eventually went to Brent Spiner.

Legacy

Writer: Joe Menosky. **Director:** Robert Scheerer. **Airdate:** October 29, 1990.

The *Enterprise* attempts to rescue a Federation crew that was forced to make an emergency landing on Turkana IV, which just happens to be the lawless planet where former security chief Tasha Yar was raised. An *Enterprise* landing party finds itself caught between the local warring factions, one of which wants Federation weapons. One of these battling factions offers up Ishara Yar, Tasha's sister, as a go-between with the *Enterprise*, but she turns out to be working to get the *Enterprise* to help destroy her enemies. Data, who had befriended Ishara, feels betrayed.

Ishara Yar [*to Data*]: The time we spent talking—that was the closest thing to friendship I've ever had. If that means anything to you.

Notes: Writer Joe Menosky scripts his first *Trek* episode with this tale. He would go on to write quite a few episodes of *Deep Space Nine* and *Voyager*.

Reunion

Writers: Thomas Perry, Jo Perry, Ronald D. Moore, Brannon Braga. **Director:** Jonathan Frakes. **Airdate:** November 5, 1990.

The dying Klingon chancellor drags Picard into the messy process of choosing his successor, so Picard becomes the arbiter of succession. Klingon Ambassador K'Ehleyr, Lt. Worf's old flame, arrives with a boy in tow, and Worf learns that the boy—Alexander—is his son.

Picard has to choose between Gowron and Duras, the two candidates for leading the Klingon council. Duras is the one who had smeared Worf's family name, claiming his father was a traitor and getting Worf shamed by the council in the past (see "Sins of the Father").

During the succession proceedings, a Romulan bomb explodes. While the *Enterprise* crew tries to figure out what's happening, K'Ehleyr learns that it was actually Duras' father, not Worf's, who betrayed the Klingons at Khitomer. Duras kills her, but not before she makes Worf promise to raise Alexander. Worf challenges Duras to a right of vengeance battle and is victorious.

Gowron is named the new Klingon chancellor, and Alexander gets shuttled off to be cared for by the human adoptive parents who raised Worf (see "Family").

Worf: A warrior does not ask so many questions.
Alexander: I don't want to be a warrior.

Notes: The always-intriguing politics of the Klingon Empire are a welcome return to the show, though shoe-horning Picard into a role in the selection of the empire's next leader seems like a naked attempt to keep the show's star in the center of things. Picard's great, of course, but Worf, K'Ehleyr, Alexander, and the others are strong enough characters to hold their own.

And let's pay tribute to the role of Worf's son, Alexander Rozhenko. Played initially by Jon Paul Steuer and later by Brian Bonsall, Alexander is a character that could easily have been an annoyance or an irrelevant presence on the show. Thankfully, he was not an annoyance (unlike the *Galactica 1980* child horde), and when he is brought back on the *Enterprise* later in the series, he serves a very sweet role of—forgive the term—humanizing Worf and letting us see deeper dimensions of our favorite Klingon.

Steuer would go on to play Quentin Kelly for three seasons of *Grace Under Fire*, eventually leaving acting to be a musician and a restaurateur, but he tragically died at the age of 33 from what was believed to be a self-inflicted gunshot.

Future Imperfect

Writers: J. Larry Carroll, David Bennett Carren. **Director:** Les Landau. **Airdate:** November 12, 1990.

While investigating an underground cave, Riker, La Forge, and Worf are knocked unconscious by gas. When Riker awakens, he finds that 16 years have gone by, he is now captain of the *Enterprise*, and he has a son named Jean-Luc (after now-Admiral Picard, of course). He is told by Dr. Crusher that he lost his memory of the previous 16 years due to an illness.

Riker begins to piece together inconsistencies and glitches in this new world of his, finally concluding that he is on a Romulan holodeck with the goal of making him reveal sensitive information. But even that revelation proves to be false, as he learns that his supposed son is really an orphaned alien who had created the entire simulation so that he could have companionship.

Data: Pardon sir, I am experiencing sub-space interference, which limits my abilities. I can't operate as quickly as I—
Riker: What did you say?
Data: I said I cannot operate as—
Riker: No, that's not what you said. You said, "I can't." You used a contraction, didn't you?

Data: Sir, I can explain if you would just give me a moment.
Riker: No, you can't; don't even try.

Notes: In the original telling of the *Buck Rogers* stories, Rogers is trapped in a cave while investigating unusual occurrences there. He is exposed to radioactive gas, and he enters a state of suspended animation from which he doesn't escape for nearly 500 years, and when he does, society has collapsed and the world is engulfed in a long brutal war. Riker was lucky.

Final Mission

Writers: Kasey Arnold-Ince, Jeri Taylor. **Director:** Corey Allen. **Airdate:** December 2, 1990.

Captain Picard brings Wesley Crusher on a mission to deal with a mining dispute in the Pentarus system. It's Wesley's last mission (hence the title), because he has finally been accepted to Starfleet Academy. But their shuttle crashes on a deserted moon, and they are stuck without food or water. The one source of water they find is protected by some sort of force field, and Picard is injured in an attempt to get around the field.

Wesley finally finds a way to switch off the force field, and soon he and Picard are rescued by the *Enterprise* after it has completed a separate mission of disposing of a radioactive garbage barge in the Gamilon system.

Picard: Oh, I envy you, Wesley Crusher. You're just at the beginning of the adventure.

Notes: And so young Wesley Crusher finally exits the *Enterprise* after a frustrating four years of being the genius kid who alternately saves the day or endangers everyone's lives with an experiment gone wrong. He's Starfleet's problem, now.

The Loss

Writers: Alan J. Adler, Hillary J. Bader, Vanessa Greene. **Director:** Chip Chalmers. **Airdate:** December 31, 1990.

When the *Enterprise* is snagged by some two-dimensional beings who are headed toward a "cosmic string" that could destroy the ship, counselor Deanna Troi discovers that she is unable to use her empathic powers. Disturbed by the loss, she quits her job.

Picard persuades her to attempt to reach the aliens, and she and Data develop a plan to break the *Enterprise* free of their grip. After they make their escape, Troi regains the use of her empathic abilities, which had been hidden underneath the aliens' own strong emotional output.

Dr. Crusher: Therapists are always the worst patients. Except for doctors, of course.

Notes: "The Loss" is not the strongest episode of the season, but it is a nice focus on Troi in a way that isn't mocking, such as when her mother visits and belittles her. To be honest, I never cared for the character of Troi. That's not because of the actor, Marina Sirtis, who does a fine job; it's just a weird position or role, being both a staff psychiatrist and a mind-reading spy for Captain Picard.

Data's Day

Writers: Harold Apter, Ronald D. Moore. **Director:** Robert Wiemer. **Airdate:** January 7, 1991.

Data takes center stage in this nice, low-key episode. Very much a "day in the life" story, "Data's Day" tells us how the android spends his time when he's not navigating the ship, painting, playing with Spot, or doing the sex thing with Tasha Yar.

This particular day includes him giving some advice to Keiko Ishikawa, the woman who is about to wed Transporter Chief Miles O'Brien. His misunderstanding of standard pre-wedding jitters introduces some unneeded tension on the happy day.

Meanwhile, a mission to transport a Vulcan ambassador to a secret meeting with Romulans apparently ends in tragedy, but the *Enterprise* crew discovers they had been deceived—the "ambassador" was a Romulan spy all along.

Captain Picard performs the wedding ceremony for Keiko and O'Brien.

Dr. Crusher: They don't do a lot of tap-dancing at weddings.

Notes: There is drama in this story, but the pleasure in viewing it really comes from seeing things through the eyes of the innocent android Data. And, again, it's nice to see what non-crisis life is like on the starship, because let's face it: most fans daydream about being aboard one.

Rosalind Chao, who portrays Keiko, has a long acting record. Most interesting is her role as Soon-Lee, a South Korean refugee in the later episodes of the Korean War but-really-it's-about-Vietnam sitcom *M*A*S*H*; her character finally married Maxwell Klinger, and she reprised the role in the short-lived sequel series *AfterMASH*.

Oh, and the *Enterprise* is once again acting as an ambassadorial Uber ride.

The Wounded

Writers: Jeri Taylor, Stuart Charno, Sara Charno, Cy Chermak. **Director:** Chip Chalmers. **Airdate:** January 28, 1991.

No long honeymoon for Chief O'Brien. Captain Picard enlists the help of Miles O'Brien to try to convince O'Brien's former commanding officer, Benjamin Maxwell, to stop attacking Cardassian ships. Maxwell claims that the Cardassians are engaging in a military buildup, but evidence is scarce.

O'Brien manages to talk his former boss out of his attacks, but not before Picard finds reason to warn the Cardassians to behave themselves.

Picard: Take this message to your leaders, Gul Macet: We'll be watching.

Notes: This episode is O'Brien's chance to shine.

Actor Marc Alaimo fills the role of Gul Macet. He would portray Cardassian Gul Dukat for nearly 40 episodes of *Star Trek: Deep Space Nine*, where the talented Colm Meaney and Rosalind Chao (and eventually Worf) would all extend their Starfleet tenure.

Devil's Due

Writers: Philip Lazebnik, William Douglas Lansford. **Director:** Tom Benko. **Airdate:** February 4, 1991.

The people of Ventax II think a god—or, more accurately, a devil—has returned to claim their world. Called Ardra, she supposedly helped make the planet peaceful and safe in return for her coming back to claim it a thousand years later. Now, one millennium hence, Ardra wants her due.

Captain Picard, not being an idiot, is pretty sure she's not a god/devil, and he sets out to prove it. In a court case, with Data acting as the impartial judge, he has La Forge recreate the supposedly miraculous tricks that Ardra has pulled off, and Riker is able to locate and take over her ship. She's just a con artist who learned about Ventax II's "bargain with the devil" and tried to take advantage of it.

Riker: We are not impressed with your magic tricks!
Ardra: I pity you. We live in a universe of magic, which evidently you cannot see.

Notes: This episode, derived from an idea for the never-realized *Star Trek: Phase II* series in the 1970s, is probably one of the weakest of the fourth season of *Next Generation*. The obvious "lesson" for the Ventaxians is clearly seen coming a mile away, as is the usual anti-religious attitude of the storyline.

Clues

Writers: Bruce D. Arthurs, Joe Menosky. **Director:** Les Landau. **Airdate:** February 11, 1991.

How reliable is your android? The *Enterprise* gets a lesson in the trustworthiness of resident 'bot Data when all of the non-android members of the crew are knocked unconscious, apparently by a wormhole. Data tells his colleagues that they were only unconscious for half a minute.

The ship leaves the star system it had been investigating and everyone tries to focus on other things, but discrepancies start to pile up, calling Data's explanation into question. Why does Worf have an injury? What made Dr. Crusher's moss samples grow faster than they should have? Further investigation shows that they have in fact lost an entire day.

The *Enterprise* returns to the star system, and they are contacted by an alien who tells Picard his plan failed and the alien race is going to destroy the *Enterprise*. The aliens are the Paxans, and they hate having anyone else in their star system. They normally push the ships away and convince their crews that it was the effect of a wormhole, but Data was not affected by their mind-erasing technology, so Picard ordered him to lie and try to convince the crew when they awoke to accept the wormhole theory.

Picard realizes the *Enterprise* crew simply didn't get rid of any anomalous clues before they underwent the mind wipe the first time; he convinces the Paxans to let them try again and do it better this time.

If at first Data doesn't succeed, try, try again.

Data: We must leave, sir.
Picard: This ship isn't going anywhere—not until I get an answer. Now, who gave you that order?
Data: You did, sir.

Notes: This is the second episode this season—the first was "Remember Me"—that tells a science fiction story by making the mystery about the reality the characters are experiencing; they are just as in the dark as the audience.

In both cases, characters have to act in unusual ways, and the resolution of the story makes it all sensible. And in both cases, they are well-executed stories, though this episode's "We'll just try harder" doesn't survive scrutiny; there are just too many little details aboard the ship that could trip up the plan that it's unlikely even a very diligent crew could figure them all out. (And wouldn't the *Enterprise* sync its clocks with any starbase or ships or space buoys or whatever it passes?) So, I'm kind of giving them a pass on that weak spot in the story, because the setup was so good.

First Contact

Writers: Dennis Russell Bailey, David Bischoff, Joe Menosky, Ronald D. Moore, Michael Piller, Marc Scott Zicree. **Director:** Cliff Bole. **Airdate:** February 18, 1991.

Commander Riker is working undercover on Malcor III, a pre-warp society, when he is taken to a hospital with injuries sustained in an accident. Though Riker has been altered to appear to be the same race as Malcor's population, medical attention will reveal that he is an alien to them. He tries to escape, but fails.

Meanwhile, Picard meets with the chancellor of the planet and invites him to join the Federation. But after the chancellor's security minister tries to frame Riker as a murderer, the leader decides his people are not ready for the Federation. However,

Picard takes back to the *Enterprise* with him the one person who is ready, the person who was heading up Malcor's now-discontinued warp project.

Lanel: I've always wanted to make love with an alien.
Riker: It's not that easy; there are differences in the way that my people make love.
Lanel: I can't wait to learn.

Notes: What to say about an episode with six writers? Sometimes it works, sometimes not. Despite the opportunity for mayhem and muddle to be created by so many cooks in the writing kitchen, "First Contact" is a perfectly passable entry in the series.

As much as I complain about the Prime Directive's ridiculous assumption that primitive miserableness is unimpeachable and people are better off there (or even better off dead) than in a better life, this show does give us at least one character who wants the better life, the more advanced technology and the more enlightened society. And the *Enterprise* fulfills that wish. One would think *Trek* futurists would be a little more confident that people will want to live in their future.

Galaxy's Child

Writers: Maurice Hurley, Thomas Kartozian. **Director:** Winrich Kolbe. **Airdate:** March 11, 1991.

Dr. Leah Brahms, a designer of the *Enterprise*'s engines, arrives on the starship, but Geordi La Forge isn't exactly getting the fan crush come to life that he might have been hoping for. She turns out to be rather cold—and married. When she discovers that he had created a holodeck version of her (the awkwardly named "Booby Trap" in the third season), she is even less kindly disposed toward the *Enterprise*'s chief engineer.

But they are forced to work together when the *Enterprise* nursemaids a space creature that decides the Federation starship is its mother. Their solution is to make the energy on which the baby creature is feeding unpalatable—and then scram.

Leah Brahms: Commander La Forge, ever since I came on board there seems to be something a little . . . peculiar about your attitude. You seem to know things about me, even though we've never met.

Notes: In the third season episode "Hollow Pursuit," Lieutenant Reginald Barclay gets into trouble when it's discovered that he has created copies of various *Enterprise* crewmembers in a holodeck program, including a Deanna Troi who is attracted to him. It is somehow fitting that La Forge, who had a hard time being sympathetic to Barclay, is caught in a similar trap in this episode.

Truth be told, I suspect that among a crew of more than 1,000 people, there would be quite a few people who would use a holodeck to give them the love lives and sexual thrills they aren't getting in their real lives. At least *Deep Space Nine* acknowledged the idea that holosuites were used for sex.

Night Terrors

Writers: Pamela Douglas, Jeri Taylor, Shari Goodhartz. **Director:** Les Landau. **Airdate:** March 18, 1991.

The *Enterprise* finds the USS *Brittain*, which had gone missing a month earlier. The crew is dead, except for Andrus Hagan, its Betazoid science advisor. Picard and his crew can't find anything wrong with the *Brittain*, and the evidence shows that its crew likely killed each other.

Deanna Troi finds herself having a mysterious dream. The *Enterprise* is also now unable to move, just like the *Brittain*, and Data says they're stuck in some sort of space rift that won't let them escape, though an explosion might set them free. While they try to get away, the crewmembers become irritable and violent, due to a lack of REM sleep. Picard deputizes Data to act as captain, and the android works with Deanna to free the *Enterprise*—and an alien ship across the rift that had been contacting her and Andrus Hagan telepathically to get help.

Data [*to Picard*]: Sir, as my final duty as acting captain, I order you to bed.

Notes: Liberal political commentator Arianna Huffington's big cause is . . . sleep. She says people aren't getting enough of it, and she's backed up by research that says insufficient sleep contributes to poor performance, weight gain, poor thinking, reduced sex drive, depression, bad skin, and forgetfulness. Maybe that's all Locutus/Picard was getting at in the first episode of this season; he was trying to help them avoid drowsiness at the office.

Identity Crisis

Writers: Brannon Braga, Timothy De Haas. **Director:** Winrich Kolbe. **Airdate:** March 25, 1991.

Tarchannen III is an abandoned colony that had been investigated years earlier by a five-person away team from the USS *Victory*; one of those five was Geordi La Forge. Susanna Leijten, another of the five, arrives on the *Enterprise* and reveals that she and Geordi are the only two of the away team who seem to still be around. The *Enterprise* goes to Tarchannen III to investigate, finding evidence that others have also landed there.

Leijten's body is found to have alien elements in it, and she is turning into another species. La Forge investigates the original *Victory* mission, and he realizes there was another presence—an alien presence—there at the time, and it has been taking over and transforming the humans one by one. The *Enterprise* crew and Leijten must go back to Tarchannen III's surface and find a now-transformed La Forge before it's too late to return him to his human form.

Leijten: I've come back, Geordi. Let me take you back, too

Notes: The character named Ensign Graham is portrayed by Mona Grudt, who, Wikipedia tells us, "is a Norwegian TV host, dancer, editor, and beauty queen who was crowned Miss Universe 1990. She also became the first and the only Norwegian to capture the Miss Universe [title]." So this was her fifth career.

The Nth Degree

Writer: Joe Menosky. **Director:** Robert Legato. **Airdate:** April 1, 1991.

While investigating problems at the space telescope Argus Array, Lt. Reginald Barclay is knocked unconscious by a nearby alien probe. When Barclay recovers, he exhibits a rapidly growing intellect that first helps save and then threatens the *Enterprise*.

Barclay not only is smarter than before, he even becomes more effective as a performer in a *Cyrano de Bergerac* play with Dr. Crusher. But things get more intense as he eventually assumes control of the *Enterprise* and takes the ship to the center of the galaxy, where they meet the Cytherians, an advanced species that explores other star systems with remote probes rather than in person. Barclay returns to his normal IQ—except for a heightened ability to play chess.

Barclay: I wish I could convey to you what it's like for me now, what I've become. I can conceive almost infinite possibilities and can fully explore each of them in a nanosecond. I perceive the universe as a single equation, and it is so simple. I understand—everything.

Notes: This is a good concept of aliens exploring via remote probes. As much as I would love to see humanity colonize other star systems, it is much more likely that we will visit them via probes and remote observation and communication. This episode also delivers a dilemma that ends peacefully, with no damage intended or extended to the *Enterprise* crew. It was all an alien quest for knowledge not too unlike Starfleet's own mission, and the two sides spend some time just exchanging information like the nerds they are.

The director of this episode, Robert Legato, was also a visual effects supervisor for the series. He would later win Academy Awards for his work on 1997's *Titanic* and 2011's *Hugo*.

Qpid

Writers: Ira Steven Behr, Randee Russell. **Director:** Cliff Bole. **Airdate:** April 22,

1991.

Rogue archaeologist and Picard's sorta-flame Vash shows up as Picard is preparing for a meeting of archaeologists. A less welcome visitor shows up in the form of Q, who wants to do something nice for the captain but of course does it in his own annoying way.

Q creates a Robin Hood fantasy, with Picard as Robin and his executive staff as the band of merry men. Q takes on the role of the Sheriff of Nottingham and makes Vash Maid Marian. After a bit of above-par *Monty Python and the Holy Grail*-level fight scenes, Picard rescues Vash, who nonetheless goes away with Q to live a life of high adventure zipping around the universe.

Picard: I've just been paid a visit from Q.
Riker: Q? Any idea what he's up to?
Picard: He wants to do something nice for me.
Riker: I'll alert the crew.

Notes: Eh, but an occasional comedy episode is a welcome respite.

The Drumhead

Writer: Jeri Taylor. **Director:** Jonathan Frakes. **Airdate:** April 29, 1991.

Investigation into an explosion in the *Enterprise*'s engine room leads retired Rear Admiral Norah Satie to believe it was an act of sabotage. She accuses a Klingon exchange officer, who turns out to have been working with the Romulans but who apparently had nothing to do with the explosion (it was, boring enough, an accident).

Picard accepts the conclusion that there was no nefarious intent behind the explosion, but Satie pushes further, looking for conspiracies. She eventually focuses her wrath on Picard, who has been resisting her increasingly wild accusations. Her superior, who arrived to attend the proceedings, is turned off by her tactics and shuts down the investigation.

Picard: There are some words I've known since I was a schoolboy: "With the first link, the chain is forged. The first speech censured, the first thought forbidden, the first freedom denied chains us all irrevocably." Those words were uttered by Judge Aaron Satie, as wisdom—and warning. The first time any man's freedom is trodden on, we're all damaged. I fear that today—
Satie: How dare you! You who consort with Romulans, invoke my father's name to support your traitorous arguments? It is an offense to everything I hold dear. And to hear those words used to subvert the United Federation of Planets. My father was a great man. His name stands for integrity and principle. You dirty his name when you speak it. He loved the Federation. But you, captain, corrupt it. You undermine our very way of life. I will expose you for what you are. I've brought down

bigger men than you, Picard!

Notes: *Star Trek* does love its courtroom episodes, almost as much as it loves having the *Enterprise* serve as an interplanetary taxi service for alien ambassadors. That said, this is a reasonably taut courtroom drama.

Half a Life

Writers: Peter Allan Fields, Ted Roberts. **Director:** Les Landau. **Airdate:** May 6, 1991.

Lwaxana Troi is back, this time in love with a scientist, Timicin, who hopes to reboot his world's dying star and save his planet. He's not having success, and he may have to commit ritual suicide as he reaches the set age for that ridiculous rite.

Timicin's people are not thrilled when he decides to skip the suicide and continue working on his experiment. Warships are sent against the *Enterprise*, and Timicin accedes to his daughter's shaming of him. He is not strong enough to defy cultural tradition, and he decides to go through with the ritual suicide.

Timicin: You see Lwaxana, I'm on my way home now—to die.

Notes: David Ogden Stiers, who portrays the Kaelon scientist Timicin, also played (and superbly so) the role of Major Charles Emerson Winchester III on *M*A*S*H* for many years. He did it so well that even now, almost four decades after that show went off the air, when I read or write the major's full name, I hear in my head his inimitable voice saying the words.

The Host

Writer: Michel Horvat. **Director:** Marvin V. Rush. **Airdate:** May 11, 1991.

Odan is a mediator who is brought in to negotiate a treaty between two groups. Dr. Crusher falls in love with him, and they have a fling while he's aboard the *Enterprise*. But when he is injured during an attack on his shuttle, Crusher learns that Odan is actually a Trill, a species that lives inside a host body. (We'll see much more of that in *Deep Space Nine*.) The host body dies, so Riker offers to serve as a host temporarily until Odan's new host body arrives.

Crusher starts to feel the ick factor rising when Odan/Riker tries to continue their love affair; she has trouble separating the idea of the Trill from the body it inhabits. The factor hits the teenager-grossout level when the new host body arrives, and it's female. Once ensconced in his/her new female body, Odan again reaches out to Crusher, but she rebuffs him.

Crusher: Perhaps it is a human failing, but we are not accustomed to these kinds of changes. I can't keep up. How long will you have this host? What would the next one be? I can't live with that kind of uncertainty. Perhaps, someday, our ability to love won't be so limited.

Notes: Aaaaaaaand finally we have controversy this season. Things had been going along pretty nicely, some good character studies, some deepening of back stories, some neat playing with SF storytelling conventions—all in all, not a stellar season, but not a bad one by any means. It also wasn't controversial. Until now.

But the controversy is in the eye of the beholder. Was this story an anti-gay story, in which one of our heroes, Beverly Crusher, rejects a female lover because of her gender? Or was it a pro-gay story, in which Crusher is shown to exhibit the feelings and thoughts that the writers want to change?

Tor.com's Keith DeCandido cited Crusher's attempt to explain her rejection of the female host and noted that her description of it as a larger failure of humanity and not just her personal taste actually created the ambiguity and opened up the episode to criticism: "Crusher generalized, thus causing the character to marginalize a segment of the human population (both homosexuals and bisexuals) by omission." Nerve.com's Nick Keppler interpreted Crusher's explanation as "meaning that the good doctor will get into bed with shifty aliens with weird ridged foreheads but for some reason draws the line at space ladies."

And yet, for nearly all of *Star Trek*'s many, many television and film series over its first 50 years, there was not an openly gay character. Kirk/Spock fan fiction doesn't count, boys.

The Mind's Eye

Writers: René Echevarria, Ken Schafer. **Director:** David Livingston. **Airdate:** May 27, 1991.

En route to a vacation stay on Risa, La Forge's shuttle is taken over by Romulans and he is brainwashed and sent back to the *Enterprise*, believing that he actually had his nice little vacation. Back at work, La Forge works on a mission to help Klingons deal with some pesky rebels attacking one of their colonies, but he does things like secretly ship Federation weapons to the rebels or try to assassinate a Klingon ambassador. Data discovers that a mysterious E-band radiation has been emitted by someone aboard the *Enterprise*, and the Klingon ambassador is implicated, La Forge is cleared, and they're all off for another adventure.

Data: One could speculate that the E-band was being used as some form of covert communication.
Riker: We need more than speculation, Mr. Data. We need to know who, what, where, when, and why—or we may be going to war.

Notes: If you watched this episode or read this synopsis and thought, *The Manchu-*

rian Candidate, then congratulations. That 1962 movie (remade in 2004 and both of them based on Richard Condon's 1959 novel of the same name) featured a U.S. soldier captured in the Korean War, brainwashed, and sent back to the United States to commit an assassination.

In Theory

Writers: Joe Menosky, Ronald D. Moore. **Director:** Patrick Stewart. **Airdate:** June 3, 1991.

After an increasingly close friendship with fellow crew member Jenna D'Sora, Data decides to try having a relationship with her and duly programs himself to have a sub-routine to handle the matter. Meanwhile, the *Enterprise* investigates a planet in a nebula, and strange things are happening on board—things such as furniture being all piled up or objects moved to the floor. Data figures out that dark matter distortions are causing the weird occurrences, and the *Enterprise* is unable to escape the nebula until Picard goes out in a shuttle and charts a safe path for it.

In the end, D'Sora is unsatisfied with Data's overly logical and unemotional responses to her presence and they break up. Data tells her he will delete the subroutine.

Data: Are we no longer—a couple?
D'Sora: No. We're not.
Data: Then I will delete the appropriate program.

Notes: This was the first episode directed by star Patrick Stewart.

Also a tip of the hat to the writers for letting the android be an android. His final decision to end the romance by unemotionally deleting a program is perfectly logical to him; it's just hurtful to humans. As Dr. Kate Pulaski would have expected and could have told them, if they hadn't gotten rid of her.

Redemption, Part I

Writer: Ronald D. Moore. **Director:** Cliff Bole. **Airdate:** June 17, 1991.

The *Enterprise* is en route to the Klingon homeworld to attend the installation ceremony of Gowron as the leader of the Klingon High Council. Gowron fears that the House of Duras will take the empire to civil war in its own attempts to get the leadership position. Worf takes a leave from Starfleet so he can join his brother Kurn and offer their help to Gowron in exchange for the return of their family's official honor.

However, Lursa and B'Etor Duras, sisters of the Duras who died in "Reunion" earlier this season, show up and say that their nephew will challenge Gowron. Picard is called upon to help decide whether the young Klingon is eligible, and he concludes he lacks experience to do the job.

Gowron is installed as leader, he restores the honor of Worf's family, and then things get more complicated yet, as the Duras sisters gather a fleet with Romulan help—a female who looks quite a bit like Tasha Yar.

Worf: I was rescued from Khitomer by humans. Raised and loved by human parents. I spent most of my life around humans. Fought beside them. But I was born a Klingon. My heart is of that world. I do hear the cry of the warrior. I belong with my people.

Notes: This season's cliffhanger episode is not the masterpiece of last season's "Best of Both Worlds," but it is an interesting episode that dives into the history of both the series' backstory (the Klingon Empire) and a major character (Worf). As such, it is a welcome entry.

"Redemption, Part I" is also the 100th episode of *Star Trek: The Next Generation*, well past anything achieved by the original series or the animated series. This is High Trek, *Star Trek* at its zenith of popularity and confidence.

SEASON FIVE

Redemption, Part II

Writer: Ronald D. Moore. **Director:** David Carson. **Airdate:** September 23, 1991.

Not only does the Prime Directive prevent Captain Picard from becoming involved in less-developed cultures; apparently Starfleet doesn't want him to be involved in advanced ones, either. What's the point of being in space?

The *Enterprise* and a fleet of available Starfleet ships form a blockade at the Klingon and Romulan border. Picard has assigned various of his senior staff to command the other ships, including Data. The *Enterprise* is contacted by the Romulan Commander Sela, who gives them fair warning that they will be attacked if they don't drop the blockade. She also says that she is the daughter of former *Enterprise* security chief Tasha Yar, who had ended up in Romulan hands when she traveled to the past (in third-season episode "Yesterday's Enterprise") and became the mate of a Romulan general.

Nice family connection to the *Enterprise*, but that and $3 will get you a cup of coffee at Starbucks. Sela finds a way to disrupt the blockade, but Data is able to disrupt Sela's interference, and the Romulans scutter away; the Duras sisters' civil war collapses. Gowron is safe in his position atop the Klingon empire, and Worf returns to duty aboard the *Enterprise*.

Worf: This boy has done me no harm, and I will not kill him for the crimes of his family!
Gowron: Then it falls to Kurn!

Worf: No! No—you gave me his life, and I have spared it.
Gowron: As you wish.

Notes: In this fifth-season opener, we learn what might have happened to Tasha Yar, who apparently shares actress Denise Crosby's inability to stay away from the *Enterprise*. We will see her again before the final three seasons are through.

Let us not leave this episode without recognizing the 3-dimensional ridiculousness of having a border "blockade" in space. This is 2-dimensional sea-based thinking, where you can have a line of ships and submarines cut off shipping lanes or block ports. But in space, think of the distances involved. The border likely runs through numerous star systems, unless it's the tiniest imaginable border (which would lead one to think the writer did a *Galactica*-style misunderstanding of star systems and galaxies, but it's Ronald Moore, so that's doubtful). The nearest star to Earth is Proxima Centauri, and it is 4.246 light years away. According to my handy online calculator, that's 2.49606e+13 miles. No, I can't decipher that too easily, either. I think it is nearly 25 trillion miles. And that's *linear*. A border in space wouldn't just go from left to right, it'd go up and down, who knows how many zillions of miles each direction. Even assuming the use of *really* great sensors and the deployment of tons of detection buoys, it stretches the imagination to believe that Starfleet would have enough resources to "blockade" even a short stretch of such a border.

Darmok

Writers: Philip LaZebnik, Joe Menosky. **Director:** Winrich Kolbe. **Airdate:** September 30, 1991.

While trying to establish contact with the Tamarians, the *Enterprise* crew is frustrated by the allegorical way in which that alien race communicates. They can make neither head nor tails of the phrases. The Tamarians similarly are unable to figure out what the heck the humans are saying, so they send Captain Picard and Dathon, the Tamarian captain, down to a planet and force them to learn how to communicate with each other.

Hearing "Darmok and Jalad at Tanagra" from the alien captain is as useless to Picard as when your grandfather quotes a Latin writer you've never heard about. But when a predator attacks, Picard and Dathon are predictably forced to take a crash course in mutual comprehension. Picard eventually gets the hang of the Tamarian way of communication, but Dathon dies as a result of injuries incurred during a fight with an alien beast.

For his troubles, Picard is immortalized in the Tamarian language with a new phrase, "Picard and Dathon at El-Adrei."

Riker: New friends, captain?
Picard: I can't say, Number One; but at least they're not new enemies.

Notes: It's "Arena" with more understanding; it's "The Return of Starbuck" with language troubles; it's *Enemy Mine* without the alien birth. Put two opponents on a planet and have them either fight it out or come to some sort of peaceful coexistence. Or fight and then coexist.

Ensign Ro

Writers: Rick Berman, Michael Piller. **Director:** Les Landau. **Airdate:** October 7, 1991.

Ensign Ro Laren, a Bajoran and former prisoner, arrives on the *Enterprise* to help deal with a problem involving the Bajorans, the Federation, and the Cardassians, who had colonized Bajor decades earlier. She rubs pretty much everyone the wrong way, but she is able to help Picard get in touch with a Bajoran, Keeve Falor, to try to learn who's behind a Bajoran attack on the Federation. But Ro is playing a double game, working with Admiral Kennelly on their own secret mission.

Picard uncovers the deception behind that Bajoran attack: It was a Cardassian attempt to get the Federation to side with them. The plot squashed, Picard then convinces Ro to join Starfleet.

Guinan: Am I disturbing you?
Ro: Yes.
Guinan: Good. You look like someone who wants to be disturbed.

Notes: The Bajorans and Cardassians would of course be central to the spinoff *Star Trek: Deep Space Nine*, and Michelle Forbes was asked to return to the role of Ro for that series, but she declined. She does return for guest appearances later in *The Next Generation*, and she continued to act in many films and television shows, including a smashing performance as Admiral Helena Cain in the reimagined *Battlestar Galactica* (see chapter three).

Silicon Avatar

Writers: Lawrence V. Conley, Jeri Taylor. **Director:** Cliff Bole. **Airdate:** October 14, 1991.

It's obsession time again, as Dr. Kila Marr teams up with the *Enterprise* to track down the Crystalline Entity, which has attacked Melona Four, a Federation colony. Picard wants to communicate with it and try to use peaceful means to stop it from attacking colonies; Marr is driven by revenge—her 16-year-old son was killed by the Crystalline Entity on Omicron Theta.

Though Marr makes some sort of a connection with Data, who is able to access the memories of the dead Theta colonists, she remains unmoved by Picard's arguments and sabotages an *Enterprise* attempt to communicate with the Crystalline thing. The Entity is destroyed, as is her career.

Kila Marr: Why are we pursuing the Entity, if not to destroy it?"
Picard: We are not hunters, Doctor. Nor is it our role to exact revenge.
Marr: What do you propose? We track it down, greet it warmly and ask it if it would mind terribly not ravaging any more planets?

Notes: The Crystalline Entity, perhaps one of the blandest villains in *The Next Generation*'s run, was first introduced in season one's "Datalore" episode. An emotionless and relentless killing force, like the xenomorph in *Alien*, can be quite a compelling and scary villain, but the Crystalline Entity fails to look or sound scary.

It looks more like a malevolent but not evil marauding chandelier.

Disaster

Writers: Ron Jarvis, Ronald D. Moore, Philip A. Scorza. **Director:** Gabrielle Beaumont. **Airdate:** October 21, 1991.

When the *Enterprise* hits a spatial anomaly, crewmembers are isolated in various parts of the ship while they try to get everything running properly once again. On the bridge, Counselor Troi is thrust into command, and she tangles with Ensign Ro, who wants to take a more aggressive approach toward saving the ship, even if it means sacrificing a large part of it.

Elsewhere, Captain Picard is stuck in a turbolift with three children to whom he was giving a tour, perhaps cosmic justice for a child-phobic captain. Keiko is ready to give birth, but she's stuck in Ten Forward and the only midwife available is Worf. La Forge and Dr. Crusher are in the cargo bay, where they have to undertake a risky action to stave off an explosion.

Troi: We will separate the ship when I decide that it's time, and not before. Is that clear, ensign?
Ro: Yes. Perfectly.

Notes: The writers shoehorn a handful of plots into one episode, which can be problematic, but it does have a nice side benefit of giving a large number of the characters a chance to be the focus of a subplot, something not usually available in a traditional *Trek* story. Though the Troi storyline is predictable (of course, put the let's-talk-about-your-feelings person in a position of making tough life-and-death decisions), it is nonetheless nice to watch Troi show some mettle. Most of the characters were stuck having to do something not of their usual duties, which helps with the drama but also the humor. Isn't Worf literally the last person you would want as your birth doctor?

And are we the only ones who think it would be interesting to see Ensign Ro in a command role? Talk about a tough female leader.

The Game

Writers: Brannon Braga, Fred Bronson, Susan Sackett. **Director:** Corey Allen. **Airdate:** October 28, 1991.

Wesley Crusher is back from Starfleet, vacationing and trying not to save the ship and all. But despite his best intentions, he is forced to do the dirty deed.

Commander Riker picked up a game from a one-night-stand while vacationing on Risa, and he brought it back to the *Enterprise*, where it is copied and shared with the rest of the crew. (Having written that sentence, am I the only one to liken the game to a venereal disease?) People using the game become addicted and fall under the sway of the alien Ktarians. Only Wesley and his girlfriend Ensign Robin Lefler stand in their way—until Lefler is captured by the game.

One-night stand: You see the disk and the cone?
Riker: Yeah.
One-night stand: Concentrate; make the disk go into the cone.
Riker: How do I do that?
One-night stand: Just let go.

Notes: Singer Ashley Judd first appeared in "Darmok" and reappears here in the same role of Ensign Robin Lefler. "Darmok" was the first screen appearance for Judd, who would go on to amass a considerable film and television resume.

Unification, Part I

Writers: Rick Berman, Michael Piller, Jeri Taylor. **Director:** Les Landau. **Airdate:** November 4, 1991.

The *Enterprise* visits the dying Vulcan Sarek after Picard is told that Sarek's son Spock is on Romulus and might have defected to the Romulans. Despite the obvious unlikelihood of Spock doing that, apparently some in Starfleet are gullible enough to believe it. But Sarek suggests that Spock is pursuing a long-held desire to reunify the Vulcans and Romulans, and he gives Picard a contact of Spock's to try to learn more.

Picard and Data put on some makeup and costumes to make themselves look Romulan and travel to that empire's home world, where they meet Pardek, the Romulan senator with whom Spock had been in touch for decades. Pardek takes them to a cave, where they finally meet Ambassador Spock.

Data: As you examine your life, do you find you have missed your humanity?
Spock: I have no regrets.
Data: "No regrets." That is a human expression.

Spock: Yes. Fascinating

Notes: This two-part episode was timed to air shortly before the debut of *Star Trek VI: The Undiscovered Country*, and there are cross-references between the two. In the film, the Federation finally initiates peace with the Klingons, bringing an end to their hot-and-cold wars and ultimately leading to Worf being on the *Enterprise*. In this episode, it is the Vulcans and Romulans who are trying to make peace. At least some of them are.

Here's a parlor game anyone can play while watching this episode. Way back in 1982, Spock died in *Star Trek II: The Wrath of Khan*. In the pages of *Starlog*, columnist David Gerrold approached it two different but related ways. First, he said, it should be a real death. Let him die, so that the death wasn't just a trick played on the viewers. The film series did and did not comply with that. Spock did really die in *Khan*, but he was more or less brought back in *Star Trek III: The Search for Spock*. Second, Gerrold built on his belief that Spock should show that he has changed since his encounter with Vger in *Star Trek: The Motion Picture*. In that film, remember, he has a mind-meld of sorts with the massive Vger consciousness and realizes that the robot intelligence has amassed vast amounts of information and energy, but it was empty and it didn't understand life. Spock seemed to realize that in ST:TMP and maybe recognized that it reflected his own conflicted concerns over pure logic and his one-half humanity. But whether Gerrold's suggestion that Spock should exhibit—even in small ways—a new understanding and appreciation of emotions and humanity and the role of occasional illogic was represented in *Khan* or later films or even in this two-part episode is something you'll have to do. Your parlor game.

Unification, Part II

Writers: Rick Berman, Michael Piller. **Director:** Cliff Bole. **Airdate:** November 11, 1991.

Spock refuses Picard's plea to get off Romulus, telling the captain that he didn't want to put others in danger like he did when he helped broker Klingon-Federation peace. Even when it turns out that the Romulan Sela has arranged a trap, Spock decides to stay and continue seeking a peaceful future.

The *Enterprise* comes across three Vulcan ships, but they are destroyed by a Romulan warbird—which is disposing of evidence that they were really a Romulan trick.

Spock learns of his father's death and mind-melds with Picard, who carries with him some of Sarek's thoughts from when they had mind-melded.

Sela: Excuse me; I'm just finishing up a speech—for you, Mr. Spock. I rather enjoy writing. I don't get to do it very often in this job.
Data: Perhaps you would be happier in another job.

Notes: Denise Crosby (Sela) returns in this episode, reprising her role as the offspring of Tasha Yar.

This episode includes a title card memorializing the recently deceased Great Bird of the Galaxy, Gene Roddenberry.

A Matter of Time

Writer: Rick Berman. **Director:** Paul Lynch. **Airdate:** November 18, 1991.

A temporal disturbance produces a small craft with someone who calls himself Professor Berlingoff Rasmussen. He claims to be from the 26th century doing research on the mission that the *Enterprise* is currently fulfilling: helping the planet of Penthara IV after an asteroid hit. However, Data discovers the truth about Rasmussen: He is really from 200 years in the past, and he has been stealing items from the *Enterprise* in the hopes of turning them into a tidy sum of money when he returns to the 22nd century. Picard refuses to release Rasmussen, and his craft autopilots back to his timeframe.

Picard [*to Rasmussen*]: I'm sure there are more than a few legitimate historians at Starfleet who would be eager to meet a human from your era. Oh, professor—welcome to the 24th century!

Notes: Guest star Matt Frewer, who portrays Rasmussen, starred in the short-lived 1980s TV phenomenon *Max Headroom*. Perhaps one of the oddest stars of a television series since *My Mother the Car*, the computer-generated TV host only lasted for two seasons and a total of 14 episodes. But he also had a longer-running British career as a video DJ, film star, and talk show host.

New Ground

Writers: Sara Charno, Stuart Charno, Grant Rosenberg. **Director:** Robert Scheerer. **Airdate:** January 19, 1992.

Worf's foster mother shows up and dumps Worf's son, Alexander, on Worf and tells him it's his turn to do the parenting; Alexander wasn't adjusting well to life with his grandparents. However, he has problems aboard the *Enterprise*, too, where he becomes something of a juvenile delinquent in the ship's school.

Meanwhile, La Forge is all excited about an experiment involving a soliton wave, something that you won't understand even after reading the Wikipedia description of it. Naturally, as with any experiment with which the *Enterprise* is involved, something goes wrong.

Alexander: You don't care about me!
Worf: That's not true!
Alexander: All you care about is your honor.

Notes: Yes, you are allowed to wonder about the professional capabilities of the *Enterprise*'s crew, after watching them deal with screwed up science experiment after screwed up science experiment. And you thought it was just Wesley Crusher's fault.

Hero Worship

Writers: Hilary J. Bader, Joe Menosky. **Director:** Patrick Stewart. **Airdate:** January 27, 1992.

A boy named Timothy is the only survivor of the research ship *Vico*. He is brought aboard the *Enterprise*, where he attaches himself to Data, with whom he clearly identifies. The boy believes that hiding his emotions will protect him from the nightmares he has been having. He thinks that he caused the destruction of his ship, though he is assured that that isn't possible.

When the *Enterprise* encounters the real cause of the *Vico*'s destruction—some sort of shock waves moving through space—Timothy points out that the *Enterprise* is about to do the same thing the *Vico* crew did before they were destroyed. Data suggests a different course, and the ship is saved.

Data: Timothy, your head movements are counter-productive. Can you be still?
Timothy: But you do it.
Data: The servo mechanisms in my neck are designed to approximate human movements. I did not realize the effect was so distracting.

Notes: Episodes don't necessarily air in the order in which they were filmed. As we saw, a previously aired episode included a memorial card for the late Gene Roddenberry, but it was actually during the filming of this episode that the show's creator died.

Young actor Joshua Harris, who portrayed Timothy, had quite an acting resume, including a regular gig on *Dallas* and guest starring stints on *Falcon Crest*, *Twin Peaks*, and other shows. He later played professional baseball with the Lansing Lugnuts, a Chicago Cubs minor-league team, for one season.

Violations

Writers: Shari Goodhartz, Pamela Gray, T. Michael, Jeri Taylor. **Director:** Robert Wiemer. **Airdate:** February 3, 1992.

Three telepathic Ullians, including Tarmin and his son Jev, are traveling on the *Enterprise*. Tarmin helps Keiko retrieve a childhood memory of a cup that was important to her, but when he pushes Dr. Crusher to let him use his telepathic gifts to help her, Jev warns him against using his powers without permission.

Meanwhile, Jev finds a connection with Deanna Troi; both have troublesome parents. She later remembers a romantic moment with William Riker, but in the memory Riker eventually becomes an aggressive Jev. Riker himself later has a memory "attack," and Dr. Crusher tests the Ullians to see if they might be causing the problem. Her tests don't clarify anything, and she, too, is mentally attacked.

Troi recovers from her attack, and Jev points to his father as the culprit. But in the end, it is the son who is caught red-handed. Red-minded?

Troi [***to Jev***]**:** It's not easy having an overbearing parent. Believe me, I know how you feel.

Notes: The forceful mind-reading in this story has been called "mind rape," and the story certainly revolves around a man taking undo advantage of the women around him. No surprise that there were so many women involved in crafting this story—a tale that is certainly common inside Hollywood and without.

The Masterpiece Society

Writers: Adam Belanoff, James Kahn, Michael Piller. **Director:** Winrich Kolbe. **Airdate:** February 10, 1992.

Should anyone be allowed to live in splendid isolation, even if it requires people who don't want to share their isolation to remain there? The *Enterprise* tries to do some do-goodery by evacuating the colony of Moab IV, which is in danger from a fragment of a disintegrated neutron star. Unfortunately for everyone involved, Moab IV is a genetically engineered society, and its leader, Aaron Conor, doesn't want to evacuate for fear of losing his people's oh-so-perfectness.

Troi begins to get involved with Conor, and La Forge works with Moabian scientist Hannah Bates to come up with a way to prevent the fragment from destroying the colony without having to evacuate it. They succeed, but Bates then tries to convince everyone that the colony still needs to be evacuated due to a problem with the colony's shield. There is no problem; she made that up. But it reveals that she (and ultimately 22 other colonists) want to leave the colony. They are allowed to do so, and Picard bemoans the fact that people have free will.

Picard: We are responsible.
Riker: We had to respond to the threat of the core fragment—didn't we?
Picard: Of course we did. But, in the end, we may have proved just as dangerous to that colony as any core fragment could ever have been.

Notes: Ugh. The Prime Directive. At the end of this episode, Picard brings up the importance of the Prime Directive, which forbids involvement in pre-warp societies. I've already shared at length my denunciation of the idiocy and racism of the Prime Directive elsewhere in this episode guide. But Picard sums up that idiocy by saying that a society that has to deal with other societies and the differences they bring would be worse off than if that society were completely obliterated? That's obscene.

Conundrum

Writers: Paul Schiffer, Barry Schkolnick. **Director:** Les Landau. **Airdate:** February 17, 1992.

When does "I was only following orders" become "I was only mind-controlled into following malevolent aliens' orders"? When the crew of the *Enterprise* all suddenly lose their memories (but not their abilities to successfully pilot the ship), they all try to fill in wherever possible and in whatever way seems logical. Thus Data tends bar in Ten Forward, Worf takes on the captain's role (until Picard re-assumes it), and Ro and Riker become a romantic-ish pair. Executive officer Kieran MacDuff, however, wants to make sure the ship completes its mission of destroying the central computer of the Lysians.

MacDuff, of course, is a plant, placed on the ship to make sure the Federation starship destroys the Lysians, the enemies of his race, the Satarrans. The Satarrans didn't have the military might to destroy their enemies, but they had hoped to use their ability to alter memories to get someone else to do their dirty work.

Riker: I don't know who any of you are.
Picard: Nor do I. I don't—I don't even remember who I am.

Notes: The conceit of this story—the sudden appearance and acceptance of an alien as a high-ranking member of the *Enterprise* crew—is quite good and is more interesting than the plot itself. The Lysian attack is necessary to give the episode a story, but pulling off the MacDuff deception is a feather in the production team's hat.

Power Play

Writers: René Balcer, Brannon Braga, Maurice Hurley, Paul Ruben, Herbert J. Wright. **Director:** David Livingston. **Airdate:** February 24, 1992.

While visiting Mab-Bu VI, Data, Troi, and O'Brien are possessed by entities claiming to be survivors of the USS *Essex*, which was lost in the region 172 years earlier. They try to convince the *Enterprise* crew to investigate the polar region of the planet, where they say their bodies are.

When their pleas are refused, they take over the ship and beam up hundreds of their compatriots, who like them are really fellow inmates on the Mab-Bu penal colony. The *Enterprise* crew is able to, first, contain the hundreds of new entities and, second, get the entities controlling Data, O'Brien, and Troi to leave their bodies. The prisoners are beamed back down to Mab-Bu VI.

Data: Lieutenant, I must apologize for my inadvertent misconduct toward you.

Worf: No apology necessary.
Data: Your restraint was most remarkable.
Worf: You have no idea.

Notes: Only in science fiction can you have an episode with "guest stars" who are actually your regular cast (acting possessed). Thus no extra actor costs.

Ethics

Writers: Stuart Charno, Sara B. Cooper, Ronald D. Moore. **Director:** Chip Chalmers. **Airdate:** March 2, 1992.

Today apparently is not a good day to die. When Worf is gravely injured in an accident in the storage bay, Dr. Toby Russell suggests a risky but potentially restorative surgery to replace his injured spine. Dr. Crusher doesn't like the idea, but after Worf is unable to convince Riker to help him commit ritual suicide, Worf elects to have Dr. Russell perform her procedure.

Meanwhile, as the *Enterprise* helps treat injured colonists, Crusher catches Russell using an unapproved drug on a patient who dies. Nonetheless, Worf is operated on, Worf survives, and Crusher tells Russell she's an awful person.

Worf begins physical therapy with the help of his son, Alexander.

Crusher [*to Russell*]: You scare me, doctor. You risk your patients' lives and justify it in the name of research. Genuine research takes time—sometimes a lifetime of painstaking, detailed work in order to get any results. Not for you. You take short cuts, right through living tissue. You put your research ahead of your patients' lives. And as far as I'm concerned, that's a violation of our most sacred trust. I'm sure your work will be hailed as a stunning breakthrough. Enjoy your laurels, Doctor. I'm not sure I could.

Notes: This is a good episode for Dr. Crusher to shine in, not only because it focuses on her work but because it focuses on a real, ethical issue in her work.

It is good to see Crusher as someone other than the on-call doctor, and instead someone who is both an expert in her field and someone who is upholding the highest of professional and moral standards.

The Outcast

Writer: Jeri Taylor. **Director:** Robert Scheerer. **Airdate:** March 16, 1992.

While helping the J'naii rescue a shuttle lost in null space, Riker becomes attracted to Soren, a J'naii who identifies as female even though her race is androgynous and believes that male or female gender identification is horrible. Soren and Riker strike up a relationship, which is eventually discovered and Soren goes on trial. Soren is forced to go through "therapy" to change her gender expression.

Picard won't allow Riker to rescue Soren from the therapy (Prime Directive and all that), but Worf offers to help out the commander, and the two of them beam down to the J'naii planet. But the post-therapy Soren rejects their rescue; Soren's no longer attracted to Riker.

Soren: On my planet, we have been taught that gender is primitive.
Riker: Primitive?
Soren: Less evolved.
Riker: Maybe so, but sometimes, there is a lot to be said for an experience that's—primitive.

Notes: As an allegory about treatment of LGBT people, this is an overdue entry into the *Star Trek* canon. As a convincing test of viewer attitudes, however, it falls short. If you are going to push the viewer to reconsider his or her views, then Soren could have been less obviously a female, and perhaps if this episode were produced today, CGI would have been used to achieve that. Others could argue that the entire story was a mirror image of anti-LGBT efforts, so Soren needed to be recognizably female to make the point of her differentiation from the other J'naii.

There is no way to do this story that wouldn't upset anyone, and at least *Trek* tried. But of course all LGBT critics had been asking for for many years was to have an LGBT crew member on the ship—specifically show that it's normal and not something that needs convoluted politics or explanations. Fans would wait another quarter century before that would happen in *Star Trek Beyond.*

Another decades-later development is the movement in recent years by some to avoid any gender identification. It's a still-developing approach, and it is occurring at the same time as the increasing visibility of transgender people seeking to be identified by their gender. One could argue this all one way or the other for days on end; I'll spare you that, because I'm mostly observing the slow-moving debates over it all. But I mention it here only because this episode, were it written and produced today, would likely have integrated at least some of this current thinking.

Cause and Effect

Writer: Brannon Braga. **Director:** Jonathan Frakes. **Airdate:** March 23, 1992.

If you hate playing cards, an endless game of poker is probably your idea of hell on Earth. Our heroes start out playing poker, but later in the day they find a spatial anomaly. A ship comes out of the anomaly and hits the *Enterprise*, causing its destruction. Aaaaaand they are suddenly back to playing cards, as if nothing happened.

The *Enterprise* is stuck in a time loop, and slowly various members of the crew begin to remember things from past cycles—Crusher, for example, can predict the cards that Data is about to deal in their poker game. After more trips through the loop, the poker players eventually realize they're being sent a signal from past loops that will help them escape the loop. They do, and they avoid the collision with the USS *Bozeman*, which has traveled from 90 years in the past, thanks to the anomaly.

Riker: How did you know I was bluffing?
Crusher: I just had a feeling.
Riker: I guess it's better to be lucky than good.
Crusher: It's the way your left eyebrow raises when you're bluffing.

Notes: As Memory Alpha notes, "Cause and Effect" mentions ejecting the warp core: "This is the first reference to ejecting the warp core; while it is mentioned many times, the procedure wouldn't actually be seen on screen until [the *Voyager* episode] 'Cathexis,' which marked the first of several times USS *Voyager* would eject its warp core. The USS *Enterprise*-E ejected its core in *Star Trek: Insurrection*."

The First Duty

Writers: Ronald D. Moore, Naren Shankar. **Director:** Paul Lynch. **Airdate:** March 30, 1992.

An accident with cadet Wesley Crusher's Starfleet squadron causes the death of one pilot, Joshua Albert. The captain of the *Enterprise*, heading to Earth anyway because of Captain Picard's scheduled commencement address at Starfleet Academy, is briefed on the tragedy. Wesley doesn't want to discuss it with Picard and his mother, but he gets some advice—or pressure—from fellow squadron cadet Nicholas Locarno, who says the team has to stick together. Locarno argues that the accident was the fault of Albert. Picard, meanwhile, learns that the squadron had been trying to perform a special move known as the Kolvoord Starburst, and Crusher is forced to decide between his loyalties to Picard and Locarno. Siding with Picard will have a heavy cost—in time and privileges—for young Crusher.

Picard: You have difficult times ahead.
Crusher: Yes, sir. Thank you, captain.
Picard: You knew what you had to do; I just made sure that you listened to yourself.

Notes: Cadet Nicholas Locarno is portrayed by Robert Duncan McNeil, who would go on to portray the somewhat similar character of Tom Paris for seven seasons on *Star Trek Voyager*. There is also the first of what will become several appearances of veteran actor Ray Walston as Boothby, a groundskeeper at Starfleet Academy. Walston was already a science fiction legend for his portrayal of the titular alien in *My Favorite Martian* in that early 1960s' sitcom.

Cost of Living

Writer: Peter Allan Fields. **Director:** Winrich Kolbe. **Airdate:** April 20, 1992.

Worf and his son Alexander are having troubles negotiating their father-son relationship, and just in time to "help" out is Lwaxana Troi, who boards the *Enterprise* to hold her wedding ceremony. Deanna is disappointed that her mother will not be having a traditional Betazoid wedding—by being nude at the ceremony—but Lwaxana says her husband-to-be would be offended.

As she awaits the arrival of her husband-to-be, Campio, Lwaxana hangs out with Alexander and teaches him the finer points of annoying his father, such as engaging in mud baths on the holodeck. Eventually, Campio arrives, but he rejects Lwaxana when she shows up at the wedding ceremony in traditional, um, garb.

Troi: It may be hard to imagine right now, but eventually most children come to appreciate their parents.
Riker [*over ship's communicator*]: Riker to Counselor Troi. Your mother has just come aboard.
Troi: On the other hand—

Notes: There is a B-plot in which the ship has some sort of parasite working its way through its systems. But this subplot is not particularly interesting compared to the soap opera of the Lwaxana plot.

The Perfect Mate

Writers: René Echevarria, Gary Percante, Michael Piller. **Director:** Cliff Bole. **Airdate:** April 27, 1992.

The *Enterprise* is transporting Kriosian ambassador Briam and his mysterious cargo to a peace ceremony with the Valtian when it has to stop and rescue two Ferengi, who are having ship troubles. The Ferengi, being Ferengi and the *Enterprise*'s security apparently being terrible, sneak into the cargo bay and release Briam's cargo, which turns out to be a woman named Kamala, an empath who creates a strong attraction to her in any males she's around. (Luckily for the sake of this story, we already know that Starfleet or the producers have forbidden any gay men from being on board the starship.)

Though Briam tries to keep Kamala hidden, Picard lets her roam the ship, causing disruption because Starfleet males evidently can't control themselves around her. Even more dangerous is the growing attraction between Kamala and Picard. But despite some debate among the *Enterprise* officers about the ethics of Kamala's position (is it institutionalized prostitution? does she have free will?), she goes through with her marriage to the Valtian.

Riker: Riker to bridge—if you need me I'll be on Holodeck 4.

Notes: Add another ambassadorial transport to your *Enterprise* bingo card.

Tim O'Connor, who portrayed the Kriosian ambassador in this episode, is a soap opera veteran who is also known for his portrayal of Dr. Elias Huer in the first season of *Buck Rogers in the 25th Century* in 1979–80. The Ferengi Par Lenor was portrayed by Max Grodénchik, who would go on to essay the role of Rom in *Star Trek: Deep Space Nine*.

Imaginary Friend

Writers: Brannon Braga, Richard Fliegel, Jean Louise Matthias, Edithe Swensen, Ronald Wilkerson. **Director:** Gabrielle Beaumont. **Airdate:** May 4, 1992.

Clara is new to the *Enterprise*. She arrived there with her father, and out of her loneliness she creates Isabella, an imaginary friend who, to her surprise, appears in the real world one day. Isabella doesn't turn out to be a great friend or future Girl Scouts pal; she's a lifeform from a nearby nebula.

Picard and Isabella have a come-to-Jesus talk about human parenting and how cruel humans can be to children.

Clara: It's just, I've never seen you before—not for real.
Isabella: Well, now you can see me for real. Doesn't that make you happy?

Notes: Alien Isabella is portrayed by actor/singer Shay Astar, who also acted in *3rd Rock from the Sun*.

I, Borg

Writer: René Echevarria. **Director:** Robert Lederman. **Airdate:** May 10, 1992.

The Federation's most implacable enemy—the Borg—become a bit more, well, placable when the *Enterprise* discovers a teen Borg at the site of a crashed Borg ship. The young Borg is still alive, so he is brought aboard the *Enterprise*, where the crew cook up a plan to essentially turn him into an unwitting agent of genocide. They plan to implant in him a program that would infect the Borg collective and destroy it.

But when the Borg begins to show individuality, "Hugh"—as he's dubbed by La Forge—wins over the crew and eventually convinces Captain Picard.

Hugh: You will be assimilated.
La Forge: Yes, we know. But before that, we'd like to ask you a few questions.

Notes: *Star Trek* tended to use the Borg for grand-scale, event stories. This episode shows the flexibility of the writers and producers, telling a small personal story that nonetheless has cosmic implications. The result is one of the best episodes of the season.

The Next Phase

Writer: Ronald D. Moore. **Director:** David Carson. **Airdate:** May 18, 1992.

While trying to help a Romulan ship that had suffered some sort of disaster, Ro and La Forge return to the *Enterprise* with the damaged Romulan graviton generator. But during the transport, Ro and La Forge are thought to have died when something goes wrong. The two aren't dead; they've just been knocked out of phase by a Romulan phase inverter machine.

Ro and La Forge discover that the Romulans intend to destroy the *Enterprise*, but they have no way of communicating with their fellow crew members to warn them. It is not until their funeral that the two are able to make themselves visible to the rest of the crew. Data figures out what has happened and the destruction of the ship is averted.

La Forge: We should develop our own interphase device. If it can teach Ro Laren humility, it can do anything.

Notes: Actor Thomas Kopache, who portrayed the Romulan Mirok in this episode, is one of only five people to have appeared in all of the *Star Trek* series (with the exception of the original series). He even had a role in the movie *Star Trek Generations*.

The Inner Light

Writers: Peter Allan Fields, Morgan Gendel. **Director:** Peter Lauritson. **Airdate:** June 1, 1992.

A mysterious probe scans the *Enterprise* and knocks out Captain Picard. He awakens on the planet Kataan, where he meets Eline, his wife, and he learns that his name is Kamin. They tell him his experiences on the *Enterprise* were only dreams, and he slowly acclimates himself to the planet and its society. He learns to play the flute, has a family with Eline, and realizes the planet is facing a massive drought due to its star's increasing radiation.

After Picard had been rendered unconscious on the *Enterprise*, his crewmembers try unsuccessfully to revive him, only to put his life at risk. They eventually trace the probe to a planetary system where the sun had gone nova a millennium earlier.

After experiencing 40 years on Kataan, Picard joins other villagers to watch the launch of a space probe, which contains the society's memories and which is to seek out others to inform them of their soon-to-be-lost society.

Picard reawakens on the *Enterprise*, where only minutes have passed while he had lived through four decades of Kataan life. When the aliens' space probe is opened, inside is Kamin's flute.

Picard/Kamin: I'm the someone. I'm the one it finds. That's what this launching is—a probe that finds me in the future.

Notes: This fantastic episode is *Star Trek* at its best. Intelligent, dramatic, thought-provoking, somewhat sad. It takes something as wide-ranging and devastating as the destruction of an entire planet's life and makes it come alive in a one-hour program. "The Inner Light" won the 1993 Hugo Award for Best Dramatic Presentation.

Time's Arrow, Part I

Writers: Joe Menosky, Michael Piller. **Director:** Les Landau. **Airdate:** June 15, 1992.

After the discovery of some items from the 19th century and the disembodied head of Data in a cave near Starfleet in San Francisco, the *Enterprise* arrives to investigate. They learn that shapeshifting aliens from Devidia II are present, and they travel to that planet to discover that the Devidians are somehow drawing human life forces out of their human hosts to make use of them.

The *Enterprise* crew tries and fails to prevent what they know will happen: Data at some point will die. When Data is transported back to 19th-century San Francisco, he discovers Guinan. Eventually, Picard leads an away team to travel back in time to try to defeat the Devidians and save Data from certain destruction.

Jack London: Isn't that what makes America great?
Data: To what are you referring?
London: A man rides into town in his pajamas, wins a grubstake at a poker table, turns it into a horseless carriage, and makes a million bucks. That's America!
Data: I believe I have given you an erroneous impression.

Notes: "City on the Edge of Forever" this isn't, but it is still an entertaining and involving dramatic tale, and a worthy season-ending cliffhanger.

SEASON SIX

Time's Arrow, Part II

Writers: Joe Menosky, Jeri Taylor. **Director:** Les Landau. **Airdate:** September 21, 1992.

In 1893 San Francisco, Picard and the away team are able to find Data, Guinan, and—why not?—Samuel Clemens. They also learn that the Devidians had gone back in time to the 19th century because they could use a cholera epidemic as cover for their preying on humans.

During a struggle over the prop that opens the portal, the android Data loses his head—literally—and Guinan suffers an injury. Picard is left in the past with Guinan and Data's head while the rest of the away team returns to the 24th century. The captain manages to insert into the android's noggin a message for his crew to discover in the future, in the hopes of both rescuing him and preventing the Devidians from destroying humans in the past (and thus in their future).

Guinan: I'll see you in 500 years, Picard.
Picard: And I'll see you—in a few minutes.

Notes: Time travel episodes—whether in the original *Star Trek*, *Next Generation*, *Deep Space Nine*, *Voyager*, or hell, even *Galactica 1980*—always provide a chance to use differences between the two time periods to comment on the "present." This episode is no different, though larding up the plot with not one but two legendary writers (Mark Twain, aka Samuel Clemens, and Jack London) is too precious. And once time travel is established as feasible, the episode's writers have basically two options when it comes to the matter of solving a problem in another time: come up with a ridiculous reason that it is not feasible (which, after *Star Trek IV: There Be Whales Captain*, simply doesn't fly) or just ignore it and hope the audience isn't paying too close attention.

Realm of Fear

Writer: Brannon Braga. **Director:** Cliff Bole. **Airdate:** September 28, 1992.

Reginald Barclay is scared witless by transporters. And, wouldn't you know it, during a transport he sees scary "worms" that no one else can detect. Barclay is part of the *Enterprise* contingent helping the USS *Yosemite*, which lost several crew-members in a transporter accident. Barclay thinks he's just suffering hallucinations as part of "transporter psychosis." But when they are able to discover the effects on his arm where a worm had touched him, the *Enterprise* crew knows something real is happening. On another trip through the transporter, Barclay captures one of the worms, who turns out to be one of the missing *Yosemite* crew. Further trips bring back all of the missing people.

Troi: La Forge said you seemed a little nervous this morning.
Barclay: I'm always nervous. Everybody knows that.

Notes: This episode is a good example of how you can have a dramatic and even unsettling story without a real villain in it. It is also, once again, a nice use of Barclay.

Man of the People

Writer: Frank Abatemarco. **Director:** Winrich Kolbe. **Airdate:** October 5, 1992.

The *Enterprise* comes to the rescue of Lumerian Ambassador Ramid Ves Alkar, whose Federation ship was being attacked. During the subsequent trip to the Rekag-Seronia system, where Alkar is to mediate in a conflict, Troi meets Alkar's elderly mother, who accuses Troi of wanting to mate with Alkar. When the mother dies, Crusher is unable to explain it, but something clearly is transferred from the old woman to Troi.

Troi then somewhat vamps it up, trying to seduce Alkar and others. But she soon starts to age, and when another of Alkar's female aides appears, Troi confronts her just like she was confronted earlier. Alkar's negotiating success is revealed to be his ability to use another person as the equivalent of a cloud storage device for his negative emotions; unfortunately, it rapidly ages and kills the other person.

Troi: Thanks for sticking by me.
Riker: I always will, even when you're old and gray.

Notes: The ambassador's ship at the beginning of this episode is the *Dorian*. So, yes, *The Picture of Dorian Gray*.

Relics

Writer: Ronald D. Moore. **Director:** Alexander Singer. **Airdate:** October 12, 1992.

It's Barclay's or Bones McCoy's worst nightmare: A man stuck in a transporter buffer for 75 years. The *Enterprise* responds to a distress call, which turns out to be from a small craft that crash-landed on the outside of a Dyson Sphere, a gargantuan structure completely encircling a star. They find that the transporter buffer still holds the data for a certain Captain Montgomery Scott. They materialize him and help him recover on the *Enterprise*.

The former chief engineer of a previous version of the *Enterprise* has a hard time adjusting to this new future—no real alcohol, for one thing—and he refers to himself as a relic. But when the *Enterprise* gets trapped while exploring the Dyson Sphere, Scotty and La Forge use Scotty's ship to help the starship escape. In return, the crew gifts him with a shuttle to use to continue his explorations.

Scotty: Laddie, I was drinking scotch a hundred years before you were born, and I can tell you that whatever this is, it is definitely not scotch.

Notes: This gem of an episode is a great character study that manages to make better use of Scotty than the "Unification" two-parter did of Spock. The recreation of the original *Enterprise* bridge is particularly poignant; far from being just a nostalgic stunt, it underscores the loneliness of Scotty, while tying together the two *Trek* series.

Schisms

Writers: Brannon Braga, Jean Louise Matthias, Ron Wilkerson. **Director:** Robert Wiemer. **Airdate:** October 19, 1992.

Call Scully and Mulder! Aliens are abducting *Enterprise* crewmembers—including Riker—and doing experiments on them. They only discover this after some of the affected crewmembers get together and share their experiences on the holodeck, and Dr. Crusher finds that they exhibit evidence of tampering to their bodies.

They hatch a plot to send Riker back to the aliens, while La Forge tries to figure out what to do with a subspace rift that opens up in Cargo Bay 4.

Data [*after sharing some of his poetry*]: Your hesitation suggests you are trying to protect my feelings. However, since I have none, I would prefer you to be honest.

Notes: Lanei Chapman, who portrays Ensign Rager, later was a regular in the series *Space: Above and Beyond.*

True Q

Writers: Matthew Corey, René Echevarria. **Director:** Robert Scheerer. **Airdate:** November 1, 1992.

The *Enterprise* is a death trap. Falling cargo containers nearly kill crewmen. The warp core nearly explodes. How did this ship pass inspection?

Both of those dangers are quashed by Starfleet intern Amanda Rogers, who exhibits miraculous abilities. So Q shows up, claiming Amanda as one of his own, or more accurately, as a Q. Picard, ever suspicious where Q is concerned, finds out that Amanda's parents were killed by a freak storm in Kansas, and Q has been sent to kill Amanda if she turns out to be a Q-human hybrid.

When a nearby planet sends a distress call, Q has Amanda make a choice: Join the Q Continuum or remain a lowly human.

Rogers: Ever since I got here, I've been fighting this. I've been denying the truth, denying what I am. I am Q.

Notes: Olivia d'Abo, who portrays Amanda Rogers, is related to Maryam d'Abo, the Bond girl in *The Living Daylights.*

Rascals

Writers: Diana Dru Botsford, Ward Botsford, Alison Hock, Michael Piller. **Director:** Adam Nimoy. **Airdate:** October 30, 1992.

Somebody's got to get those transporters fixed. Is there no quality control, no OSHA, in Starfleet? Adult crewmembers Picard, Guinan, Keiko O'Brien, and Ro Laren are, er, turned into children in the scientifically questionable transporter accident they suffer while returning to the *Enterprise* from a planetary visit.

Before Dr. Crusher can reverse the de-aging (un-aging?), the starship is attacked by Ferengi, who transport—apparently successfully—the adults to a planet but keep the kids on board. The youngified Picard leads the children—the real ones and the incredibly unscientifically artificially de-aged ones—in undermining the Ferengi to regain control of the ship.

Troi: You could return to the Academy; take another degree; brush up on your Latin.
Young Picard: And be Wesley Crusher's roommate?

Notes: This episode was reportedly very unpopular among the series' crew, and it *is* a ridiculous concept (if you didn't get that idea from my description above). It is, nonetheless, also a rather entertaining episode to watch, poking some fun at the regular characters and in particular giving us the cute turnaround of having Captain Picard, the Starfleet officer who famously didn't want children on his ship, turned into a child on his ship.

This episode was the directorial debut of Adam Nimoy, the son of *Trek* legend Leonard Nimoy. In 2018, he married actor Terry Farrell, who portrayed Jadzia Dax on *Deep Space Nine*.

A Fistful of Datas

Writers: Brannon Braga, Robert Hewitt Wolfe. **Director:** Patrick Stewart. **Airdate:** November 9, 1992.

Somebody's got to get the holodeck fixed! Forced to spend some recreational time with his son, Alexander, Worf agrees to participate in a holodeck story based in 19th century Deadwood, South Dakota. But at the same time, La Forge and Data are doing an experiment of connecting Data to the *Enterprise*'s main computer and letting him run important functions. Because that's what nerds do when they're bored. And you know what happens when an experiment is run aboard the *Enterprise*.

Something happens that causes Data and the main computer to swap parts of their programming, and he increasingly turns up as characters—dangerous characters, at that—in the holodeck story, endangering the lives of Worf, Alexander, and Troi, who has also decided to visit Deadwood.

Data: Y'all must be mistaken.
La Forge: Data, you did it again.
Data: Did what?

Notes: A cute episode, and I have to admit to enjoying almost all of the stories with Worf and Alexander. But it's also an entirely silly diversionary episode. After two of these in a row, will ST:TNG sober up?

The Quality of Life

Writers: L.J. Scott, Naren Shankar. **Director:** Jonathan Frakes. **Airdate:** November

16, 1992.

Exocomps are little machines that can not only fix problems but can learn and adapt. They better themselves, like Robert DeNiro in *Stanley & Iris*. The *Enterprise* crew learns about exocomps during a visit to Tyrus 7a to view something called a particle fountain. Exocomps are impressive little creatures, but Data becomes convinced that they are capable of much more, including sentience. They not only are able to get themselves out of danger or refuse to put themselves in danger; they have developed the ability to sacrifice themselves to save others.

Dr. Farallon: There is a big difference between Data and a tool.
Data: Doctor, there is a big difference between you and a virus, but both are alive.

Notes: One episode after star Patrick Stewart helmed an episode, this one is directed by co-star Jonathan Frakes. It is, perhaps, an overly simplistic and obvious story, but it is redeemed somewhat by Data's tying his own interest in defending the exocomps to Captain Picard's defense of Data in "The Measure of a Man" from the second season.

Chain of Command, Part I

Writers: Frank Abatemarco, Ronald D. Moore. **Director:** Robert Scheerer. **Airdate:** December 14, 1992.

Captain Jellico takes temporary command of the *Enterprise* while Captain Picard is away. Picard, along with Worf and Dr. Crusher, train for their secret mission to infiltrate and destroy a Cardassian biological weapons facility. Jellico had played an important part in the Federation-Cardassian peace negotiations, so his presence—and the *Enterprise*'s subsequent patrolling along Cardassian territory—is used to try to prevent any flareup of trouble with the troublesome Cardassians.

Jellico and Riker don't get along from the start, but worse is in store for Picard, Crusher, and Worf when they arrive at the site of the supposed bio-facility—and discover that it's a Cardassian trap. Worf and Crusher get away, but Picard is captured.

Jellico: I want this ship ready for action, and I don't have time to give Will Riker or anyone else a chance. And forgive me for being blunt, but the *Enterprise* is mine now.

Notes: Michael Dorn told this story to an enthusiastic audience at a *Next Generation* 25th-anniversary convention in Calgary, Canada: "We had been crawling through caves, in dirt, on stage 16, which we call Planet Hell because that's where they put all the god-forsaken planets we go to; and it was dirt. They just keep dirt on the stage. And we had a lot of cats at Paramount—stray cats. Cats; dirt. And we're crawling around and . . . we're all dirty, and Gates is there. All of a sudden, it's late, we're sitting there between takes, and I look over, and Patrick and I just start laughing for no reason . . . uncontrollably. I said, 'Patrick, what are you laughing at?' He says, 'I don't know how I got here. I was in a seminar in Santa Barbara, the next thing I know I'm crawling around in cat shit.'"

Chain of Command, Part II

Writer: Frank Abatemarco. **Director:** Les Landau. **Airdate:** December 21, 1992.

Picard has been taken captive by Gul Madred, who tortures him in an attempt to learn Federation secrets about the planet Minos Korva, which the Cardassians covet. Picard resists, despite an array of torture procedures used against him.

Meanwhile, Jellico refuses to admit to the Cardassians that their captive was on a mission for Starfleet; that means Picard won't get the treatment of a prisoner of war. Riker objects, and Jellico relieves him of duties. Later, Jellico must enlist Riker's help to carry out a plan to set some space mines to prevent a Cardassian fleet from taking Minos Korva. Apprised of the mining operation, the Cardassians give in, and Picard is returned to the *Enterprise*.

Madred: How many lights do you see there?
Picard: I see four lights.
Madred: No. There are five.

Notes: This unusually strong and dark episode was heavily influenced by Amnesty International, which was consulted by the writer and of which Patrick Stewart has been an advocate.

Ship in a Bottle

Writer: René Echevarria. **Director:** Alexander Singer. **Airdate:** January 24, 1993.

Really, somebody's got to get the damn holodeck fixed. Evil Professor Moriarty is more than a fictional character in Sherlock Holmes stories, he's a sentient artificial thingamabob who (that?) manages to create a consort/companion (the Countess Regina Bartholomew) and leave the holodeck altogether.

But it's a double- or triple-switch in this episode, as the *Enterprise* crew realizes that what they thought was the *Enterprise* is still just a holodeck program, and then they convince Moriarty that he has escaped the holodeck, when he's really just exploring strange new worlds within a program. Check mate.

Moriarty: A holodeck character? A fictional man? Yes, yes—I know all about your marvelous inventions. I was created as a plaything so that your Commander Data could masquerade as Sherlock Holmes. But they made me too well, and I became more than a character in a story; I became self-aware. I am alive.

Notes: This story is a sequel to the second-season episode "Elementary, Dear Data." Whether all of the explaining and holodeck trickery actually adds up in the end, I don't know. But it's a fun episode anyway.

Aquiel

Writer: Brannon Braga, Ronald D. Moore, Jeri Taylor. **Director:** Cliff Bole. **Airdate:** February 1, 1993.

The *Enterprise* is at a small Starfleet station along the Klingon border where it finds its two staff—Aquiel Uhnari and Rocha—missing; only a dog remains, along with some weird organic residue on the floor. Picard puts his service to Klingon Chancellor Gowron to good use, wielding it to pressure the local Klingon governor, who caves and produces Aquiel, who is still alive. She tells the *Enterprise* crew that she had been attacked by Rocha.

La Forge decides it's time that he finally gets the woman, so he strikes up a relationship with Aquiel, who fears that she will be blamed for Rocha's death. Meanwhile, Dr. Crusher discovers that that organic residue from the station is alive, and it takes the shape of lifeforms it touches. Is Aquiel just a copy of the original? Was Rocha a copy? And who's sleeping with La Forge?

Aquiel: Geordi?
La Forge: I can see you. Oh, and I can feel you.

Notes: Spoiler alert: The dog is a shape-shifter. So we're not the only ones who saw John Carpenter's *The Thing*.

Face of the Enemy

Writers: René Echevarria, Naren Shankar. **Director:** Gabrielle Beaumont. **Airdate:** February 8, 1993.

Troi is captured and taken aboard a Romulan warbird, with her appearance altered so that she can pose as Major Rakal of the feared Romulan secret police the Tal Shiar. She is told by the Romulan N'Vek that she has to use this guise to convince the warbird's commander, Toreth, to take the ship to the Kaleb sector. N'Vek and "Rakal" want to deliver a secret cargo: a high Romulan official and his two assistants, who are unconscious but who want to defect to the Federation.

The *Enterprise*, too, is headed to the Kaleb sector, having been tipped off by a messenger from Ambassador Spock of a meeting there. It all comes to a head when the *Enterprise* trails the warbird, and Troi has to assume command of the Romulan ship to prevent it from destroying her real ship. But she still needs to let an attack go forward, if only to hide the transport of the secret cargo to the *Enterprise*.

Then there's just the little matter of getting herself off the Romulan ship after

Toreth resumes command. Oh—and getting rid of the Romulan cosmetic surgery once she's back home.

Toreth: How is the empire threatened by the words of an old man, a devoted citizen who was merely trying to speak his mind? How did the Tal Shiar protect the empire by dragging him, my father, out of his home in the middle of the night?
Troi [*as Rakal*]: Clearly, your father was a traitor.
Toreth: No. He was just an idealistic old man. I never saw him again.
Troi: I don't need your devotion, commander, just your obedience.
Toreth: And that's all you have.

Notes: Recent episodes have involved *Trek* characters turning into children, being fooled by the appearance of aliens pretending to be long-time comrades, living an entire lifetime as another man, turning into invisible observers, turning into holodeck computers, and being taken over by body-snatching aliens that suck out their lifeblood. There is a strong through-line of—forgive the term—body alienation in these stories, playing with the definitions and appearances of characters we already know well. Whether this was done because the writers were running out of stories to tell, or if they were free to push their plots further because of the confidence that came with the show's success, is something I can't tell. But, as in this story, it often produced interesting tales.

Tapestry

Writer: Ronald D. Moore. **Director:** Les Landau. **Airdate:** February 15, 1993.

Picard is shot and killed by terrorists. But death in science fiction is never a certain thing, and he awakens to find Q, who informs him that he died because his artificial heart failed when he was attacked. Picard had lost his real heart in a barroom fight when he was a young Starfleet officer, something he says he regrets. So Q sends him back in time to undo that action.

Back Picard goes, and this time instead of getting into the fight to help his friend, he prevents the fight from taking place. Returned to his own time on the *Enterprise*, he finds that he is no longer the captain but instead a junior officer. He is told that he never managed to stand out because he avoided risk in his career. He complains to Q, is returned yet again to his young adulthood, has the fight, loses his heart, and voila, when he returns to the here-and-now he is once again captain of the *Enterprise*.

Q: The Jean-Luc Picard you wanted to be, the one who did not fight the Nausicaan, had quite a different career from the one you remember. That Picard never had a brush with death, never came face-to-face with his own mortality, never realized how fragile life is, or how important each moment must be. So his life never came into focus. He drifted through much of his career, with no plan or agenda, going from one assignment to the next, never seizing the opportunities that presented themselves. He never led the away-team on Milika III to save the ambassador, or take charge of the *Stargazer*'s bridge when its captain was killed, and no one ever offered him a command. He learned to play it safe, and he never, ever got noticed by anyone.

Picard: You're right, Q. You gave me the chance to change, and I took the opportunity. But I admit now: it was a mistake!

Q: Are you asking me for something, Jean-Luc?

Picard: Give me a chance to put things back the way they were before.

Q: Before—you died in sickbay. Is that what you want?

Picard: I would rather die as the man I was than live the life I just saw.

Notes: Well, now. As a parable about how all events of one's life—good and bad and traumatic and transcendent—go into who one becomes, this episode succeeds. But what is problematic is the experiences that were used to teach Captain Picard this lesson; and his ultimate argument about why he wants things to be the way they were originally is far from inspiring and raises more worries than is necessary.

The youthful "error" that Picard has undone and then redone is his getting into a needless and near-fatal bar fight. Why was that example chosen? It ennobles every half-drunk nitwit who gets into a bar fight over a stupid game or real or imagined insult or whatever. In real life, people get seriously injured and die because some liquored-up idiot feels his honor is at issue because someone looked at his girlfriend (or his girlfriend dumped him, or any number of other reasons that are just excuses to break the chains of decency and try to attack another person). And the writer thought that young Picard showing caution and avoiding that fight would then become a meek loser who never learned about the importance of life and death and risk-taking? As if there would never ever again be an opportunity for Picard to experience or witness (or, hell, read about and take into his thoughts) the realization that life can be ephemeral and sometimes if you want something you have to risk it?

What lesson did they think they were teaching young viewers with that particular example of Picard's youth? He didn't take a risk to save his friend's life (in fact, by taking the risk he put his friend's life in mortal danger). He didn't take a risk to protect an endangered child or save an animal's life or defeat a bully. He put his own life (and that of his friend, don't forget that) in danger over a stupid bar game at which both the Nausicaans and his friend had cheated.

Near the end of the episode, Picard (as shown in the section quoted above) says he would rather be dead than live the life of the junior officer that he had become in the alternate lifeline. Rather dead than be a junior science officer. We're sure the junior science officers on his ship would be thrilled to learn that he thinks anyone who doesn't become captain of a ship is better off dead. They can probably think he's going to be really careful about putting their lives in danger on away missions or during tense situations, right?

In short, an intriguing episode done well, but with an immoral core to the story and its conclusion.

Birthright Part I

Writer: Brannon Braga. **Director:** Winrich Kolbe. **Airdate:** March 7, 1993.

While on a visit to *Deep Space Nine*, Worf hears a rumor that his father was not killed at Khitomer, as he believed, but was captured by Romulans, which would be a dishonor in his society. He gets leave from the *Enterprise* to go in search of his father and find out if the rumor is true. This leads him to a planet near Romulan space, where he discovers a settlement of Klingons. To his relief, he learns that his father did indeed die at Khitomer. But when Worf tries to leave, he is captured by Romulans.

Meanwhile, DS9's Dr. Julian Bashir comes aboard the *Enterprise* and, working with La Forge, causes Data to experience dreaming. Data is puzzled by the experience, and believes he has been preprogrammed to dream by his creator, Dr. Soong.

Bashir [*to Data*]: Your creator went to a lot of trouble to make you seem human. I find that fascinating.

Notes: James Cromwell returns to portray Jaglom Shrek, the alien who tells Worf that his father survived in Romulan captivity. Cromwell played warp drive discoverer Dr. Zefram Cochrane in *Star Trek: First Contact*, a role he reprised in the "Broken Bow" episode of *Star Trek Enterprise*. In other roles, he also appeared in this episode, "The Hunted," and DS9's "Starship Down."

Birthright Part II

Writer: René Echevarria. **Director:** Dan Curry. **Airdate:** March 14, 1993.

Worf, stuck in the Romulan prison with the other Klingons, is disturbed that his fellow Klingons don't try to escape. He is told that they are there by choice, knowing that they would bring dishonor to their families if they returned, because Klingons would rather you died in battle than be taken prisoner. Some of these Klingons have even married and had children with Romulans.

Worf decides the Prime Directive has no role here, so he trains young Klingons in the encampment how to fight and teaches them about Klingon culture. The Romulan commander tells Worf he can either give up his agitation or be killed; Worf decides it'd be a pretty good day to die, then. Instead, he and the young Klingons he has trained are allowed to leave, and he is returned to the *Enterprise*.

Picard: You found what you were looking for, Mr. Worf?

Worf: No, sir. There was no prison camp. Those young people are survivors of a vessel that crashed in the Carraya system four years ago. No one survived Khitomer.
Picard: I understand.

Notes: I have always found it odd to have the two halves of a two-part episode be directed by different people. This is not the way every series does it; see the *Battlestar Galactica* episode guide. In some cases, it leads to a slight inconsistency in feel between the halves. And with "Birthright," not only are there different directors, there are different writers for each part.

But that's all okay, because Worf is smart enough to give the heave-ho to the Prime Directive.

Starship Mine

Writer: Morgan Gendel. **Director:** Cliff Bole. **Airdate:** March 29, 1993.

The *Enterprise* is emptied of its crew so the ship can be worked on. They might want to spend some time fixing the troublesome holodeck. But no, the ship is being decontaminated with a baryon sweep, which would kill living beings on board. Looking to avoid a boring social engagement, Picard instead returns to the ship to get his saddle so he can go horseback riding during his break.

He might have found the cocktail party more interesting than he thought, because the other *Enterprise* officers in attendance are taken as hostages. Still, things aren't all quiet aboard his ship; he discovers that a group of intruders is also there, looking to steal something from the warp engines that can be used as an explosive. Picard must elude the criminals while also trying to stay ahead of the approaching baryon field, which eventually corners him in Ten Forward.

With the help of his crew, who have finally managed to escape their captors, Picard is able to stop the baryon sweep before it can kill him.

A criminal: You're Starfleet. You won't kill me.
Picard: You sure? [*He stuns the criminal.*] It seems you're right.

Notes: Tim Russ, the future Tuvok of *Star Trek: Voyager*, appears here as Devor, one of the criminals. The role of Kira is played by Patricia Tallman, who would also show up in *Babylon 5* as Lyta Alexander.

Lessons

Writers: Ron Wilkerson, Jean Louise Matthias. **Director:** Robert Wiemer. **Airdate:** April 5, 1993.

Annoyed that the stellar cartography section is using more than its share of the *Enterprise*'s systems, Captain Picard heads down there. He finds Nella Daren, stellar cartography's stellar chief, and the two have almost instant chemistry. That is later underscored when they discover a mutual love of music.

Picard quickly begins to think about (or overthink) the complications of a captain being in a relationship with one of his crew, and that becomes even more clear when Daren is believed killed on an away mission. Though she in fact survives, their relationship is over. Picard chooses his career over the woman.

Daren [*to Picard*]: Well, Captain, now that I'm on your ship, maybe you should start expecting the unexpected.

Notes: The tale of a captain unable to really enjoy a relationship with an underling is nothing new, but it's well-told here. But you'll notice Picard never falls for a redshirt security woman; he wants a longer relationship than that.

The Chase

Writers: Joe Menosky, Ronald D. Moore. **Director:** Jonathan Frakes. **Airdate:** April 26, 1993.

Why the nose ridges? Why, even after *Star Wars* littered the interstellar landscape with radically differently shaped aliens, do so many of the aliens in *Star Trek* look like humans with bony ridges on their faces and heads? Is it just hurried makeup and budget constraints, or is it something . . . more?

Picard is contacted by his former archeology guru, Richard Galen, who wants to lure him into joining him on an adventure with an incredibly important discovery. Like a woman on the ship (see "Lessons," above), an Indiana Jones adventure doesn't succeed in peeling Picard away from his ship. But when Galen is attacked and killed, Picard is energized into figuring out the mystery to which Galen alluded. On Galen's ship, there are clues that are studied by the crew of the *Enterprise* until they determine that it involves a DNA puzzle. When they head to a planet Galen had been trying to reach, they find themselves in a competition with Klingons, Cardassians, and Romulans for the secrets Galen sought to discover.

On the planet, the DNA secret turns into a holo-message from an alien who looks suspiciously like Odo from *Deep Space Nine*, who tells them that it represents the Ur-species of all humanoid life in their quadrant. Is this laying the grounds for peace instead of conflict between the descendant races?

Picard: It would seem that we are not completely dissimilar after all; in our hopes, or in our fears.
Romulan: Yes.
Picard: Well then perhaps, one day—
Romulan: —one day . . .

Notes: Actor Norman Perlmutter portrayed Picard's mentor Galen. The character of Galen was killed too young, but Perlmutter, born in World War I-era 1914, lived to the fine old age of 102. He had a full career in acting, including science-fiction roles in *Seven Days* from 1998 until 2001, and a guest appearance in *The Twilight Zone*. In addition to acting, he directed (including episodes of the *Alfred Hitchcock Presents* television series) and produced (including *Journey to the Unknown* and *Tales of the Unexpected*).

Frame of Mind

Writer: Brannon Braga. **Director:** James L. Conway. **Airdate:** May 3, 1993.

While on a covert mission, Riker is captured and subjected to experiments that create in his mind the illusion that he is either on the *Enterprise* or in a mental institution where he is told he has killed someone. Again and again, he fights his way out of the illusions and tries to return to reality, all the while experiencing a painful feeling in his head.

When he finally succeeds, he finds that he's on a table with an attachment to his head where he's been feeling the pain. He is beamed back to the *Enterprise* after he manages to get his communicator back, and once on board he goes to dismantle the set of a play he was in—which concerned a man trapped in a mental institution.

Riker: No! Let me out of here! Let me out of here! Help me! Help me.

Notes: As we noted in our "Face of the Enemy" episode writeup, this is another story this season in which a character is somehow confronting a changed reality about himself and how he experiences what's around him. Alienation. Were the writers crying out for help?

Suspicions

Writers: Joe Menosky, Naren Shankar. **Director:** Cliff Bole. **Airdate:** May 10, 1993.

Dr. Crusher's in trouble. She has been relieved of duties, because she performed an autopsy on a dead Ferengi without permission. Apparently this is not allowed by the Rules of Acquisition. The Ferengi was a scientist, Dr. Reyga, who had invented a metaphasic shield that would allow a small ship and its crew to survive a journey into the corona of a star. But when a Takaran scientist, Jo'Bril, is selected to test the shield on a shuttle, the shuttle is retrieved with his lifeless body in it. Reyga soon turns up dead, allegedly a suicide, but Crusher suspects murder.

Despite a Ferengi tradition not to perform an autopsy, Crusher does one, and to confirm her findings, she takes the shielded shuttle into a star's corona and survives. Except that also on that shuttle is a very much alive Jo'Bril, who had faked his death in order to discredit Dr. Reyga's work. If Crusher can survive her run-in with Jo'Bril, she can get her job back.

Guinan: I've never been to a formal inquiry.
Crusher: Well, I'll see if I can arrange one for you. All you have to do is disobey orders, violate medical ethics, and cause an interstellar incident.
Guinan: Well, I guess that would do it.

Notes: Jo'Bril was portrayed by James Horan, who had spent much of the 1980s successfully acting in soap operas (*Guiding Light, General Hospital, All My Children, Another World*, and others). But he appeared a couple times in *Star Trek: The Next Generation* (this episode and in "Descent"), in the "Fair Trade" episode of *Star Trek: Deep Space Nine*, in "Tosin" on *Star Trek: Voyager*, and even appeared on the first two seasons of *Star Trek Enterprise.*

Rightful Heir

Writers: James E. Brooks, Ronald D. Moore. **Director:** Winrich Kolbe. **Airdate:** May 17, 1993.

Worf goes off on a spiritual quest to the Temple of Boreth. There he thinks he has a spiritual vision of Kahless, the long-dead founder of the Klingon Empire. He lacks a few things Worf expects, like not being able to say what the afterlife is like; but a genetic test matches him with blood from the real Kahless.

Klingon Chancellor Gowron is none too pleased by the long-prophesied return of Kahless, because he thinks it's a plot by the religious leaders to take power from him. Worf learns from the temple's chief priest that it is not a resurrected Kahless after all, but a clone. Worf convinces Gowron to appoint Kahless as a powerless ceremonial emperor to unite the people.

Kahless: Kahless left us, all of us, a powerful legacy. A way of thinking and acting that makes us Klingon. If his words hold wisdom and his philosophy is honorable, what does it matter if he returns? What is important is that we follow his teachings. Perhaps the words are more important than the man.

Notes: Broadway veteran Kevin Conway portrayed Kahless. He had also played Roland Weary in the 1972 *Slaughterhouse-Five* film.

Second Chances

Writers: René Echevarria, Michael A. Medlock. **Director:** LeVar Burton. **Airdate:** May 24, 1993.

A decade earlier, Riker was nearly trapped on Nervala IV, something he remembers shortly before he beams down with an away team—and discovers another William Riker. He is the Riker who was stranded on Nervala IV, apparently when a transporter beam was altered in an attempt to get through the local distortion field.

Before you can say *The Man Who Folded Himself*, the *Enterprise* crew is left wondering what to do with two genuine Rikers. Though, unlike the hero of that David Gerrold book, Riker and Riker don't get along. Commander Riker and Lt. Riker—the rank he held at the time of the original mission to Nervala—resent each other; in Worf's estimation, each of them dislikes the other because he sees something that reminds him of what he doesn't like in himself. Troi, on the other hand, sees Lt. Riker as a chance to have a different kind of relationship with her old flame Riker.

After a dangerous but successful attempt to rescue some important data from the science outpost on Nervala IV, the two Rikers make peace, with Commander Riker giving his trombone to the lieutenant, who has chosen to go by the name Thomas Riker, using his middle name.

Data: If you met a double of yourself, would you have difficulty interacting with him?
Worf: I think so.
Data: Why?
Worf: I am not easy to get along with.

Notes: Yet again, the writers tackle a sort of alienation story, but this is arguably one of the best of the lot. This story is filled with interesting tidbits about Riker and Troi, and some good advice from others; best of all, the writers didn't take the easy way out of having Lt. Riker fade into nonexistence, merge with Commander Riker, or be killed at the end of the episode. He goes off on his own, leaving both Rikers in existence.

Thomas Riker would appear again in the "Defiant" episode of *Star Trek: Deep Space Nine*, in which he helps uncover a secret military base, though at the cost of his freedom.

Lt. Palmer is portrayed by Mae Jemison, a real-life NASA astronaut.

Timescape

Writer: Brannon Braga. **Director:** Adam Nimoy. **Airdate:** June 14, 1993.

On a shuttle returning from a conference, Picard, Troi, La Forge, and Data are almost back to the *Enterprise* when they have to change their path to avoid temporal distortions. When they get to their starship, they find it frozen in time, being fired upon by a Romulan warbird.

They visit the *Enterprise* and the Romulan ship, seeing everyone frozen in action, including Dr. Crusher being shot by a Romulan's disrupter. One Romulan who doesn't stay frozen, however, gives away his uniqueness, and he is taken back to the shuttle, where they learn he is an alien from trans-dimensional space. He and another alien were trying to retrieve a singularity from the warbird, because it carried their offspring, and that created the cascading events that led to the frozen moment in space.

La Forge: I think this is gonna work. But it's gonna take some time.
Picard: Well, Mister La Forge, . . . it would seem that time is what we have plenty of.

Notes: This is not a time travel episode, necessarily (we'll ignore for the moment the slight reversing and repeating of time in this story). But it is a very interesting exploration of time and the consequences of altering it. And you've got to love a Starfleet officer drawing a smiley face in a time-frozen cloud of gas.

Descent, Part I

Writers: Ronald D. Moore, Jeri Taylor. **Director:** Alexander Singer. **Airdate:** June 21, 1993.

Responding to a distress signal from Ohniaka III, the *Enterprise* arrives to find an alien ship and, at a science station on the surface, some Borg. But the Borg aren't behaving like well-oiled machines; they are behaving more like individuals. In fact, Data isn't behaving like a well-oiled machine either; he displays rage and beats the bejesus out of one of the Borg.

While Data tries to figure out why and how he experienced emotion, the *Enterprise* collects its team and goes to another colony that is being attacked by the Borg. Two of them beam aboard the *Enterprise*; one of them survives and is put into the brig. He says his name is Crosis, and he follows the One. Crosis is able to activate something in Data, and the two of them take a shuttle off the starship.

The *Enterprise* follows the shuttle to a distant planet, where they discover a boisterous bunch of Borg—and Data's brother, Lore, who tells them that he and Data are together and will destroy the Federation.

Riker: They were fast, aggressive, almost vicious. It was more like fighting Klingons than—Borg. [*To Worf:*] No offense.
Worf: None taken.

Notes: At the beginning of this episode, Data is in a holodeck scene, playing poker with Albert Einstein, Isaac Newton, and Stephen Hawking. Hawking, of course, is portrayed by the real Professor Hawking. Einstein and Newton, not so much.

SEASON SEVEN

Descent, Part II

Writer: Rene Echevarria. **Director:** Alexander Singer. **Airdate:** September 20, 1993.

What a turnabout. Just weeks after she was about to lose her job, Dr. Crusher now commands the *Enterprise*. Oh, and Data and Lore are working together on a mission to defeat artificial lifeforms. And a Borg ship is firing on the *Enterprise*. Not a good day to be in charge.

Crusher is commanding the starship because Picard and others are on the planet below, prisoners of Lore and Data. La Forge's VISOR allows him to see a carrier wave traveling from Lore to Data.

Well, it's actually double-turnabout for Crusher. She nearly lost her job in "Suspicions" because of her efforts to defend Dr. Reyga, who had created a way to shield a ship so it could get closer to a star. She now takes the *Enterprise* close to the nearby star, drawing the Borg ship close enough to destroy it.

Meanwhile on the planet, Riker and Worf discover Hugh, the individualized Borg from "I, Borg," who tells them he is leader of a rebel band of Borg who oppose Lore's plans. Data's ethical programming is turned back on by the away team, and Data refuses Lore's effort to get him to flee with him; he shoots Lore instead. Hugh assumes leadership of the remaining Borg on the planet.

Hugh: We can't go back to the Borg Collective, and we no longer have a leader here.
Picard: I'm not sure that's true.

Notes: Memory Alpha tells us that the site of Lore's compound was actually the Brandeis-Bardin Campus at American Jewish University, which also appeared as Camp Khitomer in *Star Trek VI: The Undiscovered Country*.

Liaisons

Writers: Roger Eschbacher, Jeanne Carrigan Fauci, Jaq Greenspon, Lisa Rich. **Director:** Cliff Bole. **Airdate:** September 27, 1993.

Picard crash-lands on a planet with Voval, an Iyaaran shuttle pilot who apparently dies before Picard is rescued by a woman claiming to be a survivor of another ship crash. Back on the *Enterprise*, an Iyaaran ambassador makes a pain of himself after he demands that Worf be his guide. But when he finally pushes Worf too far and Worf attacks him, he is pleased.

Picard soon discovers that the woman is not what she claims to be, and that Voval didn't die in the crash. Voval and the other Iyaarans aboard the *Enterprise* are studying human emotions, and all is forgiven.

Data: I have heard that in moments of diplomatic tension, it is often helpful to find elements of commonality.
Worf: Ambassador Byleth is demanding, temperamental, and rude!
Data: You share all of those qualities in abundance. Perhaps you should try to build on your similarities.

Notes: Some of the weakest of episodes from all of the *Trek* series are those in which some aliens do stupid things with our heroes to "learn about" human emotions, or human sex, or human obedience, or whatever. This episode does nothing to change that opinion. What might make them worthwhile is if we could see what having that knowledge would do for them. Just saying it's a pure quest for knowledge is really just saying the writers were lazy.

Interface

Writer: Joe Menosky. **Director:** Robert Wiemer. **Airdate:** October 4, 1993.

Not even the news that the ship carrying his mother is probably lost can stop La Forge from his mission to use his VISOR to link him to a probe that will try to rescue the USS *Raman*. He believes his mother is still alive, but he soon runs into trouble on his *Raman* mission, including getting burned and shocked.

When his mother appears, it starts to get really weird. Despite Picard's direction to stop the mission, La Forge forges ahead, attempting to save her and her fellow crewmembers. But she turns out to be an alien (a 50/50 possibility when you see your long-lost relative in a *Star Trek* episode); still La Forge helps her/it rescue her/its fellow aliens in the gas giant below.

Picard [*to La Forge*]: You disobeyed my direct order. You put yourself in grave danger. I am not happy.

Notes: Madge Sinclair, who portrayed Geordi La Forge's mother, had earlier appeared in *Star Trek IV: The Voyage Home* as the captain of the USS *Saratoga*. Way back in 1977, she portrayed Belle in the seminal TV miniseries *Roots*, which is notable not only because *Roots* was a media phenomenon viewed by seemingly everyone and their uncle at the time, but also because *Roots* starred LeVar Burton (as Kunta Kinte).

Gambit, Part I

Writers: Christopher Hatton, Naren Shankar. **Director:** Peter Lauritson. **Airdate:** October 11, 1993.

While searching for a missing Picard, Riker is separated from his colleagues and taken aboard a mercenary ship. There he discovers that Picard is also on the ship, apparently in league with a bunch of archaeological thieves. Picard stays in his undercover guise, creating an opportunity for Riker to earn value in the eyes of Baran, the mercenary ship's commander, who is able to inflict pain on his crew thanks to some handy but nasty little implanted technology.

Picard skillfully alters weapons and other tech aboard the mercenary ship to prevent it from doing much damage, but then it comes up against the *Enterprise* and attacks it.

Riker: The captain died in a bar fight for nothing. Somebody has to answer for that. Then I can mourn.

Notes: Writer Naren Shankar is a writer and producer whose work in the science fiction genre includes *Farscape*, *The Outer Limits*, *Star Trek: Deep Space Nine*, *seaQuest 2032*, *Grimm*, and *Star Trek: Voyager*.

Gambit, Part II

Writer: Naren Shankar, Ronald D. Moore. **Director:** Alexander Singer. **Airdate:** October 18, 1993.

Picard, Riker, and—remotely—Data manage to conduct a battle between the mercenary ship and the *Enterprise* that damages nothing but that leads Baran to withdraw, thinking his ship had suffered serious trouble.

Baran has warmed up to Riker, and orders him to murder Picard. But Picard has discovered that the artifact Baran is seeking—thought to be Romulan in nature—is really an ancient Vulcan weapon. Baran sends Picard and Riker to the *Enterprise* to retrieve an item, and Picard pretends to kill Riker and leaves him there while he returns to the mercenary ship. The merc ship then undergoes upheaval as it heads to the Vulcan homeworld to complete its mission.

Picard: You were right, Tallera. The resonator cannot be stopped by phasers and shields; but it can be defeated by peace.

Notes: Robin Curtis, who portrays a Romulan in this episode, is best known to *Trek* audiences for her role as the Vulcan Lt. Saavik (taking over the role first performed by Kirstie Alley in *Star Trek II: The Wrath of Khan*) in the third and fourth *Trek* motion pictures.

Phantasms

Writer: Brannon Braga. **Director:** Patrick Stewart. **Airdate:** October 25, 1993.

While Picard prepares himself for an admirals' dinner that he'd really rather avoid, Data is having weird dreams. There are strange repairmen who disassemble Data in one of them; in another, he is cutting a cake that is made of Troi.

Then in his waking moments, Data starts to see strange things: his fellow crewmembers with little mouths on their bodies. After he attacks Troi when he sees her with one of those mouths on her shoulder, he sequesters himself in his quarters. But his attack turns out to have been crucial to discovering a problem, because Dr. Crusher treats Troi's wound from the attack and finds evidence of interphasic aliens. Data uses the holodeck to interpret the clues he received in his dreams, and the *Enterprise* is successfully rid of the creatures that were affecting the people and the warp drives.

Best of all, in all the excitement, Picard misses his admirals' dinner, which is a dream come true.

Picard: Normally I would wish you pleasant dreams. But in this case, bad dreams would be more helpful.

Notes: One of the weirder episodes in a while, "Phantasms" features Data answering a rotary phone in his torso, Riker with a tube out of his head, and the Troi cake, which is oft-commented on in episode commentaries. At the end of the episode, of course, Troi offers a non-dreaming Data a cake shaped like Data.

Dark Page

Writer: Hilary J. Bader. **Director:** Les Landau. **Airdate:** November 1, 1993.

Lwaxana Troi comes aboard yet again, helping members of an alien telepathic species to speak. But something's wrong with Lwaxana, who seems overworked and mentally worn out. Deanna Troi and Dr. Crusher urge her to refrain from using her telepathic abilities until she recovers.

But Troi is having terrible dreams, and with the help of one of Lwaxana's students, her daughter joins her nightmare world, where Deanna learns she had a sister who died when she was young, a tragedy that tormented Lwaxana ever since.

Lwaxana: Aren't you going to mingle, Mr. Woof?
Worf: I do not care for telepaths. They make me—uneasy.
Lwaxana: Don't worry. The Cairn couldn't read your thoughts even if they wanted to. Your brain isn't sophisticated enough.

Notes: Two episodes in a row feature weird dreams requiring deciphering. At least this week, Troi is the dreamer and there are no crew cakes.

The role of Hedril, one of Lwaxana's students, is essayed by Kirsten Dunst, who would go on to . . . well, everything.

Attached

Writer: Nick Sagan. **Director:** Jonathan Frakes. **Airdate:** November 8, 1993.

Picard and Dr. Crusher are captured by the Prytt while trying to meet with the Kes on the unoriginally named planet of Kesprytt, which is split between the two groups. The Kes want to join the Federation, while the Prytt don't want any outside contact whatsoever. The two Starfleet officers are outfitted with neck devices that are supposed to reveal the truth of their intentions; Picard and Crusher soon learn that they are able to read each other's mind. Through that, Crusher learns that Picard had an unrequited love for her that he buried due to his friendship with her late husband.

They are able to escape their captors, while up in orbit Riker manages to strong-arm the Kes and the Prytt into releasing them to the *Enterprise*, where they must then learn to live with the secret between them that was revealed.

Crusher: When Jack died, you felt guilty.
Picard: I felt guilty before he died. Having feelings like that for my best friend's wife—and then later after the accident, I promised myself that I would never tell you how I felt. It would be like betraying my friend.
Crusher: That's why you didn't want me on the *Enterprise* seven years ago.

Notes: Music for this episode was composed by the Emmy-winning Dennis McCarthy, whose many credits include this series, as well as *Deep Space Nine*, *Voyager*, *Enterprise*, and *V: The Final Battle*. He also produced *Ol' Yellow Eyes Is Back*, the 1991 album by Data actor Brent Spiner. It included backup vocals by *Trek* stars LeVar Burton, Michael Dorn, Jonathan Frakes, and Patrick Stewart.

Writer Nick Sagan is the son of *Contact* author and popular astronomer Carl Sagan.

Force of Nature

Writer: Naren Shankar. **Director:** Robert Lederman. **Airdate:** October 15, 1993.

Data is forced to try to train his cat, Spot, to get her to stop destroying things. Meanwhile, the destruction of space around the Hekaran homeworld by the use of warp drive is posited by two Hekarans, Rabal and Serova. Rabal and Serova are too impatient to go through Federation research protocol, so they get all activisty and attack the *Enterprise*. This is apparently the best way to get results, as Data looks into their research and basically says yep, something's there.

The Federation agrees that overuse of high-level warp fields is damaging space, and it issues a non-emergency speed limit of warp five for its vessels.

La Forge: We still have time to make it better.

Notes: This rather strained attempt to tell an environmental story is a bit of a hot mess. Why the producers felt they needed to do some stretched analogy between warp travel and environmental damage is unknown; they could have more cleanly simply visited a planet where . . . there was environmental damage. Maybe the Federation requires aspirant members to get their industrial economies onto a sustainable path before they can join. Easy. The goal here might have been good, but this episode ranks as a failure. Nice Spot subplot, though.

Inheritance

Writers: René Echevarria, Dan Koeppel. **Director:** Robert Scheerer. **Airdate:** November 22, 1993.

Doctors Pran and Juliana Tainer board the *Enterprise* to work on a project to help Atrea IV's population. Juliana reveals herself to be the former wife of Noonien Soong, the creator of Data and his brother Lore. She shares with him some tales of his childhood (apparently he didn't like to wear clothes). But Data becomes a bit suspicious, and his suspicions are confirmed when Juliana is injured—and her arm comes off, revealing her to be an android like him.

Luckily, Noonien Soong left a "Watch this when your mom's arm comes off" holographic message, in which he explains to Data that there was a real Juliana who was his wife, but after she died, he created the android Juliana, who believes she is human. When Juliana recovers from her injuries, Data lets her continue in that belief.

Noonien Soong: I programmed her to terminate after a long life. Let her live out her days and die believing she was human. Don't rob her of that, son, please.

Notes: Once again, a supposed relative of an *Enterprise* crewmember shows up and, whad'ya know, she's not who she purports to be. It almost seems as if Worf's parents were the only real relatives to visit the *Enterprise*. (Okay, I know, Riker's dad, Lwaxana, etc.; but I said "almost seems," so just go with it, okay?) So, not an original premise, but a nicely done program nonetheless.

Julilana is portrayed by Fionnula Flanagan, an actor and activist who appeared in this episode, *Star Trek: Deep Space Nine*'s "Dax," and *Star Trek: Enterprise*'s "Fallen Hero."

Parallels

Writer: Brannon Braga. **Director:** Robert Wiemer. **Airdate:** November 29, 1993.

Worf returns to the *Enterprise* after a bat'leth tournament, but he begins to realize he is slipping between alternate universes. His RNA is tested and the results show that he is indeed from a different universe. Each of the universes is slightly different; Riker captains the *Enterprise* in one; the Bajorans dominate the Cardassians in another; Worf is married to Troi in yet different one.

Having determined that Worf's problem came when his shuttle went through a time-space fissure, the Klingon is sent via shuttle back into the spacial disruption. On his way he has to dodge a Borgified *Enterprise* from yet another universe, before he can finally get to his own universe, where he invited Troi to have dinner.

Troi [*to Worf*]: I know Klingons like to be alone on their birthdays. You probably want to meditate, or hit yourself with a pain stick, or something.

Notes: A fun frolic through parallel universe possibilities. Enjoyable.

If you've always wanted to hear "For He's a Jolly Good Fellow" sung with Klingon lyrics, this is your episode.

The Pegasus

Writer: Ronald D. Moore. **Director:** LeVar Burton. **Airdate:** January 10, 1994.

The *Enterprise* tries to recover the *Pegasus*, a ship long thought to have been destroyed in the initial Cylon attack. Wait, wrong "Pegasus" episode. In this show, the *Enterprise* helps search for the *Pegasus*, a ship thought to have been destroyed in a warp core accident a dozen years earlier. But a Starfleet spy on Romulus leads them to think the ship and its experimental technology might still be had.

Riker had served on the *Pegasus* years earlier, and the *Pegasus*' former captain, Erik Pressman, tries to draw him into an undercover operation involving the retrieval and use of a Federation cloaking device. But cloaking devices are forbidden by treaty (and writers having painted themselves into a corner decades earlier), and Pressman and some of his compatriots in Starfleet Intelligence are herded off toward a court-martial. Riker takes a brief sojourn through the brig in penance for his role in the matter, but is released by a forgiving Picard.

Pressman: Now that doesn't sound like the same man who grabbed a phaser and defended his captain 12 years ago.
Riker: I've had 12 years to think about it. And if I had it to do over again, I would've grabbed the phaser and pointed it at you instead of them.

Notes: Pressman is portrayed by Terry O'Quinn, whose many genre credits include an episode of *The Twilight Zone*, a recurring role on *Earth 2*, *The X-Files: Fight the Future*, *The Rocketeer*, *Harsh Realm*, and *Millennium*.

Homeward

Writers: Naren Shankar, William N. Stape, Spike Steingasser. **Director:** Alexander Singer. **Airdate:** January 17, 1994.

A distress call brings the *Enterprise* to Boraal II. Worf's human brother, Nikolai Rozhenko, works there and has set up force fields to shelter the local population in caves in response to strong storm activity. Before transporting to the planet, Worf is altered to look Boraalan to avoid running afoul of the moronic Prime Directive.

Rozhenko, perhaps having read my many dissertations against the Prime Directive, believes it is better to save the Boraalans than to let them perish in blind adherence to a Starfleet rule. So Rozhenko creates a holodeck simulation of the planet and beams the Boraalan survivors there without them realizing the switch. The *Enterprise* helps locate a new home planet for this small band of people, and Rozhenko opts to remain with them, assuming the role of the "village chronicler," a Boraalan named Vorin. Vorin had managed to escape the holodeck and, unable to accept the

Starfleet culture, killed himself.

Picard: This is one of those times when we must face the ramifications of the Prime Directive and honor those lives which we cannot save.
Rozhenko: I find no honor in this whatsoever, Captain.

Notes: Take a deep breath. 10, 9, 8, 7, 6, 5. . . . Okay. I'm fine. You can stop looking at me with that anxious concern.

We'll give the episode credit for at least tackling head-on the cultural supremacy and even genocidal logic of the Prime Directive, which would have otherwise civilized people allow masses of others to die from easily preventable conditions just so they didn't "contaminate" them with knowledge that other people exist in the universe who are unlike them. But the actions of the character Vorin show a big part of what's wrong with that idea; Vorin is so gob-smacked by what he sees on the *Enterprise* outside of the holodeck that he commits ritual suicide. Is that likely to be the reaction of all of the Boraalans? Is that supposed to suggest that that would be the reaction of large numbers of people of any culture? Because it's not the reaction of very many people from cultures here on Earth when they have been confronted by other cultures and technologies. And shouldn't *Star Trek*'s heart always be with the people (or Boraalans or whatevers) who are excited and intrigued and inspired by seeing what is greater than all that they know?

Okay, we've backed away from the ledge now.

Sub Rosa

Writers: Brannon Braga, Jeanna F. Gallo, Jeri Taylor. **Director:** Jonathan Frakes. **Airdate:** January 31, 1994.

The *Enterprise* zooms over to Caldos IV so Dr. Crusher can go to her grandmother's funeral. She reads in her late grandmother's diary that she had been involved with a man 66 years younger than she was. Talking to the local groundskeeper, she learns that her grandma had a special candle that woke up a ghost, and when she spots the "ghost," she sees the man who would be about the age of her grandmother's boy toy.

The ghost is called Ronin, and he manipulates her to fall in love with him. When Picard meets Ronin, he is attacked by the ghost; despite Ronin's warning, Crusher helps Picard.

Meanwhile, La Forge and Data discover that there's an energy source of some sort in Crusher's grandmother's grave. They open it up and are attacked by the dead woman. Crusher shows up and does an impromptu post-mortem exorcism, and then she destroys Ronin, who was an alien who used the candle as a holder of his energy.

Crusher: You have been using me, Nana—my entire family—for centuries!

Ronin: And I loved all of them! And they loved me.

Notes: Borscht Belt comedian Ellen Albertini Dow, who portrayed Crusher's late grandmother, was a little over 80 when she portrayed the 100-year-old Crusher matriarch. Dow herself would live to be 101.

Lower Decks

Writers: René Echevarria, Jean Louise Matthias, Ronald Wilkerson. **Director:** Gabrielle Beaumont. **Airdate:** February 7, 1994.

Who will become the new ops night duty officer? Lavelle or Sito? Those two junior officers are awaiting judgment on promotions, along with two of their peers who are up for other positions. In this first of two consecutive episodes dealing with crewmembers trying to get promoted, they all find themselves interpreting every slight or praise as indicative of their personal chances at professional advancement.

Meanwhile, a Cardassian has been brought onto the *Enterprise* after being rescued from an escape pod. He is Joret Dal, a Federation operative who will need to be escorted back to Cardassia; Sito volunteers for the duty. But she is killed in the course of her mission, and Lavelle gets the promotion.

Riker: Lavelle—
Lavelle: Sir?
Riker: Resume previous course and speed.
Lavelle: Aye, aye sir.
Riker: One "aye" is sufficient acknowledgment, ensign.

Notes: Not to be confused with *Star Trek: Lower Decks*, a CBS All Access (later Paramount+) series telling the story of lower-level crew aboard a different Starfleet vessel.

Alexander Enberg, who plays the Vulcan junior officer Taurik, is the son of Jeri Taylor, who was a producer of *Next Generation* and the co-creator—along with Rick Berman and Michael Piller—of *Star Trek: Voyager*.

Thine Own Self

Writers: Christopher Hatton, Ronald D. Moore. **Director:** Winrich Kolbe. **Airdate:** February 14, 1994.

Data is injured while on a mission to retrieve a deep-space probe that had crashed on the pre-industrial planet Barkon IV. He then unintentionally exposes local villagers to the radioactive remains of the probe, and when they get radiation poisoning, they think Data caused it. He concocts an antidote and gives it to the villagers, but some of them still attack him and try to kill him.

Riker and Crusher arrive on Barkon IV, figure out that Data's body has been buried, and they beam him directly to the *Enterprise* from his buried coffin.

Meanwhile, Troi is taking tests to determine if she can be promoted from lt. commander to commander. She passes, but only after Riker nudges her to be more ruthless in her decision-making.

Troi: Tell me one thing: Is there a solution, or is this simply a test of my ability to handle a no-win situation?
Riker: There is a solution—
Troi: Then give me time to find it.
Riker: I can't; as much as I care about you, my first duty is to the ship. I can not let any bridge officer serve who's not qualified.

Notes: Data visits a pre-industrial society and literally contaminates them with radioactivity. Hmm, maybe I should rethink this Prime Directive thingie.

Kimberly Collum, who portrays the Barkonian Gia, was nominated for a Young Artist Award for her performance.

Masks

Writer: Joe Menosky. **Director:** Robert Wiemer. **Airdate:** February 21, 1994.

The *Enterprise* crew investigates a comet and finds ancient remains inside the stellar body. The structure uses the starship's own scans of the comet to transmit information back to the *Enterprise*, and throughout the ship symbols and objects from the alien civilization begin to appear. Data begins to take on different personalities, and Picard must try to negotiate with them to try to stop the alien artifacts from taking over the *Enterprise*.

Data tells him that only by building a temple can they bring about the ultimate confrontation between someone called Masaka and someone called Korgano. Data, playing Masaka, is then duly confronted by Picard, wearing a mask of Korgano.

Picard: Data, you never may become fully human, but you've had an experience that transcends the human condition. You've been an entire civilization.

Notes: As much as I am a fan of Brent Spiner's incredible talents and abilities to bring to life multiple characters in a single episode, he wears thin quickly as Masaka in this poorly conceived episode. Apparently other critics agree, and this shows up on a number of "worst episode" lists.

Eye of the Beholder

Writers: Brannon Braga, René Echevarria. **Director:** Cliff Bole. **Airdate:** February 28, 1994.

After the suicide-by-plasma of Lt. Kwan, Troi and Worf investigate his workstation, which controls the warp nacelles. There, she experiences a vision of a tragedy that happened there eight years ago while the ship was being built. A murder took place between jealous lovers, and because the person murdered was an empath, Troi and the empathic Kwan had picked up the feelings of despair he left behind.

When Troi, still under the influence of the, uh, empathic vision in the nacelle, is on the verge of killing herself—having just killed Worf because he was two-timing her—she is stopped. By Worf.

Worf: Is there someone in particular you would rather I not be involved with?
Riker: Mr. Worf, you sound like a man who's asking his friend if he can start dating his sister.
Worf: No! No, I was merely—never mind. Excuse me, sir.

Notes: Actor Mark Rolston portrays Walter Pierce, one of the crewmen associated with the suicide of Kwan. Rolston has appeared in many films and television series, but he has also carved out a nice place for himself as a voiceover actor, such as voicing Lex Luthor in *Young Justice*, or Deathstroke in *Batman: Arkham Origins*, or in a handful of video games.

Genesis

Writer: Brannon Braga. **Director:** Gates McFadden. **Airdate:** March 21, 1994.

Dr. Crusher screws up big-time. She treats Reginald Barclay in an attempt to strengthen his immune system, but the treatment has the effect of triggering other crew members to revert to prehistoric creatures.

Captain Picard and Data aren't on the ship when this happens; they have been on a side-trip to retrieve an errant missile. When they return, they find everyone has de-evolved into Steve Bannon. Well, actually Troi is becoming some kind of amphibian, Riker a caveman, Barclay a spider, and Worf whatever Klingons regress into. Oh, and Spot the cat has become an iguana.

Data is able to create a retro-virus and bring everyone back to their current, modern states of being.

Picard: What—what's that?
Data: It is large, approximately 200 kilograms. It is heavily armored with an exoskeleton. Life signs appear to be . . . Klingon.
Picard: Worf!

Notes: Dr. Crusher is conveniently immobilized for most of this episode, freeing up time for actor Gates McFadden to direct her first and only episode of the series.

Also, Data's cat Spot, which had mostly been referred to as a male cat for much of the series, is pregnant with a litter of kittens. Medical marvels never cease.

Journey's End

Writers: Ronald D. Moore, Antonia Napoli, Shawn Piller. **Director:** Corey Allen. **Airdate:** March 28, 1994.

Wesley Crusher takes a break from Starfleet Academy to visit the *Enterprise*, but he's moody and argumentative. The starship is on a mission to Dorvan V, which is one of a handful of planets that must be evacuated of Federation people under the terms of a treaty with Cardassia. However, the settlers of Dorvan V are descendants of Native Americans, and they very much don't want to leave the planet.

Wesley is accosted by a Dorvan villager named Lakantha, who gives him something to think about bigger than himself. Wesley then helps the settlers revolt against the Federation's attempts to remove them. Lakantha reveals himself to be The Traveler, and Wesley heads off with him to explore the universe.

The settlers agree to stay on the planet and give up their Federation citizenship; instead, they will be allowed to become part of the Cardassian realm. If you're thinking, "Gee, that's an obvious solution that should have been presented much earlier to the settlers" and "Federation negotiators must really suck at their jobs," then you are smarter than quite a few Starfleet admirals.

Anthwara [*to Picard*]: That is why you have come to us—to erase a stain of blood worn by your family for 23 generations.

Notes: Once again, *Star Trek*'s writers and producers demonstrate their beliefs that religion is passé—except for Native American religion (and Bajorans and Klingons). Apparently Islam, Christianity, Judaism and other faiths have disappeared, however; it's a rather selective anti-religious attitude. Intellectual rigor therefore is not a hallmark of this episode.

One of the more disturbing ideas in this story is Picard being shamed by the behavior of an ancestor of his, who fought Native Americans in the Pueblo Revolt hundreds of years earlier. The Pueblo Revolt is a real historical incident, having taken place in 1680. But are the writers serious? Do they think Picard—or anyone—has some sort of racial guilt passed down to him century after century? But, again, intellectual rigor is not to be found here.

Firstborn

Writers: René Echevarria, Mark Kalbfeld. **Director:** Jonathan West. **Airdate:** April 25, 1994.

Worf decides Alexander needs to butch it up some now that he's reached the age for declaring his plans to become a warrior, but Alexander has no desire to become a warrior. So Worf takes his son to a Klingon festival where, naturally, there is lots of fighting. When Worf and Alexander are attacked, they are saved by a stranger, a Klingon named K'mtar.

K'mtar agrees with Worf that Alexander needs to become a fighter, but the kid continues to resist. When the *Enterprise* tracks down the Duras sisters, who are linked to a dagger used to attack Worf and Alexander, they learn that the dagger has markings on it for someone who isn't even born yet. Worf then confronts K'mtar, who reveals himself to be his son Alexander from the future, having returned to try to change his younger self into a fighter so he can defend Worf from a future attack. Worf convinces him to return to his own time, and he accepts Alexander for what he is.

Worf: The path of a warrior begins with the first Rite of Ascension—
Alexander: Is that when they hit you with pain sticks?
Worf: No, that is the second rite.
Alexander: Oh.

Notes: A strange episode, but one with an ultimately uplifting resolution and message.

Bloodlines

Writer: Nick Sagan. **Director:** Les Landau. **Airdate:** May 2, 1994.

Dr. Crusher has a son. Data builds a daughter. O'Brien has a baby. Worf has a son. Troi had that weird alien pregnancy. Now it's Picard's turn, when the Ferengi DaiMon Bok shows up again (see "The Battle" in season one) seeking revenge (again) for the death of his own son during a battle with the *Stargazer*, which was commanded by Picard years earlier.

Bok has a threat (again): He plans to kill Picard's son. Only problem (well, there are multiple problems, but for the sake of the story) is that Picard doesn't know he has a son. He might have commiserated with James Kirk about errant offspring. Eventually he comes across Jason Vigo, whose mother had a relationship with Picard in the past. Picard struggles to get along with Jason, who is experiencing the effects of some disease.

Crusher reveals that Jason is not Picard's son, despite a faked DNA test Bok had set up. Bok's Ferengi companions abandon him and Picard and Jason try to figure out whether they want to know each other as friends.

Picard [*to Jason*]: Like it or not, I'm your father. I don't know what that means—I know that means something, has some connection. But one thing is clear: you'll never look at your hairline again in the same way.

Notes: A few thoughts.

First, Picard, baldness is inherited via the maternal line, so Jason probably doesn't need to think about that, unless his maternal grandfather was also bald. Just noting for the record.

Second, yet again, the rule of *Next Generation* unexpected family relations rears its head. If there's a surprise meeting with a long-lost or unknown relation, there's a good chance it's a robot/alien/dream/whatnot.

Actor Ken Olandt portrays Picard's almost-son, Jason. He has appeared in other genre series, including *V* and *Leprechaun*, and starred in the syndicated *Super Force*.

Emergence

Writers: Brannon Braga, Joe Menosky. **Director:** Cliff Bole. **Airdate:** May 9, 1994.

During a practice of Shakespeare's *The Tempest* in the holodeck, a train suddenly shows up and runs through the scene. Soon, the *Enterprise* jolts into warp seemingly of its own accord. Something weird is happening on the starship, and the crew discovers that the *Enterprise*'s systems have some sort of protected nodes that lead to the holodeck.

In the holodeck, they find themselves in an Orient Express storyline, where characters are trying to get to Vertiform City. The characters—and the ship—are creating a new lifeform, but they need vertion particles.

Picard: Yes, yes, Data, I know about the Orient Express, but what is it doing on Prospero's island?

Notes: There are some neat ideas in this episode, such as the *Enterprise* as a proto-AI (something that would have been great to explore at greater length, though it might be too similar these days to *Red Dwarf* or *Farscape*) at a time when the smartest computers were basically command-and-response machines. The idea of the ship creating a new lifeform (hey, if Crusher, Data, O'Brien, Worf and almost Picard could do it, why not *Enterprise*?) is also a worthy subject.

Then why is this episode so tiring to watch? Could it be the interminable scenes with the stupid holo-characters on the train, mouthing silly sounding mysteries that are supposed to intrigue but instead only bore? Yes, yes, that's it.

Preemptive Strike

Writers: René Echevarria, Naren Shankar. **Director:** Patrick Stewart. **Airdate:** May 16, 1994.

Ro Laren, exit stage left. Ro is given an undercover assignment to infiltrate a group of the Maquis, vigilantes who are fighting the Cardassians (and who will figure prominently in the setup for the spinoff *Star Trek: Voyager*). She assures Picard of her ability to do the job, even though the Maquis are doing the same rebellion thing that her Bajorans once did.

But when the Maquis leader is killed by Cardassians, her resolve begins to waver, and she tries to derail Picard's plan to capture the Maquis. She finally has her chance, exposing a Federation fleet that was hiding in a nearby nebula, and she escapes with the Maquis—after first telling Riker to apologize to Picard for her betrayal.

Riker: You're going with them?
Ro: It's been a long time since I really felt like I belonged somewhere. Could you tell Captain Picard something for me?
Riker: Of course. What is it?
Ro: Tell him I'm sorry.
Riker: So long, Ro. Take care of yourself.
Ro: Goodbye, Will.

Notes: This is a much better character wrapup episode than Wesley Crusher's "Journey's End." Though it is interesting that in both cases, the Starfleet member—Crusher and Ro—both betray their Starfleet orders in favor of their own sense of ethics. Had this series not been one episode away from ending, we could expect to see Worf kill the Klingon chancellor and take over the empire.

A large part of the Roddenberry/*Trek* myth is that 23rd- and 24th-century Starfleet and the Federation have resolved all kinds of problems and are run as ethically as possible. But (as anyone would expect when confronted with a superman-type perfection of character or society) there's not much opportunity for interesting stories in that, especially since these oh-so-perfect people can't interfere with anyone who's less-than-perfect. So, the oh-so-perfect people's society has to be less-than-perfect.

Ergo—Starfleet and the Federation are not as evolved as they claimed to be, as their heroes preached. Maybe they could have told us that before the penultimate episode.

All Good Things . . .

Writers: Brannon Braga, Ronald D. Moore. **Director:** Winrich Kolbe. **Airdate:** May 23, 1994.

Q shows up one last time, or more accurately, three last times. He sends Picard on a journey through three time states to try to stop the annihilation of humanity: back when Picard took control of the *Enterprise*, the "present," and 25 years in the future. It's all an attempt to see if Picard can save the human race from the harsh judgment of the Q Continuum.

All three of the Picards end up in starships at an anomaly in space, unsure of what to do. Somehow, the anomaly is the key problem he and his crew have to solve, if only Picard can learn to think across multiple timelines. In the end, Q judges him—and humanity—to have passed the test and to therefore be worthy of continued existence.

Picard: So, five-card stud, nothing wild—and the sky's the limit.

Notes: This episode won a 1995 Hugo Award for best dramatic presentation, and it was nominated for four Emmy Awards, winning one for special effects. The episode deserved the awards, as well as a number of other plaudits, for it is a fitting end to the series, one that has real drama, plays fair but creatively with the future versions of our beloved characters, and ends with the beautiful touch of having Picard finally join his senior staff's poker game.

THE NEXT GENERATION FILMS

The *Star Trek* film franchise got its start in 1979 with the original cast's big-screen debut in *Star Trek: The Motion Picture*. That $40 million-plus film failed to impress critics and Paramount bean counters, but the second film was a resounding success with both, and thus *Trek* became a movie franchise. After a total of seven films, the decision was made to hand off the cinematic activities of the *Enterprise* to the next generation. *Star Trek Generations* was the result, a film that bridged the two generations and spawned its own series of *Trek* films. Here is an "episode guide" of the *Next Generation* films.

Star Trek Generations

Writers: Rick Berman, Ronald D. Moore, Brannon Braga. **Director:** David Carson. **Release date:** November 18, 1994.

A not completely successful pairing of the two generations of *Trek*, *Generations* nonetheless charms with its *Next Gen* characters. Captain Kirk is transported (but via the mysterious space-rift Nexus rather than by transporter) to the 24th century, where he meets up with Captain Picard, and they join forces to defeat Soran, who will do anything to live in the Nexus forever, even if it destroys countless others. In the process, James Tiberius Kirk makes the ultimate sacrifice, the *Enterprise* is destroyed, and we learn that Data can swear.

Kirk: Captain of the *Enterprise*?
Picard: That's right.
Kirk: Close to retirement?
Picard: Not planning on it.
Kirk: Let me tell you something. Don't. Don't let them promote you. Don't let them transfer you; don't let them do anything that takes you off the bridge of that ship, because while you're there, you can make a difference.

Notes: It should be noted that this film cost $35 million to make, which is about $11 million less than *Star Trek: The Motion Picture* cost 15 years earlier. They both earned roughly similar amounts at the box office.

And as much as I am proudly a member of Team Picard when it comes to the Captains Olympics, there are some nice moments here for James Kirk. Sadly, as is usual with the original cast, the non-Kirk characters who are here representing the original crew are treated as sidekicks.

Star Trek: First Contact

Writers: Rick Berman, Ronald D. Moore, Brannon Braga. **Director:** Jonathan Frakes. **Release date:** November 22, 1996.

The first all-*Next Generation* film goes back in time to track down some Borg, which leads to the need to team up with Zefram Cochrane, the man who first made warp drive work. Cochrane also turns out to be a bit different from the visionary taught in schools to later generations; he's a bit more interested in money and drink than in exploring new frontiers. The milestone of Earth's first warp flight—during which they are noticed and then visited by the Vulcans—is put in jeopardy by the Borg, so the *Enterprise* crew must nursemaid the drunk, argumentative Cochrane so he will carry through with his historic act.

Troi: Timeline? This is no time to argue about time! We don't have the time.

Notes: This is the best of the *Next Generation* films, and it vies with *Star Trek IV: The Voyage Home* for best *Trek* film of all. (For the record: Both are time-travel stories.) It is smart, it is funny, it has great special effects, it is touching, and there are wonderful moments even for the supporting actors. And Alfre Woodard as Lily is simply spectacular; her scene in which she convinces Picard to give up his ship is a standout moment for both characters (and for both actors).

Star Trek: Insurrection

Writers: Rick Berman, Michael Piller. **Director:** Jonathan Frakes. **Release date:** December 11, 1998.

While away on an undercover mission, Data starts to go haywire, setting into motion a head-to-head conflict between the peaceful villagers of the Ba'ku, the *Enterprise* crew, and a rogue team from Starfleet. In the process, many horrible things happen, including mutiny, ethnic cleansing of the Ba'ku, and Worf singing Gilbert and Sullivan.

Riker: A photon torpedo. Isn't that the universal greeting when communications are down?
La Forge: I think it's the universal greeting when you don't like someone.

Notes: *Insurrection* underwhelmed at the box office, but it is a nice "quiet" movie and very much in keeping with the *Next Generation*'s TV modus operandi of following a high-octane episode like "The Best of Both Worlds" with the quiet "Home."

Unfortunately, it also played too much like a big-budget standard television episode.

Star Trek Nemesis

Writers: John Logan, Rick Berman, Brent Spiner. **Director:** Stuart Baird. **Release date:** December 13, 2002.

The *Enterprise* crew encounters a clone of its Captain Picard. The clone, a Reman who has taken control of the Romulan empire, wants all kinds of revenge for his terrible life.

Picard tries to reason with him, but the clone's lust for destruction is so great it results in a cataclysmic collision between his ship and the *Enterprise*, with Data sacrificing his android life in the process.

Worf: Captain, I do not think it is appropriate for a Starfleet officer to appear naked.
Picard: Oh, come now! A big, handsome, strapping fellow like you? What can you be afraid of?

Notes: The *Next Generation* cinematic swan song does try to push some character development (for Data), akin to Spock's post-resurrection following *Star Trek II: The Wrath of Khan*, and it might have been interesting to see how that plays out in future films. But this movie has none of the great moves of previous films (it's missing anything approaching Picard's edgy "The line must be drawn *here*!"). Its poor box office performance put a halt to the films until they were resurrected by J.J. Abrams with a whole new cast and setting.

CHAPTER FIVE

Preview of Things to Come: The X-Files Season One, 1993–1994

X marks the spot—where science and science fiction intersect with anti-science paranoia and real-life politics. *The X-Files* marks the spot where entertainment met real psychic agony, and the result was one of the most unexpected smash hits of all time on the small screen. This is the story of dark television magic.

September 10, 1993, was the day that the first episode of *The X-Files* premiered. Millions of viewers were confronted with something they'd never seen before: A program about government conspiracy featuring two attractive, quirky, likable characters who might or might not have the abilities to solve the mysteries.

For me, my revelation had come much earlier. A friend of mine worked at a major Chicago-based advertising agency. She invited me to her apartment one evening to view a new TV program that was expected to be a big hit—no, it wasn't *The X-Files*; it was some other program that I have long since forgotten. *The X-Files* was the backup, another cassette, the secondary show we'd watch after the main event. The "Oh, there's also this thing we could watch." We viewed the first show—whatever it was; it was fine, but clearly not memorable—and then we put in the cassette for the next program, and for the next hour we were mesmerized. When *The X-Files*' pilot episode was over, we looked at each other and said "That was pretty cool."

And it was.

We became two of the earliest fans of the new program, probably along with other advertising and media professionals around the country who had been sent review copies to aid them in their plans for purchasing ad time on television or for reviewing the show. Our attraction was not misplaced; *The X-Files* went on to a strong first season that set the tone that defined the series for more than 10 seasons (counting the new limited series) and two motion pictures.

The television series *The X-Files* premiered in the early 1990s, when a certain wing of the American public was both losing trust in the governing class and was worried about its own falling economic future. Make no mistake; militias and cult crazes were intimately connected to the idea of government conspiracies and alien invasions and, in general, outsider control of our lives.

What at the time seemed a fun and quirky exploration of the dark side of American political and social culture looks a bit different today. Oh, it's still fun, and it's an extremely well-made show. But we probably look at the fringe, conspiracy-spewing parts of our population with more alarm today, now that we see it in light of the face-painted, tusk-wearing shaman who became infamous for his participation in the attack on the U.S. Capitol, itself the result (but alas, probably not the end) of years of attacks on facts, reality, and the fragility of our social and political systems.

Am I getting too serious? Then let's go back to the beginning and remember when it was all just good clean fun.

THE ORIGIN STORY

Fox said no. That's Fox television, not Fox Mulder. And what the young television network was rejecting was what would one day become a cash cow for them: an initial treatment for *The X-Files*, presented by television writer Chris Carter.

Luckily, with the help of a producer friend, Carter got another chance to pitch his series to Fox, and this time—reportedly reluctantly—the network gave him the go-ahead for a pilot.

And the rest, as they say, was historic amounts of success.

The show appeared at a time when science fiction was gaining a foothold on television thanks to syndicated stars (such as the *Star Trek* spinoffs). But *X-Files* was both new and old: new, in that it wasn't like anything else on TV at that time; old, in that it had its roots in classic series of horror and science fiction. It grew those roots into something that was better and edgier than any of its antecedents.

Carter cites as his inspirations shows that he watched as a child, such as *Alfred Hitchcock Presents*, *Kolchak: The Night Stalker*, *Night Gallery*, and *Outer Limits*. The film *The Silence of the Lambs* played a unique role in shaping *The X-Files*. "*Silence of the Lambs* was an inspiration. It's not a mistake that Dana Scully has red hair like Clarice Starling in *The Silence of the Lambs*," Carter told *Smithsonian* magazine in 2008. He said there were a number of sources that helped him, "but the idea itself came out of my religious background and my interest in science. My brother is a scientist. He's a professor at MIT. He brought science fiction into my world. But I am a person of faith, and so it's the combination of those two things."

Carter, who was born in 1956, was a teenager during the political and social ferment and turmoil of the late 1960s and early 1970s. "I always liken myself to a child of Watergate, and that's where I developed my kind of distrust of the government," he told *Mental Floss* in 2014. "It was 1974 when Nixon resigned, but I still think there was a residual distrust of authority, and *The X-Files* capitalized on that."

He said the program's writers "were mining genres that had already proven in my childhood to be popular, which were horror and science fiction. We were capitalizing on it in a new way and in a new era, and I think that if I can take any credit for anything, it's that we were, I think, effective storytellers that had a relentless pursuit of excellence. . . .

"I always said that the show ultimately was a search for God, but that could be said about any show, in a way," he told *Mental Floss*. "It was about faith, and just the different aspects of faith, so I think those characters would be true to themselves."

Studio: 20th Century Fox
Network: Fox
Creator and Executive Producer: Chris Carter
Producers (*various titles and time frames*): R.W. Goodwin, Howard Gordon, Frank Spotnitz, Vince Gilligan, John Shiban, Kim Manners, Glen Morgan, James Wong, Michelle MacLaren, Michael W. Watkins, David Greenwalt
Theme Music by: Mark Snow
Fox Mulder: David Duchovny
Dana Scully: Gillian Anderson
Walter Skinner: Mitch Pileggi
Cigarette Smoking Man: William B. Davis

SEASON ONE

Pilot

Writer: Chris Carter. **Director:** Robert Mandel. **Airdate:** September 10, 1993.

Dana Scully is instructed by the FBI to team up with a troublesome agent named Fox Mulder, who pursues cases involving claims of the paranormal. Mulder, a believer in the paranormal, later informs Scully that his sister was abducted by aliens when she was 12.

For their first case together, Scully and Mulder head to Oregon, where high school students are disappearing and turning up dead. Exhuming the most recent victim, Scully discovers that the body in the coffin isn't the teenage girl's but is instead that of an orangutan. Are the kids being abducted? And why does Mulder's car keep experiencing problems at one spot on the road?

Scully: Time can't just disappear; it's a universal invariant.
Mulder: Not in this ZIP code.

Notes: This unimaginatively named pilot episode sets up the series pretty well, and it is surprising how faithfully this long-lived show follows the path laid out here. Not only do we have a mythology set up in which there are small capsules implanted in human abductees, but we meet the characters Mulder, Scully, Cigarette Smoking Man, and others. And the mood—the quiet, mysterious, ominous feeling that is established here and never leaves. This is the episode that made many viewers fall in love with the show, yours truly included.

Deep Throat

Writer: Chris Carter. **Director:** Daniel Sackheim. **Airdate:** September 17, 1993.

Deceit within a coverup within misdirection. Scully and Mulder investigate rumors of experimental aircraft and abused test pilots at an Air Force base in Idaho. While using a restroom, Mulder is contacted by Deep Throat, who warns him that he is being watched.

Mulder and Scully see strange maneuvers of aircraft over the base before they are driven away by a black helicopter. Later Mulder returns and is captured, his memory wiped of what he has seen. Scully rescues him by swapping him for Paul Mossinger, an undercover security person. Later, Mulder once again meets Deep Throat back in Washington, and the informant lets him know that "they"—presumably aliens—are not recent arrivals.

Deep Throat: Mr. Mulder, they've been here for a long, long time.

Notes: Yes, Deep Throat the character was named after Deep Throat the famous government source for Bob Woodward and Carl Bernstein in their Watergate coverage, and that source had been named for the adult movie *Deep Throat*, which was named for . . . well, look, the point is this new character served to explain the mythology backstory and give clues—sometimes vague—to Scully and Mulder.

Deep Throat was portrayed by Jerry Hardin. Veteran actor Hardin also appeared in such genre series as *Lois & Clark: The New Adventures of Superman*, *Sliders*, *Star Trek: The Next Generation*, and *Star Trek: Voyager*.

Squeeze

Writers: Glen Morgan, James Wong. **Director:** Harry Longstreet. **Airdate:** September 24, 1993.

Mulder and Scully are brought in to investigate a case in which a man was killed and his liver taken, but where no obvious point of entry into his building presented itself. Mulder concludes that the murder is similar to killings in 1933 and 1963, and each of those previous times there were three murders apiece.

They catch Eugene Victor Tooms and give him a lie detector test. He fails the questions Mulder used to tie him to the previous murders, but another FBI agent releases Tooms. Exploring Tooms' home, they discover he created a "nest" out of newspaper clippings and kept mementos of his victims. When Mulder discovers Tooms has taken Scully's necklace, he has to track him down before she becomes his latest victim.

Scully: Oh my God, Mulder! It smells like—I think it's bile!
Mulder: Is there any way I can get it off my fingers quickly, without betraying my cool exterior?

Notes: This is the first script from writing pair Glen Morgan and James Wong. The two would also go on to create the short-lived SF series *Space: Above and Beyond.*

Conduit

Writers: Alex Gansa, Howard Gordon. **Director:** Daniel Sackheim. **Airdate:** October 1, 1993.

Our heroes travel to Iowa to follow up on a tabloid report about the disappearance of a teenage girl. They find her brother writing down code that he says comes from the TV, and the code later turns out to be from the U.S. military. The kids' home is raided by the NSA and the family taken into custody.

While they work out the mystery of the missing teen and a related murder, Mulder finds himself thinking back to the abduction of his own sister years earlier.

Mulder: I want to believe.

Notes: This episode ends with a dawning realization by Scully that Mulder just might be on to something real after all and isn't just a believer in conspiracy theories.

The Jersey Devil

Writer: Chris Carter. **Director:** Joe Napolitano. **Airdate:** October 8, 1993.

Something humanoid killed a man and ate part of his body. Mulder and Scully think the killing is the doing of a female humanoid creature whose mate was killed. They track down and find the creature, who is killed by a SWAT team. Her child, however, is still alive, and is keeping watch on some new prey.

Scully: They found a body in the New Jersey woods yesterday missing its right arm and shoulder. They think they may have been eaten off by a human.
Mulder: Where in New Jersey?
Scully: Just outside Atlantic City.
Mulder: Not an uncommon place to lose a body part.

Notes: As a monster-of-the week episode, "The Jersey Devil" acquits itself just fine. But we do get some neat early insight into Scully's life (and she does have one besides her work with Mulder).

Shadows

Writers: Glen Morgan, James Wong. **Director:** Michael Lange. **Airdate:** October

22, 1993

Fans of electrical-based fiction will get a real charge out of this one: After two muggers in Philadelphia attempt unsuccessfully to rob a woman at an ATM, the muggers' dead bodies are found to have an electrical charge. While tracking down Lauren Kyte, the victim of the attempted mugging, Scully and Mulder witness their car moving on its own—and a later check-up shows that the car, yep, has an electrical charge. Tied up in all of this is a possible connection to a Middle Eastern terrorist group, an unknown government agency, and a technology deal gone wrong. And, because this is *The X-Files*, a ghost.

Mulder: Do you know how difficult it is to fake your own death? Only one man has pulled it off: Elvis.

Notes: Sometimes the scariest setups aren't supposed to deliver the scares. There's a nice twist here about a haunting that turns out to be protective.

Ghost in the Machine

Writers: Alex Gansa, Howard Gordon. **Director:** Jerrold Freedman. **Airdate:** October 29, 1993.

Facing shutdown over budget cuts, the central operating system (COS) of the Eurisko company begins to fight back, killing one of the company's leaders and waging battles against members of law enforcement sent its way.

Mulder learns from Deep Throat that COS is an artificial intelligence that the U.S. Department of Defense wants to get its hands on, but Mulder wants to destroy it. He tries to upload a virus into the system to take it out *a la* various attempts against the Borg, but the Defense Department is trying to stop him.

Mulder: He ran into a little bad luck in Atlanta, working hate crimes.
Scully: What kind of bad luck?
Mulder: He misplaced a piece of evidence—bagged and everything. Sent it to the cleaners. By the time he got it back, a federal judge had lost both his hands and his right eye.

Notes: We'll agree with others who have made the obvious *2001* HAL 9000 references. Fear (some natural, some healthy skepticism, some manufactured by luddites) of artificial intelligence is widespread, and A.I. makes for an easy target for a story like this. But most computers-run-amok stories fail (with the exception of *Terminator 2*), and this episode won't break that pattern.

Ice

Writers: Glen Morgan, James Wong. **Director:** David Nutter. **Airdate:** November

5, 1993.

Mulder and Scully head up to Alaska, where a number of scientists have killed themselves at a research station. A dog, found with the dead bodies of the scientists, is discovered to have black spots on its skin, as well as something that appears to be moving *beneath* its skin.

When the pilot who flew them to the station dies during an escape attempt, they are stuck in the cold wasteland, and Muller, Scully, and the remaining scientists need to find out what is infecting people and how to stop it. Scully eventually realizes that there are worms inside the bodies, and that the worms will kill each other if put together in the same organism. If only they could trust each other that they weren't infected.

Mulder: Before anyone passes judgment, may I remind you—we are in the Arctic.

Notes: Even though this episode was heavily influenced by *The Thing* (and its literary antecedents), "Ice" is just a delight from start to finish.

It looks like a big-budget production (and it reportedly did go over budget), and it's worth it. From the tension of having everyone mistrusting everyone else, to a threat that is unknown but virulent, to actors and direction that plays it all perfectly (even adding humor to the famous strip-search scene), this is one of the series' very best episodes.

Besides the literary and filmic influences, co-writer Morgan was reportedly inspired by the discovery of something in the northern ice that was a quarter of a million years old. And in another example of life imitating art imitating life, in June 2021 it was reported that Russian scientists had brought back to life the bdelloid rotifer, a 24,000-year-old tiny organism dug out of the Siberian permafrost. The revived tiny monster—I mean, organism—not only came back to life, it reproduced asexually. And, as a report on Al Jazeera notes, "Scientists earlier revived microscopic worms called nematodes from sediment in two places in northern Siberia that were dated more than 30,000 years old."

And there you've got your worms.

Space

Writer: Chris Carter. **Director:** William Graham. **Airdate:** November 12, 1993.

Scully and Mulder sure do get around. One week they're in the wilds of Alaska, and the next they're at NASA.

Mulder gets to meet a childhood hero of his, an astronaut with the improbable name of Lt. Col. Marcus Aurelius Belt, who runs the U.S. space shuttle program. Unfortunately for the hero-worship time, he pours cold water on the stories they've heard about sabotage of launches. Reports of a ghost outside the space shuttle don't help. And it might be a ghost that Belt picked up on his own trip to space years ago.

Mulder: The failure of the Hubble Telescope and the Mars Observer are directly connected to a conspiracy to deny us evidence.
Scully: Evidence of what?
Mulder: Alien civilization.
Scully: Oh. Of course.

Notes: The genesis of this plot is an image of a rock formation on the surface of Mars that looks sort of like a human face (frankly, it always looked kind of like an ancient mask to me, but whatever). As Nola Taylor Redd explains on Space.com, "Although NASA scientists quickly determined that the face was created by tricks of light and shadows, the imaginative public seized on the idea that it did not form naturally. Some people believe that the face is the remnant of an alien civilization, suggesting that other rocky outcroppings in the area may be a crumbling extraterrestrial city."

As much as I tend to side with science and the rationalists, I'm so sad about our collective loss of interest in exploring space that I'm tempted to say that if an easily disproved belief in a giant human face on Mars gets the hoi polloi interested in space, maybe it's not all bad.

Actor Ed Lauter, who portrayed astronaut Belt, had also appeared in the 1976 *King Kong* remake, the 1978 horror film *Magic*, *Star Trek: The Next Generation*, *Charmed*, *The Rocketeer*, and, because life is weird, *The Waltons*.

Fallen Angel

Writers: Howard Gordon, Alex Gansa. **Director:** Larry Shaw. **Airdate:** November 19, 1993.

A UFO crashes near a small town in upper Wisconsin, and its invisible pilot is on the loose. Mulder is nudged by Deep Throat to go investigate, but when he shows up to take photographs of the crash site, he is arrested and interrogated by Col. Calvin Henderson. Scully goes to get him out, and lets him know that the FBI wants to shut down the X-Files project and that the crashed ship is said to be a crashed Libyan fighter plane—because so many Libyan warplanes regularly cruise over rural Wisconsin, apparently.

Max Fenig, a UFO researcher and fan of Mulder, shares some of his evidence from the UFO crash site, and Mulder and Scully learn that local cheeseheads have been threatened by the government to stay silent about what happened.

All the while, the invisible alien is running around and finally kidnaps Max, and Col. Henderson's forces arrest Mulder once again.

Back in Washington, Mulder gets a cold shoulder from his boss, but the X-Files won't be shut down—thanks to intervention by Deep Throat.

Deep Throat: Quick response—I'd say you have 24 hours before the entire area is sanitized. After that, it will be like nothing has happened.

Notes: Threats to the existence of the X-Files project crop up here and would of course recur at the end of this season. Whereas once the X-Files was just the effort of this weirdo Fox Mulder who was the butt of jokes in the FBI and not taken very seriously, it is beginning to get some answers to mysteries that "they" don't want revealed. And clearly the ploy of having a skeptical Dana Scully rein in Mulder has backfired.

My favorite bit of trivia for this story is that Brent Stait, who portrays Corporal Taylor in "Fallen Angel," was a teacher at the William Davis Centre for Actors Study; William Davis is, of course, the man who plays the Cigarette Smoking Man.

Eve

Writers: Kenneth Biller, Chris Brancato. **Director:** Fred Gerber. **Airdate:** December 10, 1993.

Mulder and Scully look into two killings that occurred simultaneously on opposite ends of the country. Identical girls were present, apparently the result of some test-tube babying at a San Francisco clinic. Deep Throat tells Mulder about a military effort to genetically modify super soldiers, and they meet a woman who is part of the project who says the clones had great powers and, alas, killer attitudes. The X-Files agents find a couple of the clones—each of whom would be known as "Eve"—who, after trying to kill them, are put into a mental hospital.

But in the psychiatric institution, they are not the only Eves who are patients—or staff.

Scully: Mulder, why would alien beings travel light years through space in order to play doctor on cattle?
Mulder: For the same reason we cut up frogs and monkeys. Besides, they seem to have stepped up their interest.

Notes: The history of the U.S. military trying to develop special powers for soldiers is humorous at best (see the 2009 film *The Men Who Stare at Goats*), but it's worth noting that part of what made the Nazi defeat of France and its small northern neighbors so easy at the beginning of World War II was that the German forces were drugged with various pills to keep them functioning for days. A 2016 History Channel article noted: "A so-called 'stimulant decree' issued in April 1940 sent more than 35 million tablets of Pervitin and Isophan (a slightly modified version produced by the Knoll pharmaceutical company) . . . to the front lines, where they fueled the Nazis' 'Blitzkrieg' invasion of France through the Ardennes mountains. It should be noted that Germans were not alone in their use of performance-enhancing drugs during World War II. Allied soldiers were known to use amphetamines (speed) in the form of Benzedrine in order to battle combat fatigue."

Fire

Writer: Chris Carter. **Director:** Larry Shaw. **Airdate:** December 17, 1993.

Members of the British aristocracy are being killed—by bursting into flame. When one aristo comes to Massachusetts to seek safety, also making the trip across the pond is a former, er, flame of Fox Mulder's, Met investigator Phoebe Green. Scully thinks Green is just playing up the stories of the fires because of Mulder's fear of fire, but the fire-starting killer has followed the British aristocrat to Massachusetts and the fires start again. When Mulder freezes up, unable to save some children from a burning room, the killer—Cecil L'Ively, working undercover at the Massachusetts residence as a caretaker named Bob—steps in and saves them.

Scully starts to put together the evidence pointing to L'Ively as the killer, who gives himself away when confronted by Scully and Green.

Mulder, who managed to rescue the children during a later confrontation with L'Ively, decides not to pursue any relationship with Green, who didn't even bother to say adios before she returned to Britain.

Cecil L'Ively: I'm just dying for a cigarette.

Notes: *Boys From Brazil, Firestarter, The Thing*—there's been a bit of a trend this first season of episodes echoing (or homaging the heck out of) famous horror films.

Beyond the Sea

Writers: Glen Morgan, James Wong. **Director:** David Nutter. **Airdate:** January 7, 1994.

After her father dies, Scully has visions of him talking and singing to her. Meanwhile, Mulder says that a serial killer he had helped arrest, Luther Lee Boggs, says he has psychic insight into the kidnapping of a young couple—and he'll share it if his death sentence is commuted.

Though Mulder is skeptical that Boggs has any real psychic value, Scully follows one of the serial killer's suggestions and finds the couple. The girl is rescued, but the kidnapper escapes with the male. Scully gets more info from Boggs, including a warning about "the blue devil"—which turns out to be painted on the backdrop behind a walkway, on which the kidnapper is killed.

Boggs then tells Scully that he can relay a message to her father, but she says no. After all, she tells Mulder, she already knows what her father would say.

Scully [*interrupting Mulder reading a file*]: Last time you were that engrossed, it turned out you were reading the *Adult Video News*.

Notes: Near the end of this episode, there's a nice scene in a hospital room where Mulder and Scully directly deal with the issue of her skepticism and his convictions that strange phenomena are real. The show had to touch on that, because simply always having her raise objections and him always believing would have come to be schtick, not realistic characterization. And, like every development in this series, it is doled out in small drops, a little here and a little there.

Award-winning actor Brad Dourif portrayed the creepy serial killer. Dourif's many acting credits include David Lynch's *Dune*, *One Flew Over the Cuckoo's Nest*, *Alien Resurrection*, the *Lord of the Rings* trilogy, *Mississippi Burning*, Rob Zombie's *Halloween* and *Halloween II*, to name just a few.

Gender Bender

Writers: Larry Barber, Paul Barber. **Director:** Rob Bowman. **Airdate:** January 21, 1994.

Mulder and Scully investigate the death of a man following a one-night stand with a woman he met at a club. They follow clues to the Kindred, a religious commune in Massachusetts, where Scully finds herself unable to put up resistance to one of the members.

Later, Mulder goes back to the commune and witnesses strange religious activity that includes an apparent gender-switch of a sick man. Mulder saves Scully from her would-be Kindred seducer.

Later, a man named Michel is engaging in sex with a woman who is really one of the male Kindred in female form. (Still with us?) When a police officer stops them, the female attacks the officer, turns into a man, and runs away.

When we next see the Kindred commune, it is abandoned.

Scully: Take me back to the 20th century.

Notes: The idea of a religious group seducing new members is not as far-fetched as it sounds. In the early 1990s, I recall reading about a group that used sex to lure in new members. Called "flirty fishing," it was (I'll just take this from Wikipedia) "a form of evangelistic religious prostitution practiced by female members of the cult . . . from around 1974 to 1987. According to some sources, hundreds of thousands of men were 'fished' before the practice was discontinued." Other religious groups have also been known to engage in such practices, which apparently are more interesting than handing out Bibles on street corners.

The character of Michel is played by Nicholas Lea, who would return to the series in the role of the incredibly untrustworthy and incredibly sexy Alex Krycek.

Lazarus

Writers: Alex Gansa, Howard Gordon. **Director:** David Nutter. **Airdate:** February 4, 1994.

Scully teams up with FBI agent Jack Willis, a former teacher and love interest of hers, to capture or kill bank robbers Warren Dupre and Lula Phillips. But when they catch Dupre, both Willis and Dupre are shot and Dupre is killed, but Willis' body is inhabited by Dupre.

The now-possessed Willis finds his former Dupre body at the hospital and cuts fingers off the corpse so he can retrieve a wedding ring, which is not standard FBI procedure. Mulder realizes that Willis is now actually Dupre, because Dupre/Willis used a pair of left-handed cutting shears despite the fact that Willis is right-handed.

Willis tracks down Phillips and takes Scully hostage. While Mulder finds Scully's location through analysis of a ransom phone call, there's treachery in the Dupre-Phillips relationship, and they manage to do each other in.

Mulder: How well do you know him?
Scully: We dated for almost a year. He was my instructor at the academy.
Mulder: The plot thickens.

Notes: Like most actors, Alexander Allport Jr., who portrayed FBI agent Jack Willis, had many roles and probably went out for many more that he didn't get. But in the mid-1970s, he and Amy Irving did a screen test for a little movie called *Star Wars*—had they been successful, they would have been Han Solo and Princess Leia.

Young at Heart

Writers: Chris Carter, Scott Kaufer. **Director:** Michael Lange. **Airdate:** February 11, 1994.

Killers who are unkillable or nearly unkillable once again are featured in *The X-Files*. John Barnett is a murderer who Mulder helped arrest in his first FBI case, but now Barnett is leaving messages even though he is said to have died in prison. Barnett is benefiting from some top-secret research that has him aging in reverse—apparently in reverse from the very end of his life when he supposedly died.

Barnett keeps taunting Mulder, and the FBI agent finally manages to get to him at a concert hall where the killer is pretending to be the piano player. Barnett shoots Scully—don't worry, bullet-proof vest—and is in turn shot and killed by Mulder.

Mulder: Reggie! Reggie!
Reggie: Mulder—God, I hate it when you do that.

Notes: Trivia mavens on the *X-Files* wikia page note that this is the first episode of the series for which Fox Mulder is directly responsible for someone's death.

E.B.E.

Writers: Glen Morgan, James Wong. **Director:** William Graham. **Airdate:** February 18, 1994.

What ties together an Iraqi fighter jet, an American truck driver, and shooting at a UFO in Tennessee? Deep Throat, apparently.

Shortly after an Iraqi fighter plane shoots at a UFO in the Middle East, agents Scully and Mulder investigate a UFO sighting in Tennessee, where a truck driver by the name of Ranheim had shot at the flying object. While they're there, someone briefly borrows Scully's pen, and when she gets back to Washington, D.C., Scully finds that there is some sort of surveillance technology now in the pen.

Mulder shows her his friends known as The Lone Gunmen, three conspiracy theorists who help him out from time to time. Deep Throat gives Mulder "proof" about the Iraqi UFO sighting, but Mulder thinks it's fake, a distraction to get him off the trail of the Ranheim case. Deep Throat tells him Ranheim's truck is carrying an E.B.E., or extraterrestrial biological entity, that had been found at the site where the Iraqi UFO crashed.

Mulder and Scully track down the truck, only to find it's empty and a likely distraction from the real location of the E.B.E. They track Ranheim—not his real name—to a power plant, but they can't get to the E.B.E. held there and are taken captive by the plant's guards. Deep Throat shows up, freeing them from their guards but telling them about an international agreement to kill any alien biological being; he himself is one of only three people to have killed an E.B.E.

Probably has it on his Facebook profile.

Mulder: Have you heard of any classified planes being flown during the Persian Gulf War?
Byers: Why would you need to expose a secret plane to an air force that runs to Iran whenever you take to the air?
Mulder: What about UFO activity during that period?
Langly [*laughs*]: Yeah, UFOs caused the Gulf War Syndrome; that's a good one.
Byers: That's why we like you, Mulder—your ideas are weirder than ours.

Notes: As much as *The X-Files* became a ratings, critical, and cultural juggernaut, it has a terrible record of spinning off successful new shows. The Lone Gunmen in this episode appear again later in the series and eventually are given their own television program.

The Lone Gunmen premiered in March 2001 on Fox, but it only lasted 13 episodes. Starring Bruce Harwood (as John Fitzgerald Byers), Tom Braidwood (Melvin Frohike), and Dean Haglund (Richard Langly), the quirky show was lighter in mood than the dark *X-Files*, but as much as the Lone Gunmen were a great side story in *The X-Files*, *The Long Gunmen* just didn't work as a standalone show. It's not that there wasn't initial enthusiasm; the premiere episode attracted 13.2 million viewers, but its final episode could only muster 3.6 million.

For the record, the other *X*-spinoff was *Millennium*, which, though short-lived at just three seasons and 67 episodes, still had a much longer life than the entertaining *Gunmen*.

Miracle Man

Writers: Chris Carter, Howard Gordon. **Director:** Michael Lange. **Airdate:** March 18, 1994.

As a child, Samuel brings a badly burned dead man, Leonard Vance, back to life. As an adult, Samuel is a faith healer, but something is going wrong. The people he is trying to heal are instead dying, and Samuel is arrested.

The person behind the mysterious anti-healing deaths turns out to be Vance, who was brought back to life, yes, but horribly disfigured from the burning. While in prison, Samuel is killed by people working for the local sheriff, but he comes back to haunt Vance, who fesses up to his misdeeds and takes his own life.

Scully: Maybe we should head backstage and see what the reverend has to say.
Mulder: No, wait, wait—this is the part where they bring out Elvis.

Notes: Despite a month between the airing of "E.B.E." and "Miracle Man," the show picks up again without missing a beat.

Samuel is portrayed by actor Scott Bairstow, whose genre credits include *The Postman*, *The Twilight Zone*, *Android Apocalypse*, and *Harsh Realm* (another series created by Chris Carter, but it lasted only nine episodes, making *The Lone Gunmen* look like *Gunsmoke*).

Shapes

Writer: Marilyn Osborn. **Director:** David Nutter. **Airdate:** April 1, 1994.

Is it man or beast that killed a Native American man? Mulder and Scully go to Montana to find out the truth behind the death of Joseph Goodensnake. Mulder traces the strange killing to the very first X-file case four decades earlier, in which none other than J. Edgar Hoover investigated a similar happening.

The agents find evidence of animal features on Goodensnake's body, as well as footprints that really should be called pawprints, at least after a point.

Though the FBI agents have trouble getting information out of the local Native Americans, due to the troubled history between the two groups, Mulder learns about the belief in the manitou, a shape-shifter that can also transfer to a new host. It's on an eight-year cycle, and it just happens to be eight years since the last sighting.

Scully: Mulder, what this folder describes is called lycanthropy. It's a type of insanity in which an individual believes that he can turn into a wolf. I mean, no one can physically change into an animal.
Mulder: How can you just dismiss the evidence: the tracks in the mud, the shredded skin, a man with the teeth of an animal?
Scully: Mulder, even if you're right and Joe Goodensnake did somehow have the ability to transform physically into an animal, he's dead. Jim Parker shot him and in a couple of moments, his body will be burned. End of mystery.
Mulder: Let's hope so.

Notes: Though maybe not a stellar episode, "Shapes" is an attempt to expand the horror folklore that the show's writers draw upon for their monsters, and they deserve credit for at least paying attention to the Wounded Knee aftermath

Darkness Falls

Writer: Chris Carter. **Director:** Joe Napolitano. **Airdate:** April 15, 1994.

Mulder and Scully head to the forests of Washington state, where some loggers have gone missing. They find a recently cut tree with an odd green ring in it. Doug Spinney, an eco-activist who, with his pals, has been setting potentially deadly traps in the forest to stop logging, thinks the ring is left from some organism that was released when the tree was cut—in the form of a swarm of green insects, such as the swarm that got those missing loggers.

People are safe from the swarm during the day or when there's light. But when Mulder lets Spinney borrow gas needed to run a generator in their cabin, things get tense. They eventually make it to a car, but the insects enter the Jeep through air vents. Revived at a scientific facility, they learn that the government is using fire and pesticides to try to kill the insects.

Mulder: What happened to your friends?
Spinney: They didn't make it. We're not going to make it either—unless we haul ass.

Notes: Actor Jason Beghe, who played the role of Larry Moore in this episode, reportedly was a childhood friend of David Duchovny.

Tooms

Writers: Glen Morgan, James Wong. **Director:** David Nutter. **Airdate:** April 22, 1994.

Remember serial killer Eugene Victor Tooms from "Squeeze"? Well, he's out of jail, thanks to his jailers buying his doctor's claim that he only attacked Scully because he had been accused of murder. Mulder and Scully keep a close eye on Tooms as he now goes about his life, breaking up his attempts to prey on people and surveilling his apartment. Tooms then breaks into Mulder's home and frames Mulder for attacking him. FBI Assistant Director Walter Skinner, who has told Mulder and Scully they have to stick to the rules more closely, tells Mulder to stay away from Tooms.

Tooms needs just one more liver to eat so he can hibernate for another three decades, and he finally gets it by killing his doctor. But his former home, where he had his hibernation nest, has been destroyed and replaced with a shopping mall. He builds his nest under an escalator; Mulder finds him there and kills Tooms by turning on the escalator.

Judge: Agent Mulder—look at his fingers. Look at him—100 years old?
Mulder: I contend that, perhaps through genetic mutation, Eugene Tooms is capable of contorting and elongating his body in order to gain access to victims so that he may extract the livers, which provide him with sustenance for the hibernation period of 30 years. He needs one more liver to complete this cycle.
Defense lawyer: Your honor—

Notes: We see Walter Skinner (Mitch Pileggi) for the first time. Though he only appears this one time in this season, he would of course go on to be a major continuing (and popular) character in subsequent seasons and the films.

Pileggi pulled off an impressive accomplishment over the years with Skinner. More than just a boss cracking down on his feral agents, his Skinner had to be the heavy, as well as be the protector, and eventually co-conspirator, yet still make it believable that the FBI would keep him in that role.

Pileggi's other genre credits include *Shocker*, *Knight Rider 2000*, *Transformers: The Last Knight*, *Alien Nation*, *The Batman*, *Stargate Atlantis*, and hosting eight episodes of *In Search Of*. . . .

Born Again

Writers: Alex Gansa, Howard Gordon. **Director:** Jerrold Freedman. **Airdate:** April 29, 1994.

A lost little girl, Michelle Bishop, has an unexplained connection to the death of a police detective who was interviewing her; he is thrown out the window. Another officer dies while she is watching, as his scarf gets caught in a bus door. Scully and Mulder investigate the ties between the two dead men, as well as another death of a former coworker of theirs.

Michelle turns out to have been conceived at the same time of that former coworker's death, and Michelle targets his other former colleagues who had killed him when he tried to report their theft of some serious cash. Mulder and Scully manage to stop her from killing another officer, who had married the widow of the man who tried to report them. He is saved from death, but he pleads guilty to grand larceny and murder.

Detective: Excuse me, could I talk to you for a second?
Scully: I just started the autopsy.
Detective: Yeah, um—I don't think he's going anywhere.

Notes: Interesting that Michelle is the "monster of the week" in this episode, but she's really just a tool of vengeance by someone else. The supernatural elements of the story serve to back up what is at heart a very normal story of greed and murder.

Andrea Libman is the young actress who played little Michelle in this episode. Libman would go on to have a thriving career as a voice actor, working on dozens of animated projects, including voicing Pinkie Pie in *My Little Pony: Friendship Is Magic*.

Roland

Writer: Chris Ruppenthal. **Director:** David Nutter. **Airdate:** May 6, 1994.

Deaths at a high-tech research facility in Washington state seem to center on a mentally disabled janitor named Roland Fuller. Scully and Mulder interview Roland, who turns out to be something of a math whiz, but they can't directly connect him to the violent goings-on at the center until they tie him to a computer file of a dead scientist; the file has been worked on regularly after his death, and the password is the same one Roland uses on a piece of art.

When another scientist tries to kill Roland, Roland manages to fight back and nearly kills his attempted murderer. Mulder and Scully stop him from doing so, but they might not have stopped his dead brother from controlling his body.

Mulder: Now you see the way you work that toy is like what's happening to you. You're the spaceship, Roland, and your dreams are the controls.
Roland: But who—who runs the controls?

Notes: Writer Chris Ruppenthal only wrote this and one other *X-Files* episode, but he has had a long career in television as a writer and producer. He was producer (supervising, co-, or executive producer, variously) on *The Outer Limits* revival at the end of the 1990s, *Lois & Clark: The New Adventures of Superman*, *Touched by an Angel*, and *Quantum Leap*.

The Erlenmeyer Flask

Writer: Chris Carter. **Director:** R. W. Goodwin. **Airdate:** May 13, 1994.

Dr. William Secare is being chased by police, but when they get close to him, he's easily able to repel them. He's shot and jumps into the water, disappearing, but not before his pursuers notice that his blood is green.

Deep Throat tells Mulder that Secare is very important. Mulder and Scully look into it, as Deep Throat continues to egg them on. At the scene of a related death, Mulder discovers an Erlenmeyer flask with a label reading "Purity Control." A scientist tells him the flask contains some very unnatural bacteria that could be extraterrestrial. Once again Deep Throat shows up to shed some light on human experimentation that showed signs of saving terminally ill people with the alien bacteria. A killer (aka "The Crew Cut Man") is going around killing people involved in the caper, and when Deep Throat gives the Crew Cut Man an alien fetus, Deep Throat is shot by the killer. Deep Throat's last words to Scully are "Trust no one." Soon, Mulder tells Scully that the X-Files has been closed down.

Mulder: They're shutting us down, Scully. . . . They called me in tonight and they said they're going to reassign us to other sections.
Scully: Who said that?
Mulder: Skinner; he said word came down from the top of the executive branch.
Scully: Mulder—
Mulder: It's over, Scully.
Scully: Well, you have to lodge a protest. They can't—
Mulder: Yes, they can.

Notes: And so *The X-Files* ends its first season on a high—this episode being the highest-rated of the season, as well as being a complex and taut story that brings together the mythology theme with a cliffhanger and some true alien weirdness.

Audience appetites were definitely whetted for season two.

EPILOGUE

From the Past to the Future, Again and Again

Leaving *The X-Files* to the side for the moment, I want to address the question of why I paired the *Battlestar Galactica* and *Star Trek* franchises in this book. Certainly from about 1980 until the early years of the new century, I don't think anyone was considering *Galactica* to be a contender as a long-term creative and commercial franchise.

Star Trek, too, was dead in its tracks after its second cancellation following the third season of the original series. But it rebounded more quickly. Creator Gene Roddenberry was no slouch when it came to promotion, and through his speaking and writing (or, er, copyediting the wonderful book *The Making of Star Trek*, actually written by Stephen E. Whitfield, aka Stephen Edward Poe), he fed fans with valuable insight into their beloved show. Just a few years later came Filmation's animated *Star Trek*, which ran for two critically acclaimed seasons on NBC. Not too long after that, Roddenberry was involved in a multi-year, tortuous deal with Paramount to bring back *Star Trek* as *Star Trek: Phase II*, with the studio initially hoping it would anchor a new, fourth national television network and eventually deciding to make it a motion picture. And the rest was history, with each movie keeping the flame alive and Roddenberry finally launching *Star Trek: The Next Generation*, which is chronicled in these pages. That series spawned other series and movies, and the juggernaut continues today with streaming series such as *Picard* and *Star Trek: Lower Decks*.

As a result, *Star Trek* has long been noted among both popular and scholarly audiences as a major cultural influence in this country and across much of the world. So it makes sense to include at least one of the *Trek* series in this book.

Galactica, on the other hand, clawed its way back to commercial and critical success. Yes, there are plenty of fans of the original series who didn't like Ronald Moore's version, and vice versa. That's life. But there is no denying that it is a cultural touchstone, and its fandom has grown with the additional series.

After Syfy's *Battlestar Galactica* ended its run, the Syfy spinoff *Caprica* lasted one season before being canceled. Moore and Eick headed up a new *Galactica* series on the same channel called *Battlestar Galactica: Blood and Chrome*, starring Luke Pasqualino as a young William Adama. Both *Caprica* and *Blood and Chrome* were prequel series to *Battlestar Galactica*. Though *Blood and Chrome* was very much in the same vein as *Galactica*—military deep space opera—*Caprica* was an intentionally more female-centric, planet-bound series that eschewed the space battles and zooming spaceships of the other series. Alas, *Blood and Chrome* never got past its initial outing.

Glen Larson also made another attempt to create a new *Galactica* motion picture not related to the Syfy series. That went nowhere, and Larson passed away in 2014). But as of this writing, Universal is planning new *Galactica* productions, for both the big screen and the little screen. A number of names have been attached to the feature film adaptation, and they might still change again before the film gets made, so I'm not going to bother reporting the latest from *Variety*. I just want to note that the film and a separate, unrelated TV series planned for Universal's Peacock streaming service show there's still some gold in them thar hills, and maybe by the time it's all out before the audiences, every fan will find something to their liking.

Now, back to *The X-Files*. I just included the first season of that still-in-development episode guide as a preview of things to come. However, it is a show that needs no excuses to be included with such cultural behemoths as *Trek* and *Galactica*. *The X-Files* was a huge hit, minting millions for Fox, Chris Carter, the stars and producers and others involved. Catch phrases from the series became popular; the show became a touchstone to describe eerie phenomena (arguably overtaking the immortal *Twilight Zone* in that respect) and it spawned imitators and spinoffs.

All of these series have been accompanied by novelizations and original novels, comic books, computer games, conventions, endless websites (official and non), documentaries, and copious merchandise of posters, shirts, records, and whatnot.

Regardless of if you have a shelf full of Data action figures and Cylon raider models, this book is intended to be a companion with you as you experience the joy of rewatching and reinterpreting and rediscovering old series. It's easier to do now than ever before, with both pay and free streaming services offering up countless opportunities to view them.

This book won't change anyone's life, and I have not tried to use it to make a wholistic argument about life or culture. (I'm saving that for another book—literally; it's about half written.) If you are reading this epilog after having read the book, then you know I included my own views of all of the episodes herein and occasionally went off on one topic or another. This is, after all, a personal look at these programs, so it reflects my personal views. But even if you disagreed with me on every single point (even, ugh, the Prime Directive), I hope you found this a handy book to keep near your TV or computer, grabbing it from time to time to consult about an episode you're screening.

RECOMMENDED RESOURCES

Some of these sources were consulted by me during the writing of this book, and others are simply here because they impressed me when I read them, some of them decades ago. As for the novels or novelizations included here, they are superior examples of their art form, adding new information to an already-seen television episode or to the overall storyline of the series in question, and therefore I heartily recommend these (not only these, but definitely these) to fans of these series. All of these books can be found—new, used, or reprints; in print or in e-book form—by a fairly simple Google search or some hunting on your favorite online purveyor of merchandise.

Books

An Analytical Guide to Television's Battlestar Galactica, by John Kenneth Muir
By Your Command: The Unofficial and Unauthorized Guide to Battlestar Galactica, Volume 1: The Original Series and Galactica 1980, by Alan Stevens and Fiona Moore
By Your Command: The Unofficial and Unauthorized Guide to Battlestar Galactica, Volume 2: The Reimagined Series, by Alan Stevens and Fiona Moore
Earth Star: A Monograph on the 1977 Vision of Battlestar Galactica, by Steven O'Donoghue
Encounter at Farpoint, by David Gerrold
The Fifty-Year Mission: The Next 25 Years from The Next Generation to J.J. Abrams, by Mark A. Altman and Edward Gross
The Making of Star Trek, by Stephen E. Whitfield and Gene Roddenberry
Saga of a Star World, by Robert Thurston and Glen A. Larson
Sagittarius Is Bleeding, by Peter David
So Say We All: The Complete, Uncensored, Unauthorized Oral History of Battlestar Galactica, by Mark A. Altman and Edward Gross
The Trouble With Tribbles, by David Gerrold
TV Episode Guides (Vol. I), a Starlog Photo Guidebook, by various writers
The World of Star Trek, by David Gerrold

Audio

Battlestar Galacticast (podcast), by Marc Bernardin and Tricia Helfer
Messages for the Future: The Galactica 1980 Memoirs (audio CD), by Robyn Douglass

And, finally, for the "first draft of history," I suggest tracking down coverage of these series in various issues of such periodicals as *Cinefantastique*, *Fangoria*, *Fantastic Films*, *Future Life*, *Omni*, *Sci-Fi TV*, *Sci-Fi Universe*, *SFX*, *Starlog*, and the *Star Trek: The Next Generation* official magazine.

ABOUT THE AUTHOR

John Zipperer

John Zipperer is a writer and editor based in San Francisco and Chicago. He is the creator, editor and writer of *Galaxis*, a digital-only science fiction and science magazine, where many of the episode guides in this book originated. He has also created digital magazines on politics (*Zippererstrasse*) and the magazine industry (*Magma*).

He has been on the staff of The Commonwealth Club of California since 2006. As the vice president of media & editorial, Zipperer has directed the Club's print, digital, audio, video, and public relations departments. He also hosts or co-hosts 60–70 programs a year. In 2012, Zipperer launched an ongoing series of political roundtables called Week to Week. Since January 2018, Zipperer has co-hosted Michelle Meow's weekly program at the Club, showcasing LGBT thought leaders.

Before joining the Club, he was a writer and editor for technology magazines (*Internet World*, *Windows Server System*, *University Business*, and *Smart Enterprise*) and commercial real estate finance publications (*Commercial Investment Real Estate*, *Affordable Housing Finance,* and *Apartment Finance Today*). He also was the junior editor at the Hudson Institute think tank in Indianapolis. You can still find him in the pages of the monthly *Marina Times* newspaper in San Francisco. A Wisconsin native, Zipperer earned his BA in political science from the University of Wisconsin—Madison.

You can find out more at *www.weimar.ws*.

Made in the USA
Middletown, DE
03 August 2021

45331914R00148